D0368999

Nameless

Psychoanalysis has always striven to reconstruct damaged human subjectivity. However, with a few exceptions, people with learning disabilities have long been excluded from this enterprise as a matter of course. It has been taken for granted that learning disability is a deficient state in which psychodynamics play but a minor role and where development is irrevocably determined by organic conditions.

First published in German in the 1980s and published here in English for the first time, this brave and provocative book was one of the first to attempt to understand learning disabilities in terms of psychoanalysis and sociopsychology. Controversially, the author does not distinguish between a primary organic handicap and a secondary psychological one; rather, she argues that it is development from the very outset of the process of socialisation during the interaction of caregiver and infant, and therefore gives the analyst room to work on this maladapted socialisation. She illustrates the effectiveness of this theory when put into practice in a number of illuminating case studies.

Still as influential and powerful as when it was first published, this book will be of interest to psychoanalysts and clinicians from across the mental health services who work with people with learning disabilities.

Dietmut Niedecken, born in Germany, studied educational science and music at the University of Hamburg, and music therapy at the Guildhall School of Music, London. She now works in private practice with children and young people, as well as supervising and lecturing trainee child psychoanalysts.

Nameless

Understanding learning disability

Dietmut Niedecken

Brunner-Routledge
Taylor & Francis Group

HOVE AND NEW YORK

Translated from the original work:
Namenlos: Geistig Behinderte verstehen by Dr Dietmut Niedecken

First published 2003 by Brunner-Routledge
27 Church Road, Hove, East Sussex BN3 2FA

Simultaneously published in the USA and Canada
by Brunner-Routledge
29 West 35th Street, New York NY 10001

Brunner-Routledge is an imprint of the Taylor & Francis Group

Copyright © 1998 by Hermann Luchterhand Verlag GmbH, Neuwied,
Kriftel, Berlin

Typeset in Times by Mayhew Typesetting, Rhayader, Powys
Printed and bound in Great Britain by MPG Books Ltd, Bodmin, Cornwall
Cover design by Amanda Barragry

This publication has been produced with paper manufactured to strict
environmental standards and with pulp derived from sustainable
forests.

All rights reserved. No part of this book may be reprinted or
reproduced or utilised in any form or by any electronic, mechanical,
or other means, now known or hereafter invented, including
photocopying and recording, or in any information storage or
retrieval system, without permission in writing from the publishers.

British Library Cataloguing in Publication Data
A catalogue record for this book is available from the British Library

Library of Congress Cataloging-in-Publication Data
Niedecken, Dietmut, 1952–
  [Namenlos. English]
  Nameless : understanding learning disability / Dietmut Niedecken.
    p. cm.
  Translated by Andrew Weller.
  Includes bibliographical references (p.   ) and index.
    ISBN 1-58391-942-2
  1. Learning disabled children—Rehabilitation. 2. Children with
mental disabilities—Rehabilitation. 3. Child analysis. I. Title.

    RJ506.L4N5313 2003
    616.85'889—dc21

                                                  2003006510

ISBN 1-58391-942-2 (hbk)

Contents

Author's preface to the English edition

It is more than 13 years since the book presented here was published in Germany for the first time. The book has been reprinted twice, and the experiences from which it draws are clearly bound to their time. Things have greatly changed in the meantime.

The book was written in relative isolation in the 1980s. As a complete novice I suddenly found myself exposed to a working situation as a music therapy trainee in London and as a rather un-experienced music therapist in a big institution for learning disabled children and adults where those I was supposed to work with were living under humiliating and completely inhuman conditions. The shock I received from this has led my steps in theory and practice ever since. It has become an imminent catalyst for writing this book, with the intention to contribute to a change of situation.

When I started learning and working in the field of learning disability, I was personally interested in psychoanalytic reflection but, being too young, was not ready for psychoanalytic training. Therefore I started working as a music therapist. At that time music therapy was taught on a rather basic level. Despite a one-year course in music therapy that I attended at the Guildhall School of Music in London, I found that I had to find my own way if I was to follow a psychoanalytic approach in the field of learning disability.

Whilst I was writing the book I had a discussion with Mary Priestley who was at that time one of the best-known British music therapists, and the first author to publicly claim psychoanalytic understanding for music therapeutic work. When I told her what I was writing about, she was surprised since she could not believe that psychoanalytic understanding could have any place in the field of learning disability. She told me she did not believe any kind of transference work would be possible, and that 'these people' would not be able to grasp psychoanalytic interpretations. Of course, she was unaware – as I was, too – of the fact that at that time Valerie Sinason was already running a workshop on learning disability and psychoanalysis at the Tavistock Clinic. In any case such attitudes were quite common at the time. Fortunately the situation has greatly changed since.

However, I drew inspiration from two authors who had already published psychoanalytic reflections on 'stupidity' and learning disability: Karl Landauer, with his famous essay 'Zur psychosexuellen Genese der Dummheit' (1938); and Maud Mannoni, with her book, *The Retarded Child and his Mother* (1972). The latter particularly came to me as a kind of revelation; it can still be accounted one of the most important books written in this field. The impact of Landauer's exciting work became a lot clearer to me some years later when I was already in psychoanalytic training and my interest in metapsychology was growing.

During the final stages of writing this book I became familiar with the work of Christian Gaedt, a German doctor who in his own ways tried to follow the lines that had been drawn by Mannoni's pace-making work; and only after its publication I discovered the work of Valerie Sinason at the Tavistock Clinic in London. Her book, *Mental Handicap and the Human Condition*, was published three years after mine. The fact that the two books were published within such a short period of time seems to indicate that the time was ready for profound changes in social and, more specific, psychoanalytical attitudes towards learning disabled people. Since, there have been written quite a few more books on psychoanalysis and learning disability, in different countries.

While the psychoanalytic approach of Valerie Sinason is in many ways comparable to, and in some ways psychoanalytically more refined than mine, the impacts of her work and of mine are different. Her main issue is clinical work and besides some wonderful reflections on 'euphemisms and abuse' her case histories build the core of her book. My aim, on the other hand, was a more general one: I wanted to understand the socio-cultural situation learning disabled people find themselves in. I found a set of mechanisms at work which I called the 'institution learning disability'. By this term I do not mean single institutions, but the whole set-up in which learning disability is recognised, diagnosed, treated, administered. This altogether forms a total organisation which is unconsciously governed by social 'phantasms'.*

The impact of the experiences I had in big institutions, and the isolation in which my book was written, makes for its character of resistance and its fervent and often angry tone. The time at which it was written was one of general resistance and upheaval in big institutions for people with learning disability in Germany, which at that time were more prevalent in the care-

---

* I decided to use the French term taken from Maud Mannoni (1964) in order to make a clear distinction between individual unconscious phantasies and collective unconscious patterns underlying our general attitudes towards learning disabled people.

situation of learning disabled people. (In my early professional life I got to know two of them – one in the outskirts of London, where I was a music therapy trainee at the Guildhall School of Music; and one in Hamburg, where I took up my first position as a music therapist.) The situation was gradually impregnated by a growing resistance towards the unbearable conditions in these institutions – a movement which has since led to greater changes for the better. One of the people that played a major role in this book, Wilfried, is now living in a situation which is almost entirely created out of his own decisions. I have accepted the role of trustee for him and I see him from time to time. When we meet he expresses his pleasure to see me but clearly shows that I am not the most important person in his life.

It is not only the situation in which people with learning disability usually spend their lives that has greatly changed – the treatment methods have become more human too. It is a rarity nowadays that the simple behaviourist mechanisms of reinforcement, negative reinforcement or extinction are employed, and we use methods which treat clients with a lot more respect.

If this is so, why publish a book that is so outdated – yet not so outdated as to be treated as a historical document? This may seem an unreasonable undertaking. However, it is the third edition of the German version that has proved to be most successful. The book had already been out of print for a couple of years when I suddenly received two offers from publishers that wanted to reissue the book. Despite its age, the book's contents are growing in actuality.

There are two reasons why this might be the case. When my book first appeared, it was mainly appreciated for its clinical impacts. In recent times my critical investigation into the socio-cultural set-up of learning disability has been of increasing interest. It now seems that the theory of the institution 'Learning Disability' needed some time for maturation. However, at this point another objection could be raised: my main issue seems to be confined to German conditions – what I describe here as the phantasm of 'soul murder' has, in German and Austrian history, found a concrete realisation in what was called the 'lebensunwertes Leben' during the Nazi period. Many learning disabled people met a terrible fate in one of the concentration camps. What sense could be seen in transferring these experiences from my country to English-speaking countries?

While it is the sad privilege of us Germans to live with the inheritance of that 'realisation', I do not believe that unconscious death wishes are a typical trait only of the German character. In fact, they are to be found everywhere. When I was once invited by Valerie Sinason to talk at her workshop on learning disability at the Tavistock Clinic she found it easy to accept the idea. I spoke about introjection of death phantasies and their handicapping effect in the development of learning disabled children and she readily coined the term 'infantocidal introject' – which I myself have readily adopted.*

To live with the history of Nazism is one of the main tasks all German authors have to face. At least in academic and intellectual circles there is a tradition of reflection of the reasons. This has led to a growing sensibility in all traits of unconscious attitudes that might have caused that exacerbation of murderous impulses in our country, and that might lead to new catastrophes – not only in Germany. We have learnt to live what the German-Jewish poet Paul Celan describes in his poem 'Engführung' – 'The Straitening':

> Verbracht ins
> Gelände
> mit der untrüglichen Spur:
>
> Gras, auseinandergeschrieben.
>
> (Driven into the
> terrain
> with the unmistakable track
>
> grass, written asunder.)
>
> (transl. M. Hamburger)

This verse draws on two German metaphors: 'Gras drüber wachsen lassen', i.e. to make something unconscious, forgotten, and 'Das Gras wachsen hören', i.e. to be oversensitive to hidden impulses and movements. Through our history we have been forced to learn how to write grass asunder – to exaggerate, if necessary, what we notice in order to fight the tendency to make grass grow over facts, to forget, to dismiss, to render socially unconscious. In that sense my book is a testimony of resistance against any sociocultural tendencies to forget – tendencies that have also been described in the English situation in terms of language abuse and euphemisms by Valerie Sinason.

There is another important point, as to why the book should be made available to a greater public, that is more to do with the present situation: the enthusiasm of the protest generation has now begun to fade. It is being replaced by a more sober attitude, if not by discouragement, disappointment, and resignation. The reality of day centres and living communities

---

* In 'The "Organisation" of Mental Retardation' (1999) I described in some detail the formation of such introjects. A revised version of this paper has been added to this English edition as Chapter 9, 'The Infantocidal Introject'.

does not always fulfil the promises and expectations that the early days of the integration movement had led to expect. These great expectations have met with considerable resistance.

A few examples drawn from my present work as a supervisor in integrative living communities. The persons I refer to are living in a beautiful house under conditions that the people described in the book could not have even dreamt of – well-trained and friendly staff, excellent material conditions etc. And yet they do not appear to be able to appreciate this privileged situation: Alexandra, who tends to smear her faeces and vomit at any given time and everywhere; Fritz, who urgently requires a certain ritual which strains the caregiver's intolerance; without it he bursts out in dangerous tantrums; Jenny, who, when unobserved, washes the entire group laundry on top heat in the washing machine, making a complete mess of it, although there is no doubt she is intellectually capable of understanding what she is doing; Mark, a learning disabled and physically disabled man with no speech, who has a habit of masturbating provocatively in front of his (mostly female) caregivers, who do not dare to admit that they feel deeply offended and humiliated by such behaviour.

Such situations are well known to everyone who works in the field of adult people with learning disabilities. They are bound to create discouragement, if not anger and hate, if there are no means of understanding and changing the situation. The attempt to understand will unmistakably lead to the 'infantocidal introject' – and to its source, the phantasms and unconscious death wishes prevalent in the institution 'Learning Disability'. (All the examples quoted above – together with the description of how the problems were resolved or (in one case) why the resolution failed – will be described in detail in a new book.)

I wish to mention some more possibly irritating points that may arise from the outdated perspective of the book:

— The language of the book may at times appear provocative, if not violent. I have preferred to sometimes use old expressions that obviously show the societal tendencies of discrimination in the field of learning disability – i.e. 'Mongol' instead of 'Down's syndrome', with the intention of avoiding euphemisms. With the translator of the book, Andrew Weller, I had some discussions about the question of whether to use the modern term 'learning disability' or the older expression 'mental handicap'. My point was that I could not see why it should be better to be called 'learning disabled' than 'mentally handicapped', while his point was, that the latter expression would be offensive and utterly politically incorrect in the English scene where 'mental handicap' as a term was scrapped over ten years ago. I decided to use the modern term in this case, because using the old term might have led to severe misunderstandings.

— Some of the situations described are no longer typical:

• for example, suggestions to parents with newborn children with Down's syndrome, to put their child into a home, given in the fifties and sixties of the last century, have become rare nowadays. However, up until now most parents will have experienced a severe trauma when told that their child has been born to be different than expected, and this trauma will deeply influence the beginnings of their relationship with the child, giving way to an 'invasion of phantasms'.

• for example, nowadays it would be unimaginable for someone to speak of 'children', of 'boys and girls', when speaking of adult people with learning disability. One has become quite aware of such abuses, and tries to avoid them in using completely new terminology. Moreover, it has become 'politically incorrect' to use these expressions. Does this, however, alter the underlying attitudes? Or can we not find a tendency to hide away negative affective attitudes, that we assume we ought not to have, through the use of politically correct terms?

— The therapeutic techniques I criticised are much less in use now than they used to be at the time I wrote the book. However, the aim is not to show that these particular methods are inhuman, but to understand how *any* treatment technique can be – and will be – functionalised by what I call the 'institution learning disability', if it is not understood in its unconscious meaning.

— Owing to the book's age, and also to my age when writing it (I was in my early thirties), literature references are old and incomplete. Integrating new developments in psychoanalysis may have helped to improve the clinical parts of the book, and a more profound psychoanalytic reflection could reveal how the socio-cultural situation of being learning disabled is transformed through the process of socialisation into self representations. The treatment technique employed by me was mainly based on intuition and sometimes lacks the level of reflection which can be achieved by applying our psychoanalytic knowledge to such processes. I have decided not to change them, since I know that sometimes the beginnings of an idea can bear potential which can easily be lost by the process of revision.

— One especially important reproach might be made: the reader might think that faced with the often severely handicapped people I was dealing with I was simply imagining that I understood and that I was over-interpreting the events and developments in the therapy. I would like to set against this the experience that my understanding, whether it be essentially intuitive, as in the beginnings of my work, or more consciously influenced by the elaboration of my theory of 'being learning disabled', repeatedly proved and still proves in my present work (psychoanalysis with children, where I frequently treat both children and young people with learning disabilities, and supervision in this field) to be the motor of developments. I would like to emphasise here that it is not a matter of absolute inner psychic truths, which I cannot claim to know, but of models of understanding, scenic drafts, which enable me to keep a relationship going with people who have such severe learning disabilities, and which today also enable my supervision clients to find new ways of dealing with conflicts in their psychotherapeutic or care-giving work with learning disabled people – however limited and distorted these models may be. The criterion by which such models must prove their truth lies in the relationship which becomes unfruitful or even destructive when there are blockages in understanding and misinterpretations.

I am very much indebted to Volker Schönwiese, who has always believed in the future of this book; following his initiative the BIDOK project* provided the grant for the translation; I want to thank also Andrew Weller for translating the book; and I am grateful to Kate Hawes, Senior Commissioning Editor, that she has undertaken the risk of publishing this book in the English-speaking world. May it be of help to all those who are in search of it, in their work, in their private lives, or in their search for understanding of social processes in general.

Hamburg, March 2002

* BIDOK is an internet-library for people with disabilities and people interested in inclusive education. Its project manager is Volker Schönwiese. An English language version is in preparation. Its address is: http://bidok.uibk.ac.at

Foreword by Valerie Sinason

It is with a great sense of privilege as well as sadness that I write this foreword. This powerful book gains its first English translation nearly 13 years after it was first published in Germany. It is salutary and saddening to note that it is just as needed now in the UK as it was, and is, in Germany. Despite improvements in quality of life and access to ordinary services for many people with disabilities in Europe, the existential emotional predicament remains the same. At the root, the understandable widespread wish for medical science to eradicate learning disability means that those born and living 'with it' are not emotionally welcomed nor included.

Owing to the politics concerning translation, Dietmut and I were not aware of each other's work, or that our respective books (*Mental Handicap and the Human Condition*) came out in Germany and England at the same time, until almost a decade later. However, thanks to the growing international conference networking around learning disability, we met through links with Dr Johan de Groeuf (our Belgian equivalent) and have stayed in contact ever since.

Learning disabled children and adults were among the first German citizens to be gassed. Whilst German citizens born during or after the Second World War have had to deal with the generational transmission of their difficult history, those working in the field of learning disability have had an even bigger burden to face. In Dr Christian Gaedt's hospital (which Dietmut and I have both visited), elderly men and women with learning disability are able to tell the visitor about their friends and co-residents who were taken away to be gassed. There is a special memorial to them in the hospital grounds.

Dietmut understands only too well that this death-wish for learning disability was not a Nazi invention and exists in different forms all over the world, including the UK. Those who have read my work will know that I consider the hardest task in psychotherapy, and the most crucial, is to work through the client's deep fear of being murdered. The client with a learning disability needs a secure base from which to explore the primitive terror that we not only wish they had not been born, but would like to murder them now they are alive. From speaking of this painful emotional finding at the Tavistock Clinic Mental Handicap Workshop (when I worked there from 1980 to 2000), I was pleased to hear of psychotherapist Brett Kahr's term 'the infanticidal introject', something similar he had noted in schizophrenic patients who internalised their mothers' death wishes towards them. Such internalised toxic material takes great therapeutic time to work through but leads to major improvement. The author, in tackling such topics in the current Germany, understands from lived experience the impact of societal death-wishes.

Dr Niedecken is a professor of music, as well as child and adolescent psychotherapist and music therapist. She understands the feelings that cannot be expressed in words, as well as holding deep analytic understanding of both clients' internal lives and the social environment they internalise. She therefore provides moving clinical examples of the working-through of such deep material.

Using different terminology, we both deal with the therapeutic need for reduction of secondary handicap: the defensive behavioural ways that the deep pain of the primary disability is hidden by secondary exaggerations. Smearing, rocking, biting, spitting, and echolalia are all communications of pain, secondary disabilities that cover the true self from even more hurt. However, the problem with these secondary handicaps is that they make the task of staff more difficult and in the end take away from the client the communicative possibilities that would be available if he or she dared to give up these defences or modify them.

We both deal with the way there is pressure to be 'nice' by way of an apology for existing. This means that aggression is split off. For example, Heinzi always says 'I am fi-ine', but one time a roar of anger comes from him showing a true feeling. We are also aware that since our books were first printed, the new beautiful community homes provide an even more disconcerting backdrop for communications of despair.

Niedecken takes us on an important journey of baby observation to see the development of language and identity, and provides clinical examples from her own experience, as well as from literature, to illustrate her points. She rigorously examines the impact of transference and counter-transference at an institutional and national level, as well as in her own treatment setting. She examines different kinds of learning disability and how they are acquired and the way they show themselves.

She tackles the difficult issue of parenthood honestly, illustrating the way the mother is always blamed for producing a 'monster' and, from clinical experience, the way the loss of the wished-for child means a fantasy image is superimposed on the child with the disability.

She movingly shows the way the child 'mimics' the caricature his mother or society has dreamed or projected onto him and provides an academic discourse on the meaning of mimetic taboos. Children with Down's syndrome are particularly focused on here in terms of the differential societal response to them, and Niedecken focuses on the meaning in their play that reveals their awareness of death wishes.

At the root of this powerful book is the longing for the excluded to find their own name. This means claiming language and removing it from the death-projections from a frightened society. Psychoanalytic psychotherapy has taken up the torch of truth in language into this field and as a result of that it is changing around us. However, to consolidate and deepen those changes we have to look into ourselves and our most primitive fears. Dietmut Niedecken has done that and this book is an important aid to all in the field of learning disability.

Translator's acknowledgements

I should like to thank Dietmut Niedecken for her collaboration, contribution, and support throughout the period in which I have been translating her book. I would also like to express my thanks to Gabriele Weyermann for the assistance she gave me with this translation at various times. The comments and suggestions of Bobby and Paul Wright who read through the manuscript in the final stages were most helpful. Finally, I would like to thank Professor Dr Volker Schönwiese from the University of Innsbruck for sponsoring the translation in connection with the BIDOK project.

Andrew Weller, Paris, September 2000

Introduction by Mario Erdheim
Learning disability, murder and phantasm

Anyone who hopes to understand people with learning disabilities must necessarily take into account the culture in which they live. This does not simply mean 'higher' culture in the form of art, science or religion. 'Culture' is also the life process of individuals, the way they shape their lives and ascribe meaning and significance to their actions. From this perspective, 'learning disability' is not just to be viewed as medical fate but rather as a cultural phenomenon, and, moreover, one that says something about the future possibilities of the culture in question.

One of the important contributions of Dietmut Niedecken's book is her reflection on the cultural dimension of learning disability. She investigates how learning disability becomes institutionalised in a way that ensures that death wishes towards people with learning disabilities remain unconscious. The institution 'Learning Disability' (D.N.) follows the striking trend found in other institutions of making problems disappear by banishing them to the unconscious rather than working them through in reality. The author shows, by means of telling examples, how unconscious death wishes assert themselves repeatedly and lead to psychic death for those whose fate it is to have learning disabilities. Further, the fact that there has been little evolution in attitudes towards this issue reveals the underlying repetition compulsion of unconscious death wishes. Dietmut Niedecken has had to struggle against a long-standing and powerful trend.

National Socialism was not the first example of people with learning disabilities being condemned and put to death. The medical historian Kirchhoff cites an event from Luther's table talk when the latter suggested that a feeble-minded person be put to death:

> In Dessau, eight years ago, there was one such child whom I, Dr Martin Luther, saw and touched. He was 12 years old, and in possession of his sight and senses, so that one took him to be a normal child. Yet, he did nothing but eat; indeed, he ate as much as four farmers and threshers. He ate, defecated and wet himself, and if one tried to catch hold of him, he would scream. Whenever things went

badly at home, when there was trouble, he laughed and was cheerful, but when things went well, he cried. He had these two sides to him. So I said to the prince of the institution: if I were the prince or master here, I would venture to throw this child into the river Molde, which runs through Dessau, in the hope of killing him. But the Prince Elector of Saxony who happened to be in Dessau and the prince of the institution would not go along with me in this. Then I said: 'You should have a prayer read in the Christian churches asking the Good Lord to exorcise the devil'. This happened daily in Dessau and the same dual child died there the following year. When Luther was asked why he had so advised, he replied that he believed that such dual children were no more than a bit of flesh, a *massa carnis*, since they had no soul. The devil could do such a thing, just as he corrupts people of sound reason, bodies and souls when he takes possession of their bodies so that they can no longer see, hear or feel, making them deaf, dumb and blind. In such changelings, the devil is their soul.*

Dietmut Niedecken rightly points out that the hate that burns against people with learning disabilities is fed by the sacrifices that individuals feel they have to make on their behalf for no apparent reason. Luther's attitude can be summed up as follows: anyone who does not work but nonetheless wants to eat and, in addition, behaves unreasonably, must be possessed by the devil. By resorting to the idea of the devil, the age-old utopian desire of being able to eat and drink without having to work is rejected and individuals who live out this utopia are eliminated.

But hatred for disabled people has other roots too. Ethnologists are familiar with the common practice amongst many peoples of killing newborn babies, e.g. twins or misshapen children. Ploss mentions the Spartans

who, as is well-known, threw such children into an abyss; the African Nganga and Basutos put such people to death by drowning, as did the Brazilian Botokuden; neck-breaking and strangulation were practised by the East African Wanika and Waseguha, [. . .] Noteworthy is the unanimity of Slavs or Germans in exposing or murdering such children.[†]

In his moral history of Russia Bernhard Stern wrote:

Misbirths evoke intense anxiety. They are seen as the sign of a great misfortune. Among the wonders which Russian chroniclers list ahead

* Kirchhoff, Th. (1890) *Grundriß einer Geschichte der deutschen Irrenpflege*, p. 69, Berlin [my transl.].
[†] Ploss, H. (1911) *Das Kind in Brauch und Sitte der Völker*, p. 160, Leipzig [my transl.].

of wars, epidemics and revolutions, misbirths are always mentioned. Those who are disfigured, crippled, blind, deaf or even the dumb are regarded by the people as creatures bringing calamity with them. The worst crimes perpetrated against such people frequently combine a mixture of superstition and barbaric cruelty . . . .[‡]

These examples, selected quite arbitrarily, may suffice to lend historical and ethnic support to the author's thesis that attitudes towards people with learning disabilities are driven by a death wish. The attempt to justify this attitude by saying that it is a question of the survival of the fittest, and that such people are immature, is superficial, and does not take into account that which, in the text cited above, is more hidden than explained by the use of the catchword superstition – namely, fear of what is strange and different from what we are familiar with. We do not want to understand that which we would like to kill. This is just as true for people with learning disabilities as it is for Jews, Tamils and all threatening strangers. If the impulse to murder is gradually repressed then there is little chance of achieving understanding: what has been made unconscious is formed out of the Other, namely, the phantasm through which it can finally satisfy its lust for murder. There is no way of avoiding the necessity to make conscious and to remain aware of the death wish. It is a painful process, not least because one must suffer it oneself. Niedecken's book blazes such a trail. The author takes the lead by showing us what she has observed in herself and encourages the reader to become aware of, and to name, those impulses in himself or herself which so easily thwart our understanding of people with learning disabilities. She draws on psychoanalysis in a way that is unusual, i.e. as a process that brings understanding but no new reification. Her work is cultural in the sense that she reclaims what was formerly rejected and unknown and points ahead to new possibilities.

[‡] Stern, B. (1907) *Geschichte der öffentlichen Sittlichkeit in Rußland*, p. 66f, Berlin [my transl.].

Chapter 1

'Learning Disability'[1] as an institution and the forgotten human dimension

In an institution for people with learning disabilities where I once worked, I met a boy of about 16 years old who could only utter one word. He would repeat it endlessly all day long, yet it was never possible to discern any meaning in this word that could be related to the current situation. The word was 'Papi'. He always said it with the same questioning intonation and rhythm, usually two or three times consecutively. I can remember nothing more of him than this. Sometimes it goes round in my head like a well-known tune whose meaning is both known, and yet hidden, through my own carefully forgotten past. When I think about it, it seems to me that this 'Papi, Papi?' was like a question that had been asked long ago but which had never received an answer. It was as if the young boy had once stood before a door, which he clearly felt was the door to his life; as if he had knocked and given the password but the door had remained shut. It seemed to me that since that time, this boy had not been able to say anything else but this password; he felt it was the right one, the key to his life that was inaccessible to him because no one was there whom he could call 'Papi'. 'Papi, Papi . . .' it was clear that this was no longer a name; no one was being addressed; it was simply a tune keeping alive the moment when the boy had called his father by his name and had not been heard – perhaps because he was not there or because he did not know how to answer.

It seems to me that the lives of many people with learning disabilities amount to little more than this: standing doggedly in front of a closed door, endlessly repeating a password to which no one knows the answer when it is needed. Why they remain standing in front of this door, whether it is the only door there is, whether there is something that prevents them from searching further, or whether the strength of their wish to be let in prevents other attempts from being made, are some of the questions I shall be addressing in this book. Still more important for me is the question of whether there are ways of discovering the answer that is being sought after, ways of helping them open their door. This question expresses the desperate, persistent hope that I thought I heard behind the lifelong repetition of the password 'Papi, Papi'.

Of course, this hopelessness cannot easily be brushed aside. No one is being addressed with the words 'Papi, Papi'. They are, by any reckoning, meaningless; at least they have become so. They are addressed to no one and no one is expected to answer. They have become a mere tune. How are we to find an answer to a question that is not being or is no longer being asked?

So in this single, endlessly repeated word, the boy was giving expression to the most extreme contrast between hope and hopelessness. Any chance visit to an institution catering for people with learning disabilities will bear witness to such a polarity. There may be a young girl addressing all new-comers with the same ambiguous question to which they all give the wrong answer as if, by obstinately insisting on her question, an answer might finally be forthcoming. A child may be sitting around on a bench for hours doing nothing but hitting himself (or herself) in the face with awfully repetitive monotony, and yet looks so fairy-like that if only one could one would happily send him straight to paradise. Or there may be a young man at the entrance who, with a frightening grin, zealously opens the door for all those who are leaving the ghetto into the Promised Land outside as though, were he to really make himself meek and humble, someone might one day open the door to the outside for *him*, so that having humbled himself he might be exalted.[2] The demeanour of people with learning disabilities confronts us with this contrast everywhere; similarly those who live and work with them feel torn between extreme hope and hopelessness, between the euphoria of compulsive activity and giving up in resigned indifference.

The first time I worked in an institution for people with learning disabilities, a grandiose phantasm (without which I could not have done the work at all) lay behind my euphoric attempts to save individual cases from a life of institutional misery: I would be able to help and save people where others had given up long ago. In fact, after a while in the institution, I became known as the specialist for 'people who challenged the service', but the contrast between my high-flying dreams and the slowness and laborious-ness with which the therapies made progress was hardly bearable, and the struggle which I openly waged against the resignation and indifference of many colleagues and superiors was at the same time a struggle against my own temptation to sink into indifference, which, of course, made it doubly wearing.

In institutions for people with learning disabilities, the split between euphoria and hopelessness recurs not simply as an individual phantasm but also as an enactment of the whole community. At one end of the spectrum, the old-fashioned institutions represent the extreme of death phantasms and impotence. They are ghettos we would prefer to think do not exist. Once inside, the visitor is so alarmed by the misery that hits him like a formless mass that, in order to save his skin, he hurries through in a numbed state, with his senses half shut-off, trying to get out again as quickly as possible through this door to purgatory, rapidly forgetting what he has seen, back into the daylight of normality which has been altered by the experience of this visit.

The other extreme (and there are naturally intermediate stages – progressive homes, day centres, etc.) is characterised by establishments considered to be progressive and exemplary: the latest centres for early diagnosis and intervention.[3] In contrast to the paralysing depression, indifference, lack of vision in the large establishments, these are characterised by brisk activity, lavish expenditure on equipment, a lot of trained workers and team work. The newest acquisitions are put at the service of children (not the adults, of course) in a continual effort to bring them back into the realm of approximate normality by offering them as much help, as soon as possible. There is an overwhelming compulsion to succeed; failure is unthinkable. They are monuments of hope and phantasised omnipotence, the institutionalisation of that despairing hope which I thought I heard in 'Papi, Papi . . .'. Only, what has become of this hope in places such as these?

Subsequent to a job interview in such an institution, I was taken around by the senior doctor who showed me all the nicest, best-equipped, well-lit rooms, with shining wooden floors; the stylish waiting-room full of children's toys; the corridors, whose walls displayed many photographs of the successful, intensive work going on, along which the qualified staff walked briskly and with a sense of purpose to their next task. On the way back to the office a small boy stumbled clumsily across our path with his crutches. 'My name's Jörgi,' he said with an unnaturally elevated and exaggerated voice, staring at the doctor from behind his thick glasses with wide-open, but unsmiling – in fact anxious and fleeting – eyes, 'I'm doing fi-ine!' 'Yes, Jörgi, you're always doing fine, aren't you?' replied the director in a friendly manner as he walked with a light gait past the youth who was standing in his way. As we continued he said to me: 'This is one of our children'.

'I'm doing fi-ine!' – I remembered having heard that before, on my first day in the institution. In order to pamper me, I was first placed on a 'quiet' ward for well-adjusted adult men. My task was to go for a walk with a patient who, I was promised, would cause no difficulties. 'Heinzi' was his name, and I was to hold him by his hand and take him for a walk. But why? I did not know the grounds at all whereas Heinzi had been living there for many years . . . and, taking a grown man by the hand like a toddler, well, it was embarrassing. During the walk 'Heinzi' said little. At most, he replied just once to a clumsy question I had asked, in the elevated and exaggerated voice of a child who wants to make himself the adult's favourite. From time to time, he said in the same manner and without being solicited, 'I'm doing fi-ine'. But then, out of this rosy world and, once again, unsolicited and barely articulated, came a roar, the roar of a threatening, deep, powerful, man's voice: *Heinz*. 'Heinzi' looked around him for a moment uncertainly, drew in his breath, and repeated in a whisper, 'I'm doing fi-ine!' When I asked about this afterwards, somewhat startled, I was told: 'It wasn't anything important, he does that sometimes, it doesn't mean anything'.

Yes, indeed, what has become of the hope?

The initial shock over the parallel between the two scenes makes me aware that in my presentation of it the tension between hope and hopelessness, clearly noticeable in the first account, has in the meantime subsided. The intonation of 'I'm doing fi-ine' is in both cases exactly the same: unnatural, false, grovelling, an enormous lie. The 'I want to get better' which must have been underlying it, i.e. the desire and the hope, are perverted into a meaningless and hopeless formula, since the 'doing fi-ine' leaves nothing to be desired or hoped for. The transition from desperate dependence on nothing but the unremitting repetition of hope into its opposite almost escaped me while I was writing this. And yet, in retrospect, it is already slightly visible in those phantasms in which I wanted to see the boy on the bench who was hitting himself, and the humble man at the entrance gate, liberated – 'into paradise'. If I take the image to its logical conclusion, I wanted to transport the child into death, the end of all hope, and the one who humbled himself 'would be exalted', but only, as the Bible vainly promises, at the Last Judgement, and not in life. But what have they done to me that I feel I have to transport them into the beyond by writing such phantasms?

What have 'Heinzi' and 'Jörgi' done that makes them feel that they must apologise to every man and woman they meet by saying, 'I'm doing fi-ine'? 'Jörgi', at least, seems to fear he will be punished for stumbling across our path in the corridor. In this service where one is particularly impressed by the excellent equipment and by the photographs on the corridor walls of the children in care, documenting all the activity going on there, children apologise immediately by saying, 'I'm doing fine', as if they feared they might be got rid of once and for all because their clumsiness does not fit in with the image of a centre that is running smoothly and efficiently. It is as if they have to pay for being tolerated by colluding with the cliché 'this is one of our children – and our children always do well'. How else can the fervently uttered phrase be understood than as a response to the pressure to succeed exerted by an organisation created at great expense? If you are not a success and do not integrate properly, if you are not 'doing fi-ine', the child is made to understand, you will be cast out and forgotten about forever (and so 'Jörgi' will end up where 'Heinzi' already is, in the institution – a place for purgatory and the 'final solution'.

So the extremes of hope and hopelessness, of omnipotent helping and impotent sustaining are intermingled in 'Jörgi's' and 'Heinzi's' histories, in the fear of the truth of the final outcome, i.e. being cast out and forgotten about.

'If a person is not excluded,' writes Maud Mannoni, the French psychoanalyst, then, 'he will be integrated into "normality", at whatever price –

without any questions being asked with regard to the meaning that madness or retardedness may have for some people. In this way, illness becomes institutionalised.'[4]

What does Mannoni mean here by institution? Institutions are bound by fixed systems of rules in the service of hierarchical interaction-structures that can no longer be seen in terms of their interactional meaning, but rather as naturally unmodifiable. However, this is what 'learning disability' looks like for us, too. One principle of progressive teaching on learning disability is that one should not speak of 'patients' since people with learning disabilities are not ill. The word 'patient' suggests a hierarchy – it would be better to speak of *die Geistigbehinderten*[5] as it is a question of the natural, unalterable reality of their otherness. Do such linguistic nuances really dispense with hierarchy? Hardly. What is dispensed with, however, are the terms of interactional interdependence: one cannot only *be 'geistig behindert'* but one can *become* so; and the word 'patient' signifies less 'being ill and inferior' than 'someone who is suffering', from the Latin 'patiens' = suffering. For illnesses, there are causes; *'Geistigbehindertsein'* (having a learning disability) is the direct result of some kind of organic defect that we think does not concern us. We might feel a sense of responsibility for the suffering of *'geistig behinderte'* (those who have become numbed, who have learning disabilities) but the term serves to keep this potential awareness unconscious.

In what follows, I will at times have to violate some of the well-intentioned progressive uses and abuses of language met with in the field of learning disability in order to bring certain institutionalised, warded-off experiences back into the arena of language and discussion. Indeed, the dreadfulness of the word 'Mongol'[6] is somehow much more telling and says so much more about the fate of people branded with it than the increasingly abstract and inaccessible terms that have currency today in the progressive teaching on learning disability. Who, for example, is able to make head or tail of a term like 'trisomy-21'?

'Mongol' has a very precise meaning which those of us who are 'blessed with late birth'[7] (Federal Chancellor Helmut Kohl) do not want to know too much about: it refers to what in Germany was once publicly called *lebensunwertes Leben*,[8] with all the attendant consequences. True, 'Mongols' and other 'learning disabled people' are no longer subjected to the final solution of the gas chambers; but here, too, we have simply 'come to terms' with our frightful past (whatever that means) but cannot, of course, 'overcome' it by trying to make cosmetic revisions of the official phraseology. 'Jörgi's' look expressed mortal fear, and my phantasies humanely and elegantly transported the subservient man at the entrance gate and the child on the bench who was hitting himself into the beyond. Murder is no longer committed openly but what led to the crimes of National Socialism has not lost its power because the phraseology has been revised. It persists – subliminally, imperceptibly, carefully covered up[9] – in the phantasms that dominate our thinking and feeling about 'people with learning difficulties'. We will learn more about these phantasms shortly.

One of them is contained in the following words of Bertolt Brecht, 'the womb which this crawled out of is still fertile'.[10] Bertolt Brecht tells us more than he perhaps intended; for, in his phantasy, it was a womb that gave birth to the monster-child of National Socialism. The cause of the unspeakable murders, Brecht leads us to understand, is the female sex. Like all phantasms, this one also contains a distorted truth, namely, that one of the most important sources of the collective murderous and suicidal tendencies of our Western enlightened world that culminated in Hitler's fascism is the polarity between feminine impotence and masculine omnipotence, the subjugation of women by men. Theodor W. Adorno and Max Horkheimer[11] referred to this in the *Dialectic of Enlightenment* (and their thesis has been taken up and discussed critically in feminist research).[12]

The womb gave birth to a monster and was the origin of the most monstrous guilt. Even today mothers who bear children who have learning disabilities experience themselves, at least in the initial moments of recognition, as begetters of monsters, as failures, as guilty, whereas fathers, hiding behind their work, are often content to leave them with these feelings – 'people with learning disabilities' are women's business, i.e. mothers' business. Having for hundreds or thousands of years been unable to develop their mental faculties, women have learnt in our society, where productivity is what counts first and foremost, that their children – male, if possible – are their achievement, their *raison d'être*. When, due to an impairment, a child cannot provide them with this identity, he or she has no reason to exist and they themselves have no proof of their own value, indeed, of their own right to exist (the womb is 'still' fertile: is Brecht hoping to get rid of it?) Worse still, the 'monster' child is an image of a woman's 'failure', her 'guilt', and as such it has to be hidden, swept under the carpet. When mothers – and fathers too – are confronted with the shock of the diagnosis, they often consciously feel an impulse to kill their children. This is not due to personal badness but is rather a reflex-response to the phantasm that Brecht formulated. This phantasm is probably the central motive for our attitude towards people with learning disabilities – and their mothers. It is the attribution, the projection, of our monstrous collective guilt, the unspeakable failure of our enlightened awareness, onto individuals. Just how efficiently this works and what consequences it has, we shall have to look at more closely.

The institution 'Learning Disability' is thus based on the projection of collective death wishes onto individuals. Such tendencies do not manifest themselves today as they did 45 years ago. Now it is more appropriate to speak of soul murder. 'The misfortune of the disability has to be brushed aside! No one seems to worry about the fact that we are making the child feel insecure by giving him the feeling that we would prefer he was different from the way he is.' – 'I was born with a spastic paralysis. Today, the diagnosis would certainly be "cerebral palsy" – so the boy must be treated immediately, given therapy, in order to give him every chance of rehabilitation. It does not seem to occur to anyone that I myself might not find the spastic paralysis so terrible and, therefore, do not need to be rehabilitated.'[13] People with learning disabilities are not so articulate; language is more or less inaccessible for some of them. Unlike the physically disabled person cited above, they are unable to tell us that instead of having a sense of solidarity with the child for the suffering he or she experiences in society on account of his or her disability, we tend to identify with society and its norms. We assume that the child *must* either want not to be disabled, or at least to be less disabled, before this desire is attributed to him during the process of stigmatisation. The only thing that seems to matter is adapting the child to the current dominant norm; the alternative, exclusion and death, seems all too inevitable. Faced with seeing an adult with learning difficulties brooding for long hours, still in need of diapers, and hardly able to make himself understood, who would not think about neglected toilet training, insufficient language initiation, and ask himself what this pointless suffering is for? Is this woman's life worth living at all? If we had the chance to ride a carousel with this same woman whom we regard as being unable to get anything worthwhile out of life, then we would discover how much joy and laughter and liveliness she can have while going round and round at speed – much more, in fact, than we can allow ourselves (of course, we are only riding the carousel to give 'this person' a treat!). And, anyway, why should there not be people who enjoy spending their whole life on swings and carousels?

Mannoni attributes our understandable readiness to identify with norms against people with learning difficulties to the anxiety that 'these people' arouse in us. 'The activity of carers is in every respect defensive in nature [. . .] Consequently, re-education, advice and every sort of caring activity primarily has the aim of covering up the carers' own anxiety'.[14] I would add that it is not only the anxiety of carers but the anxiety of each and every one of us which is acted out by those who work with people who have learning difficulties. But what is the anxiety about?

First, it would seem to be anxiety that we may ourselves become failures if we get involved with the 'failures' in our society. This is suggested by the phrase 'these people'. Particular emphasis is laid on the demonstrative pronoun 'these', thereby deflecting our attention away from the persons themselves, whom we consider to be so different from us and with whom we have very little in common except our human birth. The rest of us who are, so to speak, 'normal', get by in life on our own and are relatively productive thus ensuring our survival in society. All of which, of course, is impossible for 'these people'. They are visibly dependent and, consequently, come across as being immature. Our relations with them are determined by difference, or rather, by our *emphasising* this difference which must be preserved at any price. I once had the experience on a ward of seeing a young woman with a learning disability being forbidden to smoke by the carers who themselves were smoking. Obviously, the fact that she was smoking meant the difference between 'this woman' and them had become negligible to a threatening degree. The young woman reacted with depression – and so really became a 'typically' dependent person with learning disabilities.

'These people' are not like us: this statement serves to keep people with learning disabilities at arm's length – rather like bizarre objects which we observe from a safe distance with scientific or charitable interest, whose peculiar ways of expressing themselves either amuse or frighten us. By mimicking or pitying them, we bolster the sense of our own normality and ordinariness. For us they are like lepers whom we keep at a distance with such phrases or tokens of pity. Sometimes, they are referred to as 'these pitiable people'. We only approach 'these people', if at all, under safe and hygienic conditions, in an aseptic atmosphere, without feelings, in order to protect ourselves against the danger of contamination.

Fear of contamination? The prejudice that learning disability is infectious is surely – so we like to think – a thing of the past for enlightened people. Without doubt there are still people who peddle such old superstitions: for example, that learning disability is contagious or God's punishment for the 'sins' of the parents and so on. Such horror stories have, however, long been discredited. Anyone who still clings to them today is beyond help. Admittedly, enlightened people also use this defence revealing their latent fear of contamination. We are very careful to erect barriers around ourselves and the effort and energy invested to this end is indicative of the intensity of the underlying anxiety.

'These people' – an expression, then, revealing underlying anxieties – are lacking something which is essential for us because it enables us to struggle for our survival in society, that is, physical and mental integrity and the ability to function fully. This makes them dependent which is a threatening – indeed, as recent history shows, a life-threatening situation. They are abandoned to the mercy of the environment (i.e. our world) which is something we prefer to ignore because it touches too much upon our own underlying anxieties of failing, of not being able to stand on our own two feet, of becoming dependent ourselves, of being at the mercy of a rather merciless world, of being pawns in a system that classifies people according to their utility in the production chain.

The defence of emphasising difference is also based on the anxiety of falling through the sieve of normality, of seeming different by social stan-dards from 'the perfectly normal person of average size' (Bertolt Brecht), and of not belonging. Fear of standing out and, therefore, of dropping out.

On the other hand, we would very much like to be something special, something better; and, of course, we are 'something better' than 'these people'.

What is emphasised about the so-called difference of people who have learning disabilities is always their 'childishness'. 'These people', it is said, are like 'eternal children'. Even today, in some institutions adult patients are still referred to as 'children', 'girls' and 'boys'. Parents often feel responsible for their children who have learning disabilities even when the latter are well into their adult life; it is as though they were still small children.

Now adults with learning difficulties often do act in a way that is redolent of infantile behaviour. Some do not want to be alone, clinging to their carers, or they want to drink 'inordinate' quantities; some like smearing, splashing and playing around with materials which normally have other functions for us; some experience towering anger and are unable to suppress it to conform with adult conventions of politeness; some are sexually exhibitionist in a way that is embarrassing for the rest of us who have learnt in early childhood to hide our pleasure in our own bodies under clothes. In short, people with learning difficulties seem to represent everything that is unruly, impulsive and excessive in ourselves which we have had to learn to keep under control in order to manage adequately in life. It is as if they embodied our unbridled drives. At the same time they are the spectre of the punishment we fear if we were to get more in touch with our own drives and infantile needs of being helpless and dependent. We are thus reluctant to be reminded of our own infantile needs which have remained unsatisfied along the way and we have to protect ourselves against 'contamination' by employing selected or reactivated defences.

Obviously we have not succeeded completely in giving up childhood needs for unconditional love, immediate satisfaction of impulses and constant holding. True, these needs seem unrealistic, 'they are not adapted to this world', but it is precisely for this reason that even with our reality-oriented minds we are unable to be free of them. They are the forgotten human dimension in ourselves and we encounter them again in the aura surrounding 'people with learning disabilities'. The primary function of the institution 'Learning Disability' is, therefore, to warn us to renounce those early longings once and for all.

Along with this demarcation there is the attempt to make people with learning disabilities fit in with our normative existence so that they no longer embody the repressed longings in ourselves and challenge our self-control. This implies that the institution 'Learning Disability' fulfils a second function as well: what we are no longer able to accept and experience in ourselves, we recognise in them but in the form of behavioural disorder, a refusal to accept the norm, something needing to be treated. In our dealings with them we repeat the defensive struggles that we had to make early on in our lives for our own sense of belonging. Insofar as people with learning disabilities serve as a projection screen for our own wish to deny ourselves ubiquitous and normal needs, the theatre of our own defensive struggle is displaced outside ourselves. It is thus less dangerous and its unquestioned continuity, from which we all suffer, is thereby ensured.

The institution 'Learning Disability' imposes itself through 'institutional counter-transference' to employ Jürgen Trapp's term.[15] In psychotherapy, counter-transference refers to the therapist's responses to the patient's interactions. When it is understood and mirrored, counter-transference is the means by which rigid psychic structures are loosened. By taking on the role assigned to him (or her) and in line with his own institutional therapy defences,[16] a therapist may, if he is inexperienced or lacks sufficient understanding, collude with the patient's acting out, thereby repeating the latter's early traumatic experiences. Here is an example.

Six-year-old Andy is showing symptoms of acute sickness and refuses to eat anything other than spotlessly white noodles and chocolate. Consequently, the centre he is at sets out to achieve the specific goal of developing healthy 'eating habits'. Behind the attempt to coerce the child into behaving normally there is a wish not to have to put up with his refusal to do what we all learnt to do long ago, i.e. to eat what is put on the table, both in the literal and, especially, in the figurative sense. This wish is so strong that the issue as to why Andy prefers such unhealthy food to the enforced healthy diet is not addressed at all. The key to understanding this is not difficult to find. Andy's father, a high-ranking employee, with refined manners, who only wears pin-striped (noodle-striped) suits, is known to be unable to tolerate disorder and dirt any more than his son can tolerate a blemish on his white noodles. On one occasion when Andy was sitting at the lunch table with his hands still slightly dirty from playing, the father threw up in disgust. It is hardly surprising then that the child tries desperately to be just as clean as his father by resorting to magic rituals – eating spotlessly clean noodles. His liking for chocolate, clearly a sort of dirty, faecal equivalent that his father approves of, is a substitute for his infantile love of 'dirt', which his father finds intolerable, and his delight in making messes, and is also an attempt to win his father's approval.

It is not only that the aim of the therapy is to get rid of his symptoms and the meaning behind them but also that the therapeutic staff turn the meaning of them against him. He is forced – he cannot understand it in any other way – to dirty himself, to be revolting, to 'make his father sick'. Now his liking for spotlessly white noodles can be understood as an attempt to incorporate his father in order to become clean and strong like him. So the pressure to eat different food must seem to him like an order: you are to remain a revolting, dirty and unacceptable child forever. The treatment aim is thereby reversed. The carers' defensiveness corresponds to what the child has always expected. Together they enact his interactional stance – something about me is wrong and dirty and is completely out of step with this world – not with the help of the father's professionally determined behaviour patterns but their own. Or, in psychoanalytic terms, the carers are acting out their counter-transference responses to Andy, without being aware of what the child is triggering in them and without recognising the repetition involved in the enactment.

In psychoanalysis repetition compulsion and acting out have become common terms describing a phenomenon that is by no means only valid for people with learning disabilities. When something triggers the unconscious conflicts and traumas of our childhood again, we continually re-enact them in our environment. Unconscious feelings and longings are transferred onto others who generally respond to them unconsciously with counter-transference. The latter is a compromise between the behaviour corresponding to the scenario in question and their own behavioural capacities to which we in turn react with counter-transference. The alternative to this often painful repetition is a change of strategy, i.e. the joint attempt of the partners of the interaction to agree on finding other ways of satisfying desires in such enactments and to develop negotiated alternatives. The attempt must be a shared one for it is much more difficult to break free from compulsive repetition when it always recurs in an identical way. This is particularly true when specific forms of counter-transference become institutionalised in role patterns, as is often the case in the institution 'Learning Disability'. Care, diagnosis, therapy, educative measures all offer role patterns – and I will demonstrate this in the following chapters – by means of which, what appears to be compulsive and natural to the condition of 'learning disability' is in fact created. Institutional counter-transference refers to all those ways of reacting which are institutionally determined responses to what is incongruent, incommensurable and difficult to integrate in the behaviour of those in care.

This is perhaps a good moment to make a brief digression on the theoretical assumptions underlying my work. They are derived from psychoanalytic interaction theory as developed by Alfred Lorenzer,[17] as well as the theory of the social production of unconsciousness described in Mario Erdheim's (1982) book with this title. In his books on materialistic socialisation theory, Lorenzer enables us to get away from taking a one-sided view of child development, either from the social perspective, or from the perspective of organic determination, and to understand the interface between them. In the early interaction between the child and his primary carer, the care-taking arrangements are affected by both the child's organically pre-structured drives as well as by social factors and, through the development of 'specific interaction forms', are reduced to a formula that is meaningful and practical for *this particular* child in *this particular* environment. In these interaction forms, the child's innate biological needs are registered in the gestural form that their specific social realisation acquires. If development proceeds smoothly, the child can repeatedly experiment with them, modify them, and differentiate them by playing with other children who are growing up with him. Lorenzer also describes[18] the possibility of damaged interaction forms which are of particular concern to us since interaction theory allows us to take a view of learning disability which does not simply view it as a consequence of organic damage. From this perspective, it seems much more like the product of a specific process of socialisation between a child with specific physical impairments and an environment that relates to him in a specifically pathogenic way. I have sometimes been reproached for over-emphasising the so-called environmental factor whilst denying organic factors. If this present study were to be understood in this way, it would be a misunderstanding. Understanding learning disability as a product does not mean denying reality but rather learning to see organic reality as being interwoven in a complex way with social factors, instead of seeing it as ineluctable biological fate.

The production of damaged interaction forms is concomitant with unconsciousness. Successful interaction products are characterised by the fact that, at any given time, they can be consciously employed as symbols and used playfully and thoughtfully by the subject in his encounter with the world, whereas damaged interaction forms assert themselves behind the subject's back and, not infrequently, against his conscious will in a seemingly compulsive manner. We are indebted to Erdheim for pointing out that such compulsive unconscious activity is not just a matter of individual eccentricity but is systematised, and that this system imposes itself in the form of social unconsciousness. It is already clear from Lorenzer's description that damaged interaction forms not only make one ill but also create a critical potential that may be useful in drawing attention to the social conditioning of damaged subjectivity. Erdheim shows how, in puberty and adolescence, psychical structures of early childhood are reactivated and become virulent due to this critical potential. Institutions, and particularly schools, aim to defuse and channel this potential that is directed against them in ways that are socially acceptable. In institutions, there is a conflict between unsatisfied longings that are breaking out anew and specific forms of counter-transference which require the definitive rejection of that which cannot be integrated. What Erdheim has described as the adolescent growth spurt is not experienced by people with learning disabilities which, of course, does not mean that the latter do not experience puberty. This phase does not contain for them the potential for change that it involves for other young people; their development has already been arrested much earlier at the level of 'learning disability'. The institutionalisation of 'learning disability' takes place considerably earlier, during a stage which Erdheim, in one of his lectures, compared with adolescence, i.e. during the early mother–infant relationship. This stage is also characterised by a shaking up of well-established defence structures, by instability and great critical potential. Through its institutions society also intervenes in ways designed to defuse and channel this energy. One of the aims of this book is to promote the liberation and activation of the critical potential that is dammed up or extinguished by the institution 'Learning Disability'.

The institution 'Learning Disability' is organised on three levels. Nobody is born with learning disabilities, even if it is common to hear people speaking of 'infants with learning disabilities'; it is not possible to speak of mental differentiation with newborn infants. As with every aspect of mental development, learning disability is constituted first of all in the relationship between the infant with its specific capacities and limitations and the mother (child-rearing fathers are naturally included). In this relationship the environmental attitude towards the mother and infant is formative in as far as it supports them or neglects them.

Diagnoses, social phantasms about 'learning disability', as well as institutionalised techniques of rehabilitation and integration, function as organisers of the institution 'Learning Disability'. Diagnosis has the role of concretising self–other perceptions in the early mother–infant relationship. At the same time, the exoneration from guilt it offers the mother under certain circumstances allows the real guilt, namely, the continuing existence of society's murderous tendencies to be made unconscious on a social level and to be off-loaded onto the mother. Secondly, the phantasms – a conglomeration of societal attitudes to 'learning disability' which are primarily conveyed by the mother – determine the child's development. I must point out that this is not, as one would like to believe, the mother's personal problem, however much these phantasms become fused in her unconscious with neurotic attitudes to what seem to be personal phantasies.* The third organising factor, new treatment technologies, helps to bring better organisation into the reality of those receiving therapy, as diagnoses and phantasms show.

Anyone who tries to free themselves from institutional counter-transference and to get away from the prefabricated images of our relations with people with learning disabilities, who respects their wishes and habits, trusts and affirms their own initiatives and freedom of decision, supporting them in their way of doing things instead of deciding for them, is often faced with insuperable difficulties. Common defensive mechanisms can no longer be used to cope with threatening counter-transference feelings. The capacity to identify with people with learning disabilities, which is vital if we want to understand and make contact with them, triggers and stirs up all the anxieties which were hitherto bound by the institution

---

* Mannoni speaks of 'motherly phantasms' – I myself prefer for the reasons I have already stated to speak of 'social phantasms'.

'Learning Disability'. Excessive anxiety of failing, of being overwhelmed, of being devoured by the extreme helplessness, neediness and distress of others are states against which the institutional caring roles no longer provide protection. In the workplace, where colleagues and superiors often react with mistrust or even disapproval, there is often good reason to be afraid of failing or of being dismissed.

Some form of defence or drawing of boundaries is necessary in order to fend against this whirlwind of feelings which are thus released. And unfortunately, here, too, institutional counter-transference has ready-made roles into which it steers 'deserters'[19] – without their noticing it – in order to defuse their resistance to societal soul murder.

Here is another clinical vignette. Janice is taking care of Jenny, a seriously depressed young woman in an English institution for people with learning disabilities. In addition to the weekly music therapy sessions, she fetches her for walks, accompanies her to the library and so on. Jenny is visibly flourishing, has started speaking and eating again (which she had largely given up) but is now beginning to bombard Janice with all her long-buried desires. Things begin to go wrong when, several times a day, outside the agreed times, she starts looking for Janice in the music therapy room and responds with vehement outbursts of despair and anger when Janice says she has no time. In the end, Janice does not know what else to do but to break off the relationship with Jenny.

In retrospect, Janice believes that given the unbearable conditions in the institution, Jenny had sensed that she was afraid she would not be able to meet her needs permanently and, in particular, had sensed her constant latent withdrawal due to this anxiety. She also thought Jenny sensed that she felt guilty about this latent withdrawal and was over-taxing her capacities in the therapeutic and caring work. Consequently she felt Jenny was reacting with intense anxieties of loss and clinging so that what was to prove a very difficult and destructive rupture for both of them, but particularly for Jenny, now seemed unavoidable.

When I started working as a music therapist, I tended to believe that it was only really possible to help autistic children. (I soon noticed, moreover, that I was not the only one to think this and that the small number of children there who were diagnosed as autistic were often tied up in multifarious therapeutic activities although there was a general lack of therapy places, which I found puzzling.) So I took ten-year-old Thomas into therapy. It took quite a long time for us to establish contact and I was very happy when we managed to do so. However, Thomas was brought to one of the next sessions wearing an epileptic's helmet. I had never seen one before and I felt numbed with fear. Of course, I knew that Thomas suffered from epilepsy, but since this fact was likely to frighten me and, above all, to weaken my almost magical sense of hope regarding the diagnosis 'autistic', I had denied it as much as possible up till then. The helmet suddenly broke through my defensive denial and from then on my anxiety that he might have a fit dominated everything. It is not difficult to understand why Thomas allowed no more contact. Soon after that I was only too ready to break off the therapy on the grounds that it was 'leading nowhere' – in reality, of course, it was because I could not stand the anxiety. It is when realities that hitherto have been denied by the therapist force themselves upon him or her with alarming intensity, when patients make the whole extent of their needs felt, that relationships are broken off. Consequently, the attempt to break away from well-worn paths ultimately only leads to a new form of familiar miseries; the institution 'Learning Disability' once again gains the upper hand just when its authority is beginning to be challenged.

Others are more prudent, preferring only to get involved in relationships where they feel reasonably safe. For example, Rezia looks at me slightly reproachfully when I speak of 'Mongols' – I should not be using such an unpleasant word. I sense that there is something defensive about this. Indeed, as I read through Rezia's reports (she has regular play sessions with a girl M. whom we will get to know in the section 'Little Mongols' in Chapter 4), it strikes me that although, generally speaking, she responds to M. lovingly and affectionately, at times, she thoroughly misinterprets, dismisses or totally ignores M.'s very pressing and cryptic questions about being a 'Mongol'. Clearly, to be able to do her work Rezia has to deny the most threatening aspect of the child's reality. Without this denial, her own anxieties of failure and not belonging would break through, and so she now leaves M. to cope with this question alone. For M., however, this defence means that the question that concerns her most urgently and threatens her most, that is, her identity in this world, not only remains unanswered but can no longer even be asked.

Once again, institutional counter-transference catches up with the 'deserter'. Omnipotence and warded-off helplessness are present in all these examples; they are just not organised in the same way as standard defences. Deserters want to do something completely different, they want to help in situations which others do not want to deal with, and, in so doing, want to show that they are different, less dependent. So they look for an unusually gifted person with learning disabilities like Jenny who has a fascinating diagnosis and hope to achieve a kind of magic cure demonstrating that they were right in spite of all expectations to the contrary. The others look after those who can be induced to collude with their denial of the diagnosis. Omnipotent phantasies of this kind are of course unavoidable for the deserters and are not simply to be dismissed as personal problems. They are the counterpart to the power of the institution 'Learning Disability', which they are not responsible for, but for which they must nonetheless take responsibility if they want their critique to carry weight. Deserters draw on these grandiose phantasies for the courage and energy needed to take a stand against the general indifference to misfortune, and to stand up for the despised and rejected. They are a substitute for the much-needed solidarity from the environment that is often lacking whenever there is an attempt to break away from the paths of conformity; and, given the institutional pressure of institutions and homes, they tend to make it difficult, if not impossible, for others to show solidarity. By trying to do things differently, deserters run the risk of being isolated by management and others who feel their institutionally established defences are being challenged. Owing to anxiety, they may become know-alls, arrogant, judgemental and lacking in understanding. Instead of emphasising the difference between themselves and people with learning disabilities, they now stress the difference that exists between them and the 'old-fashioned' management; the latter, mobilised by anxieties of failure and guilt, then react by excluding them. Deserters often exhaust themselves so much in such battles that they hardly have any strength left for their work. They are not aware that this is also a means of avoiding the demands patients make on them, for they are convinced their struggle is justified. If this comes up for discussion, for example, in a supervision session, then they will tend to react with strong feelings of guilt, which are difficult to work through.

'Voluntary' resignation due to exhaustion is often the depressing outcome of an attempt to improve the lot of people with learning disabilities single-handed. Furthermore, the tense situation between the supporters and detractors of institutional counter-transference can very easily lead to resignations in which the outsider's own wish to escape clearly plays a part.

Claudia, who had for some time been doing auxiliary work in a residential home, applied for a post that had recently become available. During the application process, she adopted a hard and critical attitude, making herself so unpopular with the permanent staff that they opposed her application and struck her off the list of auxiliary helpers, even though this meant being understaffed and having more work to do themselves.

Martin hoped to continue working in an institution after finishing his 'community service'.[20] But while his application was under consideration, he ruined his chances by acting heroically. He attended a meeting as a declared member of a working group. This group had so far remained anonymous, for good reasons: they seriously criticised, albeit justifiably, the institution's management. As a result, of course, his services as an auxiliary worker were no longer required.

It is clear that provoking dismissals in this way serves to relieve the persons concerned from guilt feelings. The confrontation between their idealistic phantasies of saving others and the corresponding reality is not the main factor in their failure; rather, it is the 'malevolent' institution or home that has stood in their way and turned them down.

Now, if deserters are forced to face up to the failure of their attempt to break away, it will be seen that behind the guilt feelings plaguing them, lie unconscious grandiose phantasies. They phantasise that they are lone heroes and saviours who should answer for, and collectively prevent, enacted soul murder. At the same time, the guilt feelings point to universal death wishes. During periods when my work seemed to be going nowhere, I often phantasised that my patient had died – it would be better for him since he is only suffering anyway, I tried to convince myself, unable to admit that I wanted him to die because I hated him for confronting me with my own real limitations. When I was then troubled by guilt feelings, I often first tried to explain them superficially, telling myself that I did not have enough time or understanding. It is always painful and embarrassing to catch oneself sharing societal tendencies one would like to fight against. Nevertheless, it is only through a process of painful recognition, and by taking responsibility for what is inexcusable, that we can achieve a new line of defence that is not determined by the institution 'Learning Disability'.

Anyone who respects people with learning disabilities and stands up for them is constantly obliged to come to terms with the shameful and anxiety-producing feelings that the encounter with them triggers. This cannot be done successfully alone. Lone fighters become deserters and are thus integrated into the institution 'Learning Disability'. Collective guilt can only be resolved collectively, through solidarity.

My aim in writing this book is to draw attention to the nameless suffering of people with learning difficulties in the hope of putting an end to their isolation and, at least, of establishing a collective sense of responsibility in its place. I do not have decades of experience to draw on; consequently, my study can be little more than an outline for an eventual alternative approach to working with people who have learning disabilities. It should be regarded as a beginner's statement that will need developing both in theory and in practice.

The act of writing itself releases considerable feelings of anxiety, anger and guilt in me. This cannot be denied and I do not wish to do so. On the contrary, I see it as an indication of how we all participate in what I call the institution 'Learning Disability'. Allowing myself to be moved by the predicament of people with learning disabilities in our world and trying to communicate this concern, is the only way I can hope to avoid misusing them for therapeutic or research purposes. On the contrary, I wish to take them very seriously and let them discover their own needs. Anything else would simply be putting up new wallpaper in a dilapidated house.

This is, then, a passionate and committed book – a sad, but also a hopeful book. I very much hope that I can articulate this commitment in a convincing way and that my enthusiasm may be catching.

Chapter 2

The interface between institution and fate

Diagnosis as a Trojan horse: guilt-exonerating but equally a handicapping label

What is meant by learning disability? This seems an easy question to answer, but when we look at it more closely it is surprisingly difficult. It is usually evaluated in terms of impaired intellectual capacity. However, I have known young people who attended secondary school although they were considered by everyone around to have learning disabilities. On the other hand, I have also known children and young people whose school performance would not have been good enough even for a special school for those with learning disabilities, but whose eyes shone with such intelligence that specialists diagnosed them with little hesitation as 'school refusers', and a transfer to a special school was avoided. Equally, I have known children at a special school who seemed to be completely empty-headed but who were able in the presence of their mothers to do their homework at the level required by a normal primary school.

The diagnosis that doctors, psychologists and even teachers make is only superficially determined by the impairment of performance. It is merely taken as an indication of a suspected or obvious organic 'defect', awaiting medical corroboration. There are many such 'defects' and organic impairments: chromosome abnormalities (the most well-known is 'trisomy-21' or 'Down's syndrome'); hydrocephaly; or metabolic disturbances which, if not treated, or treated too late, can lead to brain damage (many metabolic illnesses are untreatable to date and lead to awful illnesses where deterioration is progressive); various more or less unspecified forms of brain damage (due to oxygen starvation, brain traumas, encephalitis, infections contracted in the womb); and lastly, inherited genetic damage. Such organic impairments are assumed to be the cause of what appears to be learning disability.

By far the most frequent diagnosis is at the same time the vaguest: 'mild, moderate and severe learning disability', probably resulting from 'brain damage of unknown causes in infancy'. In such cases it is only retrospectively – after the child's disability has been noticed – that an assumed oxygen starvation at birth, an unnoticed encephalitis, or something vague of this kind, is held to be responsible for what is often only presumed to be brain damage: a very uncertain diagnosis made primarily for want of knowing what else to call it. This vagueness is what makes it controversial. In their book *Schwachsinn unklarer Genese* the authors[1] present a long list of arguments challenging the assumption that perinatal brain damage can have such grave consequences for mental development: for instance, the developing child's brain capacity for compensation, the relatively large tolerance for conditions of perinatal oxygen starvation etc. According to the authors' alternative thesis, in most cases involving unspecified 'debility of uncertain causes', there exists an early childhood psychosis, probably a consequence of hereditary damage. The authors make this assumption because there is a high incidence of near-psychotic or psychotic disturbances in these children's families.

Certainly, this alternative thesis that 'debility of unknown causes' can generally be traced back to hereditary damage is also founded on rather doubtful arguments. For instance, the social causes of learning disability, which are regarded by the authors as a mild form of early childhood psychosis, are seen as being of secondary importance; moreover, the psychosocial burden of children who grow up in a family with one or more severely mentally disturbed members does not strike them as worthy of mention. The authors' argument is all the more problematic in that there are clear racist undertones: for instance, the view that learning disability which, according to statistics, is found predominantly in families with low social status and in fringe groups is the result of hereditary damage, implies that low social status is a consequence of 'inferior genes' or, at least, is often related to it.

In the large majority of cases of learning disability it is unclear which organic conditions can be said to be responsible for the disability. As I will endeavour to show, this is not due to a lack of diagnostic possibilities but rather to a misunderstanding concerning the validity of diagnoses generally. While on the one hand the diagnosis 'learning disability' is based on demonstrable as well as only presumed organic facts, which are viewed as causal, on the other, it relies on the observed mental and psychic structure of those diagnosed. When organic findings and learning disability coincide, then it is often said that the child had learning disabilities from birth. But no child, however severely organically damaged it may be, is born with learning disabilities. Even a child with Down's syndrome, or one adversely affected by German measles, or a child with an inherited disease, first has to develop psychically, albeit under difficult circumstances. The general assumption that organic defect is the ineluctable cause of a learning disability is based on making a direct correlation between diagnosis and prognosis. However, as the controversy between brain specialists and geneticists indicates, this correlation cannot be proved and is merely assumed – an assumption that has unfortunate consequences.

In his article 'Geistige Behinderung – Formierungsprozesse und Akte der Gegenwehr',[2] Johannes Elbert outlined a theory of the emerging 'handicapped self' which does not view diagnosis in the usual way as an observation of an unalterable state of affairs but rather as an observation of the basic conditions of a development involving learning disability – a provocative thesis. 'The pronouncement of a diagnosis and prognosis,' he writes, 'constitutes the key moment in the formation of learning disability for [. . .] it abruptly disrupts the reciprocal relationship between the mother and her child. This disastrous situation now forms the starting point of the specific process of the socialisation of people with learning disabilities,[3] which is determined by the prognosis.'

In a 'functional' society such as ours, oriented towards 'achievement,' it is inevitable that for parents, the prospect that 'my child will not be fully functional' signifies illness, trauma, and the cruel dashing of their hopes and wishes. 'On days when medical and psychiatric findings, on the one hand, and your own conviction on the other, leave you in no doubt that your child is "stupid", your world collapses [. . .] you put a coat of armour around your broken heart [. . .] disappointments, the child's lack of responsiveness, spoilt family projects, all this kills your spontaneous motherliness.'[4] This aptly describes the catastrophic situation Elbert refers to.

However, diagnosis is not always the starting point of the process. Mothers often have to do the rounds from one paediatrician or specialist to another in an effort to get someone to pronounce a diagnosis at all, and in most cases are then quite frankly relieved that their anxiety about their child has at last been given a name. The diagnosis is then experienced as a prop, something tangible that provides structure in the chaos of their anxiety and despair, enabling them to seek help, and also as a kind of statement exonerating them from 'guilt' for their child's difficulties.

The following two statements by mothers, which are by no means unusual, appear to contradict Elbert's thesis: 'I am for letting the parents know as soon as possible if a disability is suspected. It is simply irresponsible to leave parents to cope by themselves for years in a state of uncertainty and doubt. This wasted energy should be used to help the child. At the time, the truth may seem harsh and brutal, but on the other hand time has been gained to prepare oneself for life ahead with a handicapped child and to find ways of managing conflict positively.'[5] The second is: 'It was only when an objective disability was confirmed that I managed to get out of a numbed emotional relationship to my child and to start actively building a positive one.'[6]

Here are some scenes from the book . . . *und halte dich an meiner Hand*.[7] Markus was twelve months old, had given up his diapers only a week before and to our delight had begun to crawl. And then, one evening, I found him in his cot gasping and convulsing. Everything was convulsing, arms, legs, eyelids, mouth, his whole face. I was petrified with fright and anxiety.

By the time our doctor arrived, Markus had stopped convulsing and was unconscious; his arms and legs were limp. It was around midnight when we got him to the University clinic and the doctor said, 'If he pulls through, you must be prepared for total idiocy.'[8] Let us try for a moment to put ourselves in these parents' shoes. It was their first child, so they were very anxious. They knew his life was in danger and were totally confused and at a loss. Naturally, under the circumstances, they clung to the doctor's every word. They saw him as being the only person who could eventually relieve their anxiety. Here was a situation in which they were highly sensitive to every word which was uttered, where their last hopes depended on what the doctor said – a doctor in whom they now had to trust unconditionally since he was the specialist with their child's life in his hands – and the doctor, himself stressed by their panic and expectations, told them: 'If he pulls through, you must be prepared for total idiocy.' The parents were left to cope with this information by themselves. Their child remained in hospital while they themselves were worrying if he was going to survive at all; and they had more time on their hands than was healthy to digest the terrible information which they had to accept as the truth (for where would they muster the strength from now to question the competence of the doctor on whom their child's survival depended totally?). Once the child had got over the shock of his severe convulsions (in other cases, birth, illness, accident, operation or body pains) and come through all these traumatic life experiences, he had to face being welcomed at home by parents whose energies and confidence had been seriously undermined and who were therefore unable to help him work through the anxiety, loneliness and pain he had gone through – something that was essential if he was to recover from the trauma. Instead, he was welcomed by parents who themselves had not recovered from the shock, who had been tortured day and night with the 'truth' of the diagnosis and who now, utterly exhausted and anxiety-ridden, could not help reading into every sign of anomaly confirmation of how right the doctor must have been. Every such 'sign' drives them deeper into accepting with resignation the fatal diagnosis/prognosis but, alas, the child, who is in a state of severe shock, cannot help giving such 'signs'. In this way a 'truth' is confirmed which is no truth at all, since forecasts of this kind cannot be made with such authority. However, as a result of the destructive interplay of the effect of shock with the prognosis, such forecasts can come to have an aura of truth if the parents are unable to find the strength to challenge this pseudo-authority. This is approximately how the catastrophic scene can be pictured. The image may seem over-dramatised. If we continue to follow Müller-Garnn's description, then it is clear that the trauma of the diagnosis had a destructive effect for years to come, which can only be understood if one takes this dramatic start to life into account. As expected, Markus turned out to have serious learning disabilities and was unable to speak. In addition, as a small child, he already showed signs of behavioural difficulties: for example, he would run off at every opportunity, loved opening and closing doors, had an excessive interest in pieces of thread, strips of torn cloth and similar things; and sometimes he even attacked his mother physically. The mother-author describes all this as if they were typical symptoms of 'total idiocy'. What she does not realise is that all these preferences and peculiar habits have a common theme: the creation and destruction of links and relationships. This is understandable since the diagnosis 'suffers from learning disabilities, total idiocy' implies that the child's doings cannot be expected to have any meaning – for how can a 'total idiot' be said to act meaningfully? However, when the parents are prevented by the diagnosis from understanding the potential meanings in such symptomatic behaviour, with the result that the child no longer can have the experience of being understood, any eventual development from symptomatic to symbolic expression is made harder or blocked altogether. Such a development is made all the more difficult for him since he himself has to learn how to cope with the organic defect.

The author also tells us in her book what may have led to her son's intense interest in links and their opposite – running off, tearing things, shutting doors, and so on. Namely, that Markus was the 'soft touch' with which she had induced her reluctant friend into the marriage she had long been hoping for and that after a difficult start the couple had enjoyed an increasingly harmonious married life by mutually caring for their son. For the parents, it was their little disabled son that united them. This appears to have been the unconscious phantasy that allowed the parents to avoid working through the shock caused by the child's severe convulsions and the diagnosis. Instead, it encapsulated it, enabling them to cope with their difficult task.

The diagnosis thus actually became a handicapping definition for the parents in their relationship to their son, coming between their perception and recognition like a screen. Owing to their child's life-threatening situation, the delayed effect of a shock had not been worked through because no one had the idea that in such a hopeless situation the parents might need help too. Ultimately, they were the ones who should have helped their child overcome the trauma of his severe epileptic fits.

Of course, the handicapping function of the diagnosis is not absolute. The child finds its space, and contradictions arise which are apt to arouse both doubt and hope in the parents.

'Now we had to teach Markus,' says the mother, 'how to hold a drumstick in his hand and to make sounds on the xylophone with it. As has already been said, for a person with severe learning disabilities, doing two things consecutively, one after the other, is virtually impossible. To our delight, Markus got the hang of it after a while and managed to play a rhythmical ding-dong on the instrument.'[9]

Two pages earlier, the mother describes a game Markus played with the family dog in which the boy was able to do several things consecutively perfectly well without his mother teaching him, thereby showing that for someone diagnosed as being a 'total idiot', he possessed a remarkable degree of empathy.

'Tobby (the dog) had run off with his "favourite" long strip of cloth. Markus ran after Tobby trying to get it back but with no success. Then he picked up an old bathrobe girdle that happened to be lying there in the garden and dangled it in front of Tobby's nose like bait. Tobby snatched at it while letting go of Markus' strip of cloth. Markus bent down (not quickly, but just like anyone might have done) to pick it up. But Tobby beat him to it. The whole scene was repeated once more with Tobby getting there first at the last moment. But then Markus did something clever: once again, he held up the long girdle as a decoy but this time he tugged on it a bit, not letting go until he had recovered his strip of cloth.'[10] That Markus needed a long time to learn how to play the xylophone can clearly not be explained by a lack of intellectual capacity when we know he is capable of much more complex actions. It is more reasonable to suppose that he set greater store by recovering his strip of cloth than by making sounds on his xylophone. Moreover, it must have been important that the dog, at least, did not assume that 'doing two things in a row' was beyond Markus, but rather regarded him as a serious adversary.

The mother probably noticed the contradiction, too, which may have led her to doubt the diagnosis. But doubt is unbearable insofar as it is likely to bring back the encapsulated shock of the diagnosis as well as all the despair, anxiety and hope against which the statement 'this task is beyond the capacities of a person with severe learning disabilities' represents a bulwark. The mother has to be able to protect herself against these feelings, and the only authority capable of offering protection is clearly that which so omnisciently predicted the state of 'total idiocy'. If the doctor already 'knew' then, he must also know now how to integrate this insecurity with the phantasmatic encapsulation of the wound that has not been healed. So doubts can be undermined and rendered ineffective by ever-changing definitions. The author quotes from a lecture given by a Viennese paediatrician:

A paediatrician reported amongst other things that 'all children with brain damage have four axial symptoms in common'. [. . .]
These children are clever.
To achieve their aims, the children develop such a degree of finesse that one is constantly tempted to attribute it to intelligence, although it is nothing of the kind.
The doctor recounted that he had children in his home who could not manage steps by themselves but who could clamber over chairs and tables if they wanted to get some chocolate in the tall kitchen cupboard. He had children who were unable to use cutlery for eating but who could tune into the *right radio station* at exactly the *right time* if they were expecting a programme to play *their* kind of music. [. . .]

> From my experience of Markus I could recognise all four axial symptoms. I was now able to understand better some aspects of his behaviour and to assess them more objectively.[11]

Why is this not considered as intelligence? Is it because intelligence is only what corresponds to *our* goals? *Why* 'these people' clearly invest less interest in our goals is a question that is not asked but dismissed by means of a circular argument alluding to learning disability. On account of its perplexing illogicality, the prejudice is dressed up as 'objective' medical theory and has to be learned by heart as a 'third axial symptom'. Backed up by such definitions the diagnosis is protected against any conflicting observations that might put its validity in doubt. The frequently observed phenomenon, which Elbert also refers to in his important essay, that in order to achieve their goals, people with learning disabilities are able to mobilise energies and intelligence to an extent that far exceeds diagnostic and prognostic expectations is, since it is undeniable, simply incorporated as a typical symptom into the diagnostic bias. In any case, asking *why* is no longer a possibility for parents who, as a result of the severely traumatising diagnosis, find themselves dependent on medical opinion. Although the latter does not always obstruct their own perceptions – Frau Müller-Garnn, for instance, has described the contradictions in detail – it can obscure the way they understand them.

It is true that the manner in which the diagnosis was pronounced, as described by Frau Müller-Garnn, was particularly insensitive. Some parents have a different experience and quite often the feelings of shock arising from the diagnosis may well have been displaced retrospectively, in their memory, onto the way it was expressed, although this may not have been so cruel in reality. But it is not a question of imputing personal failure to particular doctors or accusing parents of misrepresentation. Just as our experience of the world depends on how we structure it – through guilt feelings and anxieties of failing – it is not possible to shield parents from the shock of the diagnosis. The phantasm of a *lebensunwertes Leben*, which aims at getting rid of those who are less productive, is the precursor of such a destructive constellation of relationships between doctors – sometimes psychologists too – and parents, that whatever a doctor says, and however empathetically he or she says it, it always seems unbearably harsh. As Erdheim has pointed out, phantasms are means of making dominant and repressive social structures unconscious. By assuming intellectual supremacy over individuals, doctors ensure that 'certain mechanisms, which are made to look natural, guard these norms against damaging attacks'.[12] In the system of phantasms sustaining the institution 'Learning Disability', individuals have the onerous task of making diagnoses. For while, like parents, they are caught up in the unconscious belief that what they see has to be accepted as ineluctable fate, they inevitably play a fundamental role in the creation of the institution 'Learning Disability'. They are expected to 'know' something which, since they are not omniscient, they cannot know but can only fear or presume. Parents, whose unconscious anxiety is released by the phantasm of the *lebensunwertes Leben*, have a deep need for certainty, for an authoritative, quasi-objective 'this is how it is and this is how it will be'. Living for years with uncertainty plunges them into unbearable 'self-doubt' (Häusler) undermining the very basis of their relationship to their child. Withholding the diagnosis initially from the parents out of a sense of misguided consideration is no solution either. J. Ruppert gives an account of the birth and the first days of life of their daughter Gabi who had Down's syndrome:

> I blurted out the first questions which, I believe, every mother asks: 'Is my child alive? Is he healthy?' Strangely enough, an answer was not immediately forthcoming. The midwife approached my bed, leant forward and, instead of answering my question, asked me in turn: 'How are you feeling then?' She looked at me in a peculiar, empathic way. Then I saw my baby. I felt tremendously happy and tears of joy ran down my cheeks. [. . .] These tears [. . .] were, however, misinterpreted, for when I heard the next words: 'Yes, we know, too, that she is an extremely weak child, hardly viable; in a few minutes she will be examined again carefully and then we will know whether there has been heart failure as well', I was jolted out of my dream [. . .] the words 'hardly viable' brought me down to earth with a bang.
>
> I saw in my mind's eye the body of my weak baby before me; I saw the absent expression on her little face. Never before had I seen a newborn baby with such a strange expression. I raised my head and caught sight of [. . .] a sheet of paper pinned to a board on the wall.
>
> I only saw one word, written by my doctor. I read the word 'Mongol'. Why, though, did this unknown word make me sweat and shake so?
>
> Was it possible that I had ignored or perhaps forgotten this word which was now burning in my mind?
>
> 'Excuse me, Doctor, what does Mongol mean?', I brought myself to ask.
>
> She was noticeably shocked.
>
> 'Actually,' she said in a calm and friendly manner, 'those notes up there are not intended for patients but only for doctors.'
>
> With that, the matter seemed settled for her, but for me it was not.
>
> 'Of course, I understand and respect that, Doctor, but, just now, I would kindly ask you not to look upon me as a patient.'
>
> She turned away towards the door as if she was about to leave and then said: 'You have probably noticed that your child looks different from other infants. It has slanting eyes, slightly protruding cheekbones

and the back of its head is flat and sloping. These features are described as Mongol.'

'There's one more question, Doctor, that is important. Does the word Mongol only refer to the appearance or does it mean something else as well?'

All of a sudden she was in a hurry. As she was going, she said audibly, 'But, please, don't worry about it, it merely refers to the appearance and the shape of the skull.'

Although I am usually critically minded, always prepared to go into a matter thoroughly, being unsatisfied with superficial answers, in this case I let myself be placated with what amounted to only a partial explanation. I felt sure something was being withheld from me; I had become mistrustful, but where was my old need to know everything in detail? [. . .] Did I really want to know more?[13]

Something else was going on here between the mother and the doctor. The mother quickly forgot the meaning of a word she was probably perfectly familiar with and displaced it onto anxiety sweats and shaking, while the doctor, clearly sensing this tendency to defensive denial, colluded with it. She may have rationalised that she wanted to spare the mother but we can read between the lines that she clearly felt the task was beyond her and wanted to escape.

The mother's anxiety about the exact meaning of the diagnosis was certainly increased by the anxious behaviour of the midwife and doctor. From that point on the relationship between the mother and her baby was dominated by it. For three years she avoided the truth (her husband and eldest daughter had known about it for a long time but avoided speaking about it, thereby colluding in turn with the mother's defensive denial). The anxious not-wanting-to-know, which is unmistakable, was thus passed on to Gabi, the 'Mongol' daughter, who in turn reacted to new situations, new people and noises very anxiously. The mother unconsciously connected these anxieties with Gabi's early severe nutritional disturbances and slow development (not, however, with her own severe depression during the first few months of Gabi's life) as well as with the curious and rejecting looks of strangers. With everything, that is, which she had to deny because it made clear the meaning of the unknown word 'Mongol'. She could not see, though, the connection between her daughter's anxieties and her own; for example, that Gabi vicariously feared all situations where there was a danger that others might not collude with the defensive denial. The child clearly tried to protect herself and her mother from such situations. Not surprisingly, Gabi probably feared that the breakdown of denial posed a danger for her and the fact that she had no words to express this anxiety made it even worse. As with Markus, the child was prevented by other people's symptoms from expressing something essential for which it could find no other means of expression; its capacity for symbolic expression thus being impaired.

When Gabi was three years old her mother's denial broke down, something her anxieties had been designed to prevent.

> 'Let's face it,' the husband told his wife condescendingly, 'Hitler knew what he was doing when he introduced euthanasia. Such a creature is not worth raising; it should not be allowed to live.' [. . .]
>
> Naturally, my little girl did not understand what he said but her facial expression changed and she stopped smiling at us in such a friendly way. [. . .]
>
> I didn't cry, I stood there numbed. [. . .]
>
> After a while, I went calmly over to my child, took her in my arms and carried [. . .] her home. Taking the child by the hand wasn't enough for me; I took her in my arms.[14]
>
> When we got home, I gave Gabi something to play with and went straight over to our bookcase. There were usually two reference books there; I took the second volume out and looked up the meaning of the word 'Mongolism'. 'Mongolism = Mongoloid degeneration. Form of idiocy, so called, because those afflicted have Mongol characteristics.' That was it then.[15]

The mother's first impulse is a death wish – which was precisely what Gabi had been so afraid of – an impulse to carry out the death sentence which had been pronounced in such a drastic manner by society and at the same time (since she is the one to carry out the murder) to kill herself.

> It occurred to me how the mothers of animals would probably behave in a similar situation. The mother would kill the weakest of her offspring in order to spare it from hunger and the cruelty of stronger animals. I decided to take leave of this world with my child. Where there was no place for this little girl in need of love, there could be no room for her mother either.[16]

In the end she did not carry out her plan, for which she is thankful to a girlfriend who happened to come by just as she was about to administer the ready-prepared poison to Gabi and herself. However, Gabi, whose sensitivity to her mother's moods and feelings was very acute, cannot have failed to notice how dangerously close her latent anxiety was to being realised. A little later, out of this constant state of anxiousness, she developed a severe phobia in street traffic (where she had experienced that traumatic encounter). Shortly after the mother's defensive denial had collapsed, the family moved house. This had been for Gabi's sake, because her father had been teased about her in his previous job and had changed job to escape this.

With remarkable patience and affection, Gabi's parents managed to help her overcome her phobia. Nevertheless, the connection with this experience was never made clear (the father did not know that the mother had wanted to kill herself along with Gabi) and consequently Gabi's fear of death, her anxiety about not being allowed to live as she was, also remained unconscious and unthinkable.

The diagnosis also had a destructive effect here in that it influenced the child's perception of her mother. The label 'totally idiotic' or 'Mongol' undermines the parents' confidence in their child's capacity for development, whether consciously or unconsciously, and ensures that certain autonomous manifestations of the child have little chance of being understood and of developing further; instead they are subsumed under the label 'typical learning disability'.

And yet it is important for the parents of children with learning disabilities to be given a diagnosis; many demand it and are relieved when they hear it. Telling the parents what the diagnosis is does not only have destructive effects; it also brings relief and provides the stability that enables many parents to begin functioning again. 'It was only when a real disability was identified that I was able to emerge from a numbed relationship to my child and to start actively building a more positive one.' It is hurtful as well as destructive for the relationship with the child when parents feel they are being given false hopes or that their feelings and worries are not being taken seriously, particularly when they are already having great difficulties with their child on a daily basis. They are then thrown back upon their own resources, left to struggle alone with a situation which is beyond them, and often get the feeling that they are failures, bad parents who are 'doing something or other wrong'. Furthermore, they feel that they are 'responsible' for their child's predicament. Parents of autistic children or of children whose disability cannot easily be traced to an early and identifiable organic impairment, frequently experience a phase of uncertainty like this. They then have to go through a tortuous and humiliating odyssey of medical consultations until a label is finally found to describe what is worrying them.

An example of such an odyssey-like search for a diagnosis is described by David Melton in *Todd*, an account of his ordeal with his son who had mild learning disabilities. Todd was born prematurely and his mother was concerned about him right from the beginning.

> Instinctively, she felt something was wrong. 'No need to worry,' said the doctor, 'all mothers tend to be over-anxious about their children.' The doctor did not seem concerned at all and so, for a while, Nancy was reassured. She was amused by his stories of over-anxious mothers. But once he had gone, her fears returned. The first night [after the birth, D.N.] she could not get to sleep. [. . .]

Breast-feeding was unsuccessful. At meal times Todd was hungry and at first he enjoyed his feeds. But he quickly grew tired and fell asleep. [. . .]

After five days Todd weighed half a pound less than he did when he was born. This was an alarming sign. Nancy did not have enough milk and Todd was unsatisfied.

'You do not need to worry about that at all,' the doctor told us, 'Todd will put the weight he has lost back on again, and then you can take him home with you.'[17]

After this preliminary period during which they felt rather foolish for worrying so much but also felt rebuffed, Todd's parents began paying exaggerated attention to every symptom, every illness, and every slightest sign of retarded development. 'Day by day, Nancy observed Todd's development with uneasiness.'[18] Her watchfulness was marked by uneasiness, anxiety and feelings of hurt – feelings that come across strongly in the report. Todd's parents' sense of self-worth was fragile – at one point the father describes himself as a failure – and consequently was easily offended by the doctor's words which were meant to be reassuring. But although the intensity of their concern and uneasiness may be exaggerated, it is not unjustified. When the doctor said there was no need for concern, he was unwittingly colluding with them: the anxious parents were hoping for an omnipotent opinion that would relieve them of their anxiety. This is why they wanted to hear 'there is no reason to be concerned'. But they also needed the doctor to take their own observations seriously and to tell them there was indeed some cause for concern. They had omnipotent expectations that he should *know* where they themselves could only fear, suspect and assume. In his role as the person responsible for making the diagnosis, the doctor could not sidestep these omnipotent expectations: he acted omnipotently by colluding with the ostensible nature of both wishes, and stated that there was no cause for concern. Even if this is what the parents wanted to hear, they still could not accept it. By acting omnipotently the doctor made them feel dispossessed – their own observations had no meaning. This is intolerable, and not only because it is hurtful: in the early stages of baby care it is essential for the parents to be able to trust their own observations – how else can they be certain of understanding their baby's needs correctly? The way is thus paved for a future subliminal power struggle. Henceforth, the parents constantly feel the need to have their own observations confirmed by someone else. However, since they clearly continue to hope their child is all right, in spite of their underlying, torturous self-doubts, most doctors again feel they are expected to 'know' that the parents' anxieties are unjustified.

In his book *The Doctor, His Patient and the Illness* Michael Balint describes how, for many patients, withholding the diagnosis does not reduce their suffering but makes it worse:

When a patient, after a series of careful and conscientious examinations, is told that nothing is wrong with him, doctors expect that he will feel relieved and even improve. Admittedly this happens fairly often, but in quite a number of cases just the opposite occurs and the doctor's usual reaction to this – in spite of its frequency, always unexpected – event is pained surprise and indignation. This could perhaps be avoided if doctors would bear in mind that finding 'nothing wrong' is no answer to the patients' most burning demand for a name for his illness. Apart from the almost universal fear that what we have found is so frightening that we will not tell him, he feels that 'nothing wrong' means only that we have not found out and therefore cannot tell him what it is that frightens or worries him and causes him pain. Thus he feels let down, unable to explain and accept his pains, fears and deprivations.[19]

Todd's parents, too, did not get better but worse when they were told that there were no grounds for concern; their worries were multiplied rather than being alleviated. This had consequences. Todd was clearly a particularly delicate child and his parents' anxiety and restlessness would probably mean that almost every future illness would assume catastrophic proportions. This is how the mechanism described by Balint in his general practice with adults functions. He writes:

Sometimes one can observe that some of the people who, for some reason or other, find it difficult to cope with the problems in their lives, resort to becoming ill. If the doctor has the opportunity of seeing them in the first stages of their becoming ill, i.e. before they settle down to a definite 'organised' illness, he may observe that these patients, so to speak, *offer or propose various illnesses* and that they have to go on offering new illnesses until between doctor and patient an agreement can be reached, resulting in the acceptance of both of them of one of the illnesses as justified.[20]

Todd's parents complained to doctors variously of inguinal hernia, infections, feverish cramps until inevitably a generally retarded development had set in and they finally obtained the diagnosis they had been expecting for so long, i.e. 'infantile brain damage'. Only then could they become active and request assistance. The parent–child relationship becomes more stable when the parents' anxiety has been given a name, which in turn enables them to ask for support. It is as though the diagnosis has a kind of magic effect.

At first sight, the histories of Markus, Gabi and Todd look very different. In Markus's case, announcing the diagnosis was really destructive and marked his future development decisively. In Gabi's case, the disturbance remained latent; the defence against knowing the diagnosis had the effect of undermining the foundations of the mother–child relationship, which then became dominated by permanent anxiety of a threatening catastrophe – the breakdown of this denial. For Todd and his parents, however, the diagnosis seemed to have a different meaning altogether. For them, the process of trying to get someone to make a diagnosis was akin to a long trek through extremely uncertain territory. There were several reasons for the uncertainty. First, the parents were anxious, not without reason, that premature birth and its attendant complications may have damaged their child. Secondly, the child had suffered perinatal brain damage that certainly could have been compensated for if the parents had simply had sufficient self-confidence and security (compensation was obviously still possible at seven years of age). Finally, the parents were angry about the pain the doctor caused them by not taking their anxieties seriously. The diagnosis always has a stabilising effect: the parents of a child who is diagnosed early and unequivocally benefit from the quasi-magic security that it offers, even if the primary feelings are initially ones of shock. 'When one knows what's wrong,' say many parents, then it is possible 'to adapt oneself to the reality of living with a disabled child.'

To quote Balint once again, 'the function of the diagnosis is to supply the name by which the uncanny, malevolent and frightening something can be called, thought of, and perhaps dealt with.'[21] This almost mythical formulation seems thoroughly in tune with the expectations many parents have of a diagnosis: it is not just a matter of rational anxieties but much more of something nameless, of the 'forgotten human dimension' which is stirred up, of deep and intolerable fear of failure. When the diagnosis is made at an early stage, parents are often thankful to be spared feeling responsible for their child's disability, whereas parents who have to wait a long time for a diagnosis to be made often go through a hellish period of blame, accusations, self-accusations and feelings of guilt. Long after the diagnosis has been announced, it is noticeable how they have become over-sensitive to everything that is capable of arousing their guilt feelings again. Even in the way Todd's father recounts his son's history, one can sense how fragile the stability procured by the diagnosis is. When reading this book, I find myself forced into affirming that the parents were right to insist on obtaining a diagnosis, that the doctor who was dismissive of their anxieties must have been incompetent and that the diagnosis finally procured was certainly correct.

This feeling of constantly needing to confirm the diagnosis and the parents' innocence is one that I recognise from many conversations I have had with the parents of such children. The distress and anxiety which can affect parents, and especially the mothers of handicapped children, as soon as they fear they are being blamed, makes itself clearly felt in my counter-transference.

The diagnosis I am supposed to endorse states: 'there is nothing that can be done; it is an organic defect'. The grief-stricken parents eagerly and thankfully take in this information. It is a relief to them when they can tell themselves that their child's difficulties are the result of a defect for which they are not responsible. It is therefore imperative for them that the diagnosis establishes an organic cause. A purely descriptive diagnosis such as 'general retardation' or 'autistic characteristics' is insufficient; only the addendum 'probably due to brain damage of uncertain causes in infancy', or whatever else it may be called, has the magic effect required.

Certainly, one may wonder why so many parents constantly need to have this corroboration and why case reports like Todd's make such a direct appeal to readers to be witnesses of the parents' innocence. One of the truisms concerning the institution 'Learning Disability' is that the parents of people with learning disabilities cannot escape guilt feelings unless they obtain a diagnosis, based on the paradoxical formula, organic = not guilty, psychic = guilty, which exonerates them from guilt and grants absolution. This truism is dangerous and remains a Trojan horse that has not yet been seen through.

What I found most preoccupying and worrying while I was working on this book was the concern that there was a risk of colluding with society's tendency to attribute blame and thus with the general hostility towards women and mothers. I was aware that making a critique of the magic unconscious functioning of the diagnosis in making the institution 'Learning Disability' unconscious was quite likely to reawaken in mothers the old guilt feelings and self-doubts that had been more or less subdued thanks to the diagnosis. It is not enough for me to show solidarity as a feminist. I cannot circumvent the reality of society's tendency to attribute blame; nor can I escape the fact that I myself am by no means an exception, that is to say that the projective mechanisms upon which such blaming is based operate in me too.

There is another reason as well why the issue of guilt feelings is particularly close to my heart. This book is the product of my own personal struggle with guilt feelings occasioned by my work as a novice in the field of learning disability. The idea for the book emerged from the first intensive experience I had of learning disability when I worked as a music therapist in a large institution for people with learning disabilities at the start of my professional life. I worked there for two years, which was all I could stand. When it became clear that I was going to leave, I began writing up the case histories of the therapies I had carried out there from my notes: accounts of broken-off therapies. In so doing, I became painfully aware that by leaving the institution I was leaving behind patients without always being able to ensure that their therapies would be continued.

Two accounts of broken-off therapies are included at the end of this book. I had misgivings about doing this whenever someone said to me –

and this has occurred several times – that, in the final analysis, I had damaged the two children concerned, Inge and Filippa. Having to consider this possibility has been painful. It is not true that Inge or Filippa were unhappier after their therapy was broken off than they were before, but they felt their pain more acutely because the causes of it could no longer be taken at face value. Further, I console myself with the thought that, without therapy, Inge would probably not have discovered her songs (she still sings them), and Filippa might never have learnt that she is not always and hopelessly wicked and bad. However, in the end it only helps a little to be able to tell myself that I am not to blame but rather that I was a victim of overwhelming circumstances for which one individual cannot be held responsible.

It is difficult to accept the idea that I alone am to blame because I was unable to cope with the burden of responsibility which society placed upon me in my work with people with learning disabilities. How much more difficult it must be, then, if your own child is involved. Not only are the inner bonds greater and stronger but mothers (fathers escape this more easily) are exposed to the pressure of blame. Even for mothers of 'normal' children, this is apt to create a constant fear of being judged by others as well as by their own inner critical agency which is often no less severe. The fear of being a bad mother is awfully powerful and widespread (Brecht pointed out what the principal source of this was in his phantasmatic formulation): when a mother is in difficulty, she is sure to receive disapproving looks from those around. Everyone else is glad that they are not the ones whom people are shaking their heads at or making indignant remarks about. Under such circumstances, realising that one cannot cope with the task of caring for a child who is endangered, impaired or already has learning disabilities is unbearable because mothers, unlike a therapist, cannot escape by looking for another job.

Mothers are expected to sweep the oppressive burden of their guilt feelings under the carpet with the rationalisation, 'it is organic, hereditary or a result of misfortune'. That they are quick to make use of it is quite understandable. The diagnosis fulfils its function of removing the blame so well that today many mothers say that they feel no guilt at all. 'At first, we certainly wondered if we had done something wrong,' says one mother of a 'Mongol' child with severe learning disabilities, 'but then things were explained to us and since then I know that no one is to blame for it and I have no guilt feelings.'

A little later in the conversation, when she mentioned that she had not had a genetic test done, the same mother said, 'we deliberately decided not to have this test. If we had learnt that it was hereditary and that my husband or I had passed it on, then it would have been clear who was to blame. That's why we don't want any more children.' (So there is a sense of guilt after all?) I have often been struck by this contradiction in talks I have had with mothers and fathers. The diagnosis enables them to distance themselves from guilt feelings, but anxiety lurks beneath the surface at all times, pressuring them constantly to cling to the diagnosis as if it afforded official proof of their innocence.

Back in my student days, I was asked to give a couple's six-year-old daughter regular private lessons to prepare her for primary school which the parents thought she would not be able to cope with. The mother gave me a thorough account of the child's history and development, as well as of her own lengthy search for a doctor who would make a diagnosis, whereas all the others had declared she was neurotic. She finally found out that the child had brain damage and was now telling me the whole story as if she was expecting me, a mere student, to endorse the diagnosis. But at the same time she revealed details that were intended to make me doubt the diagnosis. For instance, the child, who was diagnosed as retarded due to perinatal brain damage, had initially shown no signs of retarded develop- ment but later, at the age of three, following the birth of a little brother (whom the mother worshipped), had stopped walking and even speaking to some extent. When I naively took up the story and asked whether the retardation might not be related in some way to a reaction of jealousy concerning the brother's birth, the mother was visibly shaken. The next day she rang me up to say that she had spoken again with the doctor who insisted that I should not read 'anything psychological' into this.

The relief from blame procured by the diagnosis was so tenuous that the innocent question of a private trainee teacher was sufficient to destabilise the mother anew. This was a situation that was destined to make her even more dependent, not only on the doctor who had to absolve her once again but also on me as the representative of a latent environment that was apt to attribute blame. Throughout the time I was working with the child, the mother constantly employed all means at her disposal to convince me that the diagnosis was right, as if I was in any position to judge. The diagnosis was only effective in relieving her from guilt feelings as long as those around her believed in it. So together with bringing relief, or rather as the condition of it, the diagnosis created a permanent dependency, making the couple comply with the treatment suggested by those who claimed 'to know'.

Admittedly, this is an extreme example. I am inclined in this case to suppose that the doctor made the diagnosis more out of kindness than conviction, for there were so many contradictions. But I am very familiar with this constant need to have the diagnosis endorsed, even with parents whose child has the apparently unequivocal diagnosis of 'Mongolism' or 'Down's syndrome'. It is striking how frequently such mothers recount scenes in which the old prejudice that the mother's 'bad lifestyle' during pregnancy might have been the reason why the child has Down's syndrome is evoked and they then expect me to say that this is untrue – as if there was anything else one could say. It is as if they do indeed still nurse doubts about their responsibility.

I have repeatedly had the experience of mothers telling me things that call the diagnosis into question. It is as if they hoped I would make the contradictions that exist between their own perceptions and the actual diagnosis disappear by listening to them and approving of what they say. At the same time, it seemed to me that initially I should try to preserve their unconscious knowledge of what has been suppressed by the diagnosis without responding at all. The guilt-exonerating effect of the diagnosis is instability, making parents dependent; the inherent contradictions mean they constantly have to expend energy for defensive purposes. This instability has a system to it. Dependency makes one blind and uncritical; parents who become unconsciously dependent on others as a result of the diagnosis and the relief from guilt it affords become submissive. They then acquiesce to the norms compelling them to turn to new treatment techniques – the third organising factor.

On a conscious level, the power of guilt feelings stems from the blame attributed by others but there is another much more dangerous source which is linked to this.

> A mother was waiting at a bus stop with her disabled child in a pram. When the bus arrived, a friendly person helped the young mother lift the pram onto the bus. Only when he was inside did the man realise that the child was disabled and promptly carried the pram out again single-handed saying, 'We can't have a child like that on public transport'. The mother got off, the doors closed, and the man left with the bus.

However improbable it may seem this scene is not an isolated case; I have heard several others like it. Here is an allegory: the friendly person who lent a hand was a man belonging to the master race who would not be seen on a bus with a child like that; the passengers in the bus were the silent majority. The bus left, the mother was left behind alone with her child feeling hated and despised.

It is probably the case that through such drastic scenarios – but also through more subtle and yet no less violent ones – all mothers of disabled children experience that there is no place for their child. Or, to put it more clearly and frankly: 'Such a creature isn't worth raising; it shouldn't be allowed to live'. Society delegates its murderous phantasies onto individuals:[22] finding herself cursed by a member of the master race, left alone with her child, abandoned and exposed to her feelings with only her child to offset her horror and hatred, what was she expected to feel? How could she feel anything but hate and death wishes toward the child? All the more so since she also had to struggle with the fellow-passenger in herself – two years earlier, she herself might well have remained seated in the bus while this was happening to another passenger. We have all grown up in the tradition which not so long ago led to the extermination of a *lebensunwertes Leben* and this tradition is by no means a thing of the past as we discover when our own child is burdened with the diagnosis 'disabled'. 'Only someone who, while sitting at their abnormal child's bedside, has asked themselves in despair whether the child should be allowed to live or not, knows how dreadful the temptation is.'[23] This 'dreadful temptation' is the dangerous unconscious source of guilt feelings: the more the mother's death wishes are stimulated by those around her, the more they become unconscious and then find their outlet in substitutive ways. The tradition of murder thus lives on in this 'dreadful temptation' which is delegated to certain individuals. The other passengers turn away with indifference as the bus continues on its route, leaving the mother and her child in the lurch.

Society 'delegating' its murderous phantasies onto individuals: this is how I understand the burden and isolation facing the mothers of children with learning disabilities. Not only do they receive no help in managing their own murderous impulses – 'the dreadful temptation' – but through such scenarios, society off-loads its collective death wishes on to them as well. It was the hatred of an entire nation that led to unspeakable crimes but it is mothers who are required to carry it now and this they cannot do. Guilt feelings are thereby intensified immeasurably (guilt which is not theirs alone to carry, as we all share in it).

The diagnosis is supposed to help one with these guilt feelings. It rightly states that parents are not to blame if their child is born with impairment or has suffered a trauma. However, the guilt feelings do not stem so much from the phantasy of having caused the handicap, even if some parents later try to explain things to themselves in this way. The death wishes are too threatening, too subject to taboo, and too much of a burden to be carried alone to be seen as the source of the guilt feelings. The equation, organic = not guilty, psychic = guilty, is unsatisfactory and does not really help since the death wishes are not in fact organic but of a 'psychological' nature. So the diagnosis merely serves to suppress or split off the guilt feelings, to rationalise them or to project them, for instance, onto a doctor's bad advice or treatment or onto the medication taken during pregnancy (such projections sometimes have an element of reality to them). Making an established defence mechanism available provides some relief but at the cost of restricting the capacity for perception and weakening the ego. This explains parents' instability and constant need to expend energy defensively to convince themselves that the diagnosis is correct and that they are not to blame. It also explains their dependence on the authority that makes the diagnosis and grants absolution. The diagnosis-absolution in fact creates the opposite of a genuine relief from guilt. What is proposed is that mothers be exonerated from the responsibility which society has off-loaded onto them as individuals but, in so doing, it is recognised, albeit unconsciously, that there is individual responsibility which needs exonerating. These are the contents of the Trojan horse that continue to go unrecognised.

The doctors who have the thankless task of making the diagnosis are viewed with barely veiled aggression in the accounts of parents I have cited. While, on the one hand, they are invested with quasi-papal authority, on the other, they come across in parents' phantasies as unempathic, indifferent or cruelly judgemental. Frequently, what parents experience on the one hand as good, helpful and guilt-relieving and, on the other, as bad and judgemental, is represented by two different doctors, or by a doctor and a psychologist/therapist.

This split is also part and parcel of the diagnosis/prognosis making process. What comes across to parents as coldness or hardness may amount, for those whose thankless task it is to make a diagnosis/prognosis, to no more than a slightly tactless or sharp remark made after showing considerable patience or restraint in the face of a highly charged emotional situation. Hermann Lüdeke describes[24] in an essay how the relatives of patients with apallic syndrome tend to forget numerous lengthy discussions during which the doctor has shown considerable empathy in an effort to be supportive and make things easier for them; they then interpret a casual remark, made out of fatigue, as irrefutable proof of the doctor's heartlessness. His explanation for this is that the overwhelming despair of relatives is such that they need someone to blame so as not to have to take responsibility for their own death wishes. This is no doubt true, but the other side of the story is no less true. Lüdeke himself speaks about the anger doctors feel towards their apallic patients because they cannot bear the way the latter expose the limitations of their medical expertise so drastically. Most doctors feel that, when they are talking with parents, they ought to suppress their feelings of anger and fears of failure, as well as their own death wishes towards the patient. It is when their self-control has weakened that they give vent to their feelings by dropping a casual remark out of exhaustion. For the doctor, this may seem a rare and insignificant slip when seen in the context of his daily efforts to keep his self-control. However, parents see this as confirming what they have already sensed subliminally for a long time. It causes considerable anxiety because it corresponds dangerously to their own fears of failure, their hate and their own death wishes.

Splits occur everywhere when a child is diagnosed as having learning disabilities, whether it be between different medical authorities or between parents and the medical profession or between parents/doctor and the environment (which attributes blame). With the best will in the world, neither the doctors who make the diagnoses nor the parents are able to avoid them. In the duality of such defensive splitting where there is no space for the child as an autonomous subject, the latter becomes a subjective-object for others who have to defend themselves against archaic and deeply unconscious anxieties. At the same time, reality – and this is the characteristic of defensive splitting – has no space here. Specialists have their limitations; they cannot always cure, do not know everything and can often only hypothesise. They cannot help the fact that the diagnosis 'suffers from learning disabilities' will always be intolerable in a society that values productivity and achievement. Parents, mothers are left so alone with the responsibility for their child that they can never manage responsibly by themselves in our social reality. Splitting reduces everything to the polar dualities of impotence–omnipotence, innocent–guilty, good–bad. The institution 'Learning Disability' is organised around such splits and diagnosis has a primary organising function.

These mechanisms are not only at work in the parents of people with learning disabilities: anyone involved with people with learning disabilities will find themselves affected by them. It took me a long time, too, to learn to consciously face my death wishes and to recognise their origin, and it remains a difficulty. When I started working with people with learning disabilities, I found myself caught up in some malevolent enactments of soul murder which I was only able to understand retrospectively with a great deal of guilt, shame and sadness.

On one occasion, I stopped treating a very well-adjusted boy when a caseworker asked me to take into therapy a severely disturbed child instead, as he believed him to be in much greater need of help. I was only too happy to do this: the boy's happy adjustedness had been boring me for some time. There was no change in the therapy, the boy showed no personal motivation, obediently carried out everything he thought I wanted him to do, beaming at me all the time. Trying to appease my sense of guilt for having broken off the therapy, I told myself that the boy was really severely brain damaged and was as happy as he could be within his limited possibilities – therapy was unnecessary. I became aware much too late that I was acting out a death wish by breaking off the therapy, that the boredom I felt stemmed from my hate, that I needed the diagnosis to keep these feelings unconscious, and that I had dropped the child cruelly. The boy suffered in his own adjusted way from the interruption of his therapy: whenever he saw me, he would come up and stand beside me, all smiles, looking at me with large, unswerving, blinking eyes. It was too late when I noticed that there was nothing happy in the expression in his eyes and never had been; the expression was imploring and fearful. Fear of my hatred. Scared to death. And I had become the instrument of this hate, allowing his fear to grow. Because I could not stand his adjustedness, I had taken flight behind the diagnosis; what I found unbearable about him was the consequence of brain damage. I did not understand that his adjustedness was a kind of mimicry of his nameless dread of being abandoned. So I was guilty precisely because I made use of the guilt-exonerating diagnosis – and needed the Trojan horse all the more.

In spite of all these inevitable difficulties and complications, it is not only unavoidable, but also necessary and right, that diagnoses are made and communicated to parents. Parents have a right to know what can be said and what cannot; they must be told what the possibilities and uncertainties are. If those whose task this is understood the dynamics operating between them and parents, then it is possible to imagine diagnostic interviews where the initial shock could be cushioned. The destructive dynamics mentioned above could then be worked through, to some extent at least, for the benefit of the child and we might acquire a more critical appreciation of our social reality. It would undoubtedly be a difficult and time-consuming task and would demand a closer examination of the counter-transference on a personal level. Both these things could only be achieved in a professional setting where there was freedom and support for confronting one's own fears of failure.

Chapter 3

The process of developing learning disabilities

The true symbol of intelligence is the snail's horn with which it feels and smells its way. The horn recoils instantly before an obstacle, seeking asylum in the protective shell and again becoming one with the whole. Only tentatively does it re-emerge to assert its independence. If the danger is still present it vanishes once more, now hesitating longer before renewing the attempt. In its early stages the life of the mind is infinitely fragile. The snail's senses depend on its muscles, and muscles become feebler with every hindrance to their play. Physical injury cripples the body, fear the mind. At the start the two are inseparable.

. . . The suppression of this potential by the direct resistance of the natural environment is carried a stage further as internal organs begin to atrophy with fear. [. . .] A preliminary groping of this kind is always easily thwarted; it is always backed by good will and faint hope but not by unflagging energy. When facing in the direction from which it is finally scared into retreat, the animal grows timid and stupid.

Stupidity is a scar.[1]

In the literature on learning disability I have rarely come across a more empathic description of what developing learning disabilities means than in this snail aphorism in *Dialectic of Enlightenment* by Horkheimer and Adorno – a book in which people with learning disabilities, left behind without hope by the enlightenment, are otherwise not mentioned. The snail, a slow, exposed and totally defenceless creature, seems to me to be an apposite picture of the defencelessness of a child with learning disabilities who slowly and hesitantly tries to grow, but finds that everywhere his sensitive antenna meets with resistance which he cannot understand but which hinders his endeavours to grow.

What are these obstacles and what effect do they have on the little human being who is developing learning disabilities? 'Physical injury cripples the body, fear the mind. At the start, the two are inseparable.' Initially, in the earliest stages of life – in the womb and following birth – body and mind are still one and not separated. At this stage, moreover, the body–soul–

mind unity of the child is just as fragile, unprotected and vulnerable as the snail's horn. The embryo and the infant experience bodily hurts as nameless terrors, and psychic pains are expressed physically in the form of colic pains, eczema, diarrhoea, stomach pylorus spasms, and so on. Only when body and mind are differentiated does learning disability come about and it is futile to try and separate what is psychic from what is organic. 'Learning disability' is the product of a process, a conflict, and this is what I now want to examine more closely.

The creation of potential space – coenaesthetic experience and mimetic competence

Developing learning disabilities can most easily be described as a process if one compares the socialisation of children with learning disabilities with those who have a 'normal' development. At the outset, all children are highly vulnerable and dependent on their environment but some children are more sensitive than others on account of an organic impairment. This helplessness and vulnerability has often been observed and discussed and is nothing new. We are less inclined to take into consideration the fact that contact with such a needy and vulnerable little person also makes the first caretakers sensitive and vulnerable. This mostly means mothers, whose sensitivity is further increased by the often overwhelming experiences of pregnancy and birth, hormonal changes and the radical change of lifestyle which responsibility for a newborn baby implies. In most cases, this sensitivity is not very noticeable because development takes place relatively smoothly and mothers can use their heightened sensibility to be more closely attuned to their child's needs. If we look more closely, however, it is noticeable how the 'mother–baby relationship' theme affects mothers. Even the mothers of children who have grown up often react with unexpected sensitivity, which shows, even years later, how deeply the experience of motherhood affected them.

When an infant is born, it emerges from an infinite, boundless world of rocking equilibrium into our finite, structured world full of contrasts. Its needs for warmth, nourishment and holding are no longer immediately satisfied, and it is confronted with a great deal of sensory stimulation from within and without. It is true that things do not always proceed so smoothly in the womb and that the foetus has already had to tolerate interruptions to this state of harmony and boundlessness. Out of this, the first structures of experience are formed. We now know that the sensorium of the newborn is already very efficient. Nevertheless, it may be assumed that perception in this period is directed above all towards inner stimuli, fluctuations in balance, warmth, hunger and so on. Only after the third or fourth week do external senses (hearing, seeing, touching) acquire significance. At a certain level, however, the newborn baby perceives far more than is usually supposed. Experiences in primal therapy, bioenergetics and similar psychotherapeutic methods have shown that the birth process and experiences during the first few weeks of life can be physically relived and recalled in detail. René Spitz has called this inwardly directed perception 'coenaesthetic reception'.

> Particularly during the first six months of life, and to a certain extent even later, the perceptual system, the sensorium of the infant is in a state of transition, from [. . .] coenaesthetic reception to diacritic perception. Later the perceptual system differentiates itself into a diacritical *perception* which overlies coenaesthetic 'reception'. The sensorium plays a minimal role in coenaesthetic 'reception'; instead perception takes place on the level of deep sensitivity and in terms of totalities, in an all-or-nothing fashion. Responses to co-reception also are totality responses [. . .]. That is why I have adopted the term soma-psyche for the infant's psyche at this archaic level. [. . .] The psychic manifestations of this system are the sensations, affects and certain attributes of dreams [. . .]. The quality of the perceptive system is best described by the adjective 'sensitive', for here we are dealing with vague, diffuse sensations such as gastro-intestinal, sexual, precordial sensations and so on . . . [. . .] the fact that perception, the sensorium, is not yet functioning [intensifies, DN] the power of coenaesthetic 'reception'.[2]

Coenaesthetic experience is a deeply physical experience that directly concerns bodily well-being. It is often observed that an infant reacts very sensitively to what, for adults, are barely perceptible fluctuations of mood in his social surroundings, with restlessness, crying and psychosomatic troubles (spitting, colic). During my period of infant observation with Lynn (in the context of my training as a child and adolescent psychotherapist), I was able to observe the onset of a case of colic. Lynn, who was only a few weeks old, began having wind and crying out with pain after breast-feeding. Her mother tried to comfort her by fondling her and talking to her but as nothing seemed to help she gave the baby her breast again. This helped at first but only for a short time and again the mother did her best to soothe the crying infant. This went on for a while. I noticed how, gradually, the mother's calm and soothing way of holding her baby and the increasingly inconsolable crying which went on and on were beginning to make me feel uncomfortable too. Finally, a co-inhabitant, who had been sleeping and was still drowsy, was alerted. Feeling rested, she came up to the mother and child sympathetically and asked, 'What's the matter with her?' She took the crying bundle from the mother and immediately Lynn calmed down. Such sensitivity, such finely tuned body reactions to what, for us adults, are barely perceptible changes of mood, are, as Spitz points out, 'overlaid' in the course of socialisation by those perceptual forms which are normal for adults in the Western world. This overlay reinforces the protective barrier, the defence: whilst the baby would not be viable without coenaesthetic receptive capacity, by the same token, in our culture, dominated as it is by functional rationalism, we would not be viable either if we had no defences against this early sensitivity.

In the earliest stages of life, the infant's entire activity is aimed at achieving a continuum in which there is an absence of want, an equilibrium of warmth, satiety and security called homeostasis. Michael Balint describes this initial environmental relationship as plastic:

> [. . .] There is one more phase prior to the emergence of primary objects which might be called the phase of the undifferentiated environment, the phase of the primary substances, or [. . .] the phase of the harmonious interpenetrating mix-up. [. . .] The best illustration for this state is the relationship we have towards the air surrounding us. It is difficult to say whether the air in our lungs or in our guts is us, or not us; and it does not even matter. We inhale the air, take out of it what we need and after putting into it what we do not want to have, we exhale it, and we do not care at all whether the air likes it or not. It has to be there for us in adequate quantity and quality; and as long as it is there, the relationship between us and it cannot be observed, or only with great difficulty; if, however anything interferes with our supply of air, impressive and noisy symptoms develop in the same way as with the dissatisfied infant [. . .].[3]

This picture furnishes us with a more plastic understanding of the process of coenaesthetic reception: just as we breathe in the air around us and can recognise and differentiate between good and bad environmental influences – pure fresh air or stale, polluted air – so the baby simultaneously breathes in the mood of his environment and absorbs influences therein which do him good or harm.

'The air is not an object but a substance, like water or milk, [. . .] sand or plasticine. Their chief characteristic is their indestructibility.'[4] Bodily needs are in themselves a disturbance for the baby, the destruction of its vital need for homeostasis. Hunger hurts, as does coldness, dampness and not being held. The mother is the one who is supposed to smooth out all these disturbances. For the newborn baby she is like air; it does not see her as an independent person, does not thank her for her attention and is constantly demanding more. She must be able to tolerate this and should not expect any reciprocity from it initially. On the contrary, she must be able to discern from its undifferentiated expression of unpleasure what its precise needs are. She must not confuse coldness or not being held with hunger; if she feeds her baby when all it wants is to be held, she can provoke spitting or colic. In order to be so finely attuned to its needs, she has herself to be functioning at the level of coenaesthetic reception. Only in this way can she infer what her child's needs are.

When the mother–infant relationship goes well, the mother's handling and responses occur on quite a different level to that which we are accustomed to in our world where functional ways of thinking and acting predominate. Caring for the infant requires from the mother something Ernst Kris has called 'regression in the service of the ego'. Regression, i.e. a falling back on one's own infantile coenaesthetic ways of experiencing, on the capacity to give way to phantasies and forms of play, to let oneself be led by impulses and perceptions that are hardly accessible to conscious thought, being able to put oneself in the place of an infant and, by identi-fication, to empathise with its needs. All this should happen 'in the service of the ego', that is, while maintaining adult awareness and self-assertion and not in a state of intoxication or with severe psychical disturbance as in regression. As we are dealing here with a highly differentiated form of perception and interaction, the term regression is misleading for it suggests a return to infantile, undifferentiated experience. Erdheim,[5] accordingly, has suggested that such phases, in which established defence structures are disintegrating, should not be seen as regressive, as their progressive char-acter and their potential for achieving a new orientation and new integra-tion might easily be overlooked. He proposes instead that we use the term 'liquefaction'. It seems to me, at any rate, that the term 'regression in the service of the ego' corresponds entirely to reality, namely, the cultural reality that the dissolution of functional defensive modes causes anxiety about not being able to survive in this world and of losing the status of adult self-determination – a very real anxiety which only too frequently wrecks the opportunity that may be present in such phases of liquefaction. Anxieties of losing oneself, of becoming helpless and dependent, arise in such situations, and it requires considerable energy and ego strength to tolerate the perceptions and sensations that are aroused through identification with the dependency and neediness of the newborn baby. It was not a matter of coincidence that Kris came upon his idea of 'regression in the service of the ego' by studying the areas of competence which are specific to artists.

In order to achieve such mimetic responsiveness to her child's needs, the mother must, once again, partially give up the protective defence of the diacritic outer layer in favour of coenaesthetic experience. This makes her unstable and loosens her defences, and it is the task of the environment to compensate for this loss by protecting and supporting her. Mimetic behaviour, admittedly, is under taboo – in *Dialectic of Enlightenment* Horkheimer and Adorno have described this taboo as the basis of our Western enlightened culture – and so it leads a shadowy existence in the areas of play and art. Anyone who behaves mimetically, beyond these specific areas, is likely to make himself a laughing-stock. For example, if one argues emotionally, 'unobjectively', in a scientific discussion, one is likely to be looked down upon with a condescending smile. Again, it is not a coincidence that such disparagement is mostly directed at women: stunted mimetic competence is delegated to women and the mimetic taboo is reinforced through this contempt, compounded by women's own self-contempt. So the situation of a mother of a newborn baby is paradoxical: she is expected to be competent in a way that simultaneously demonstrates her 'typically feminine' functional 'incompetence'. I myself am very familiar with the feeling of shame that makes it difficult for me to use baby language with an infant in the presence of another person and I am always full of admiration when mothers manage to avoid speaking with their child in Latin or Greek, so to speak!

I would like to illustrate the term 'mimetic behaviour' by taking the example of the roller coaster. The frenetic ride arouses anxiety and thrills, i.e. feelings of being scared to death are aroused which can be warded off by a lightning mimetic response to the movement based on coenaesthetic recognition of its direction. Conscious decision making and acting would be far too clumsy and too slow to match the speed and anxiety (admittedly, there is no real danger of being thrown out of the car by making a false movement; however, if your movements are not synchronised you will not enjoy the ride). We are familiar with mimetic behaviour from the animal world. When a chameleon merges with its environment by changing its colour, this is its way of dealing with the permanent latent danger in which it finds itself. Similarly, when an animal freezes in the face of its enemy, it feigns death; when a cat puffs itself up and gambols, it is mimicking the danger it imagines itself to be in; it tries to mimic and match the powerful and dangerous opponent it is up against. In the mother–infant relationship there is also a danger: the infant is in danger of dying when its environment cannot sense its needs. It cannot look after itself and so the mother must be able to sense mimetically all the dangers threatening it – starvation, freezing to death and injuries of all kinds.

If there is a successful interplay between coenaesthetic reception and mimetic behaviour, then the infant gradually learns through the mother's care to differentiate disturbances in its inner equilibrium. It will start crying in different ways. By her care the mother shows it, 'this is hunger, my breast can satisfy it' or 'this is wetness, I can get rid of it'. Through her mimetic behaviour the mother takes on the mirroring function; that is, insofar as she empathetically meets the need her infant is signalling to her by crying, she mimics and reflects his bodily experiences and bestows meaning on his crying.

Three-month-old Lynn was unhappy whenever her mother pulled her baby jacket over her head. It bothered her and she would start crying. Her mother would say to her: 'Yes, I know, you don't like this at all but it's got to be done! . . . Oh God, Oh God, nothing's right? Is it such a nuisance for you; does it really make you so angry?' Was Lynn really angry? Surely she was too little to have such a structured emotion. A few weeks later Lynn no longer reacted to the same situation as if it were a catastrophe. True, she still looked unhappy, making faces, but her mother's words seemed to make her feel so secure now that she did not need to cry as the unpleasantness was just a passing thing.

One day when Lynn was three months old her mother took her off her lap and laid her on a blanket saying, 'Yes, I know you don't like this, but it has to be done!' She went away; Lynn was unhappy and started crying. I then said to her, 'This is a real bore, isn't it? These dumb adults are always doing what they want with you!' Lynn smiled as if she had understood and somehow she probably had 'understood'. She already knew the word 'dumb' (stressed) – she had heard her mother using it frequently in connection with unpleasant interactions in which she experienced something that could justifiably be called 'anger' or 'rage'. And now, as I was speaking to her, she could recognise her feeling in the tone of my voice and in my expression: they acted as a mirror and her smile showed that she was happy to have her feelings mirrored and recognised in this way.

The mother is always there as a mirror for her child from birth on, registering his expressions. With her voice, her face, her movements and actions, she responds to her child's experience and names it so reliably that the child gradually begins to recognise himself therein as a subject with wants, preferences and aversions. It is a mirror with blind spots and a frame limiting the visual field: when the mother asked three-month-old Lynn if she was really so angry this was already an interpretation. She might just as well have asked, 'Are you really so anxious?' The fact that she named one affect and not another, which both develop out of the infant's crying, was an impingement on Lynn's development. By emphasising her crying as an urgent means of defence, she affirmed her autonomy but her fears of being left at someone else's mercy as well, and her fears of dying, were left unexpressed. In such cases of impingement the mother's individually and culturally determined limitations are revealed. Frustrations can also arise when something that is important for the child remains unnamed and the affect is not designated. If, however, the frustrations remain within tolerable limits, then, in due course, the child gets to know his own boundaries and those of his love-object. He learns that mirroring and satisfaction are not always there as a matter of course and that he must appeal for them; and also that, at times, they are slow in coming. He learns that his crying has an effect on the world, that there is an interaction between the environment and himself. The sense of self and the perception of the world around thus gradually take shape and, out of the primary substances, the world of objects emerges more clearly.

The emergence of the world of objects, i.e. the perception of people and things which, unlike air, have sharp boundaries and firm contours, can only occur if the child has learnt to distinguish and recognise specific interaction forms in his contact with the environment. It was Alfred Lorenzer[6] who introduced the term 'interaction forms' into psychoanalysis to describe the subject's development as a process of interaction. Such interaction forms are recurrent patterns of satisfaction and frustration of the child's different needs; they are memory traces in which the child preserves representations both of the satisfying person as well as of his own bodily sensations in connection with the satisfaction of which it has a memory trace. If such memory traces are formed then the infant is in a position 'to hold tension in abeyance [. . .] to wait for and confidently expect satisfaction.'[7]

The mother no longer represents 'air' for the child but, to use Mahler's somewhat infelicitous formulation, a 'need-satisfying part-object'. At this stage – Mahler calls it the symbiotic phase – something new becomes important in addition to care and attention, i.e. playing. The reliability of satisfaction, the child's trust and the repeated satisfying interactions with the mother allow him – when he is not hungry or tired – to gradually discover and create a third area between him and his mother, that of playing, in which interactions are no longer governed by vital needs.

Lynn (who was now about three months old) was lying in a rocking cradle. Her mother was standing some distance away, ironing and tele- phoning at the same time. Lynn was peaceful, rested and awake; her mother's voice in the background gave her a feeling of security. And she was alone, alone with herself and with this thing: a mobile was hanging over her in such a way that by struggling and thrashing with her arms she could almost catch hold of it. The fascinating thing was moving – Lynn was moving too – struggling and thrashing energetically with her arms, not very precisely, but somehow her own movements and the fascinating object, which she was following with her eyes, were related. Lynn was being active and her mother was busy with her own things. Nothing could distract Lynn from this fascinating thing. Neither hunger nor any of the people who, unlike the object above her, would approach or move away from Lynn, independently of her thrashing movements. However – and she knew this vaguely already – she could use her voice to call them if she needed to. Even the thing moved away and came back again. The object was perhaps enabling her to repeat and experiment with experiences she had had with her mother and with hunger; she was beginning to get used to approach and distancing patterns as a 'sensuous-symbolic interaction form'.[8] With her senses, touching and seeing, she could experience the movement of the mobile and symbolically this stood for the coming and going of hunger and her mother's satisfying care. At the same time the mobile was also some- thing new, offering new experiences. So in this space created by the absence of hunger and the mother's audible presence and simultaneous absence, Lynn was able to begin to explore the world on her own.

The objects – transitional objects, including non-mothering persons – that the child plays with, become a third party in the mother–child inter-actions, originally organised as a two-person relationship. They are objects with contours, boundaries, existing independently of the child's will, yet they are also affected by his playful activity. These transitional objects thus emerge gradually from the boundless expanse of the 'primary substances' and the early mother–child relationship into the child's perceptual field. It is through such tertiary objects or persons that the child can gain a more realistic perception of himself and his mother. The child no longer feels he omnipotently controls his mother as an instrumental organ or part of himself; nor does he feel he is a powerless being, unable to defend himself against the failures of an omnipotent mother. He has acquired space to play in, and this gradually grows as he explores his environment through playing.

This development from a two-person to a three-person relationship does not occur without conflict of course: the child must put up with a good deal of disappointment with regard to his own imperfections as well as his disappointment and rage towards his mother who is neither omni-potent nor permanently available for him. The child psychoanalyst D. W. Winnicott[9] says that at this stage the child must 'destroy' his mother in order to situate her outside his narcissistic-symbiotic omnipotent phan-tasies and to be able to see her more realistically. By occasionally biting the breast, pulling her hair and, later on, thrashing around, the child tries to break free from the powerful spell of his symbiotic relationship with his mother. She has to be able to react appropriately to his aggression, neither shrinking away guiltily nor sanctioning his attempts to break away. This is a difficult hurdle in the development of the mother–child relationship. The fact that the environment constantly attributes blame, either latently or explicitly – with the result that the mother tends to be left alone to deal with the almost impossible task by herself, rather than getting the support and structure she needs – and that there is a taboo on mimetic behaviour, means that the mother cannot easily find an outlet for her aggression. Sometimes this aggression is reinforced by society's tendency to subjugate women-mothers.

It is therefore not only essential that the child's aggression can find an outlet in the relationship and be responded to, but also that the mother finds ways of expressing her own aggression so that the child can identify with her as he struggles to master his own feelings. When the mother shows the child that she cannot fulfil his wishes indefinitely and, above all, that she does not want to, whilst showing him that she can understand and accept them, she is saying to him: 'Here I am, I can't take you in my arms just now, but I do understand that you are very angry with me'. If the mother can handle it well, the child's disappointment becomes dis-illusionment: his wishes are not automatically fulfilled by an omnipotent mother–child pair, but two separate individuals relate to each other with desires, emotions, signs, gestures and words.

During this phase of child development, third parties, i.e. anyone who has a role to play in the child's life outside the symbiotic mother–child relationship, take on great significance. It is generally at this stage that the father appears as the most important object relationship after the mother. The father provides the child with a model of a relationship with the mother in which he does not lose himself symbiotically and where he can assert his autonomy aggressively and libidinously. By identifying with him and his protection, the child can distance himself from his mother and relate to her in quite a different way, i.e. as an autonomous person. This phase of separation and individuation is only partially achieved, or not achieved at all, by people with learning disabilities, and the widespread tendency of fathers to leave the mother to cope with this task alone is a significant contributing factor. This has grave consequences for the child's development, since this move towards a triangular relationship is the foundation stone for lively, autonomous learning. Symbols, words, songs, even thoughts and phantasies are also 'third parties'. Such symbols represent persons and interactions. They enable a child to imagine a person or an object in their absence. From this, autonomous thought processes as well as more realistic and critical perception of self and the environment can develop.

In any case – and this is important where the development of learning disabilities is concerned – even before the resolution of the mother–child symbiosis, or even when the level of autonomous, playful activity and thought is not attained, there is already a form of learning of the kind which behaviourism calls conditioning. In conditioning, specific stimuli come to be connected with certain responses. The newborn baby learns, for example, that certain specific experiences signify that it is going to be breast-fed and so it feels soothed in advance. Or, later, the small child learns that behaving in a certain way in given situations is rewarded – he does not know why this is so but he knows exactly what is to be gained thereby. That is, he remembers that certain kinds of behaviour are necessary in order to obtain or avoid something, unlike in playful learning where he does things for his own pleasure of discovery or through autonomous insight into the necessity of his actions. The omnipotent environment makes the dependent child act in a given way by means of conditioning that is rooted entirely in the omnipotent–impotent polarity of the two-person relationship. Consequently, for children with learning disabilities who, in terms of their social development remain stuck in this mode of relating, and who are rarely successful in making steps towards separation, this seems to be the only promising form of learning. Numerous learning and therapeutic approaches are based on this assumption.

The withholding of potential space

A child creates space for itself during the first two years of his life and the mother (the first object) also needs space in order to enable the child to achieve this. She must herself be free in the sense of having sufficient social freedom, time and external support. If these minimum environmental conditions are lacking, it may deprive both mother and child of the space they need and lead to learning disabilities. This has been shown by Spitz in his lengthy studies of foundling hospitals and children in homes: he observed that the less social contact the children enjoyed, the more clearly they showed signs of retarded and disturbed development or died as babies or toddlers.[10]

The extreme conditions of privation and emotional deprivation Spitz came across in homes and foundling hospitals are probably rare today. Sometimes, however, in lower-working-class families who live in conditions of extreme poverty and isolation, circumstances prevail which are equally detrimental for the child.

Space can be lacking; it can also be destroyed, usurped or undermined. The process of developing learning disabilities can be most easily observed where space is entirely or largely lacking or denied in situations of deprivation. Today, this is certainly not the most frequent form of learning disability but it allows us to recognise and understand what occurs in a much more complex form when the needed space is destroyed or usurped. I am now going to present the case of a girl who grew up in an extremely deprived lower-class family.

Eileen was the eighth of nine siblings; her family lived in extremely impoverished circumstances; her father was a labourer and her mother had to undertake cleaning work on top of her housework with nine children, in order to supplement their income. So there was not much time available to look after Eileen and there was in fact not enough room for her in their two-roomed apartment. Several of Eileen's siblings later ended up at a special school for people with learning difficulties. Eileen was a very quiet baby who slept a lot and was undemanding for which her completely overworked mother was only too thankful. Apart from some rudimentary care, Eileen seemed to need nothing. She could leave her lying in the next room while the other children clamoured for attention, with the result that the mother had no time to think about whether Eileen in fact needed more than just the occasional quick bottle-feed. The fact that she was so quiet made her the weakest of all the siblings and it was necessarily the child who spoke up most who got the most attention from mother. Because she made few demands, she received little and enough basic trust between Eileen and her mother was never developed for Eileen to be able to learn to play. At some point her backwardness was noticed, she was diagnosed and put into a home.

It is well known that the disadvantageous social situation of lower-class families can have a handicapping effect on the development of children. Statistics show that the large majority of children with learning disabilities come from the lower class. In his book *Dummheit ist lernbar*[11] Jürg Jegge has described the conditions that cause lower-class children to attend special schools as 'impoverished cultural stimulation', i.e. an impoverished culture of relationships characterised by the helplessness of parents who do not know how to help their child with his difficulties and hindrances and by the lack of basic trust between parents and children which leads to a weakened autonomous impulse in the child.

Lack of holding, lack of stimulation, the mother's helplessness and insufficient basic trust, are also characteristics of the conditions under which Eileen grew up. In the lower classes, society intervenes massively and directly in infantile development – not, as is the case in the middle classes, by making the mother feel guilty, but rather by a real restriction and impoverishment of the general conditions determining the child's world. As Eileen was an infant with little vitality she could not make much use of the little her environment had to offer her and was already quite unable to demand more than her stronger siblings. Later on, 'brain damage of unknown causes in infancy' was suspected. What is certain is that Eileen could not get by on the amount of attention she was getting and she developed severe learning disabilities. She learnt to walk but otherwise acquired few capacities with which she could exert influence on her environment. It is quite clear that she did not acquire the sense that she could accomplish anything in the world. Her mother's care was not tuned to Eileen's inner rhythm but much more to her own stressful condition. So Eileen's potential for acquiring experience or memory traces of satisfying relationships was far from adequate. Interaction forms, however, are a prerequisite of basic trust and a capacity for orientation in life. Eileen did not learn to have confidence in her mother; she could not expect satisfaction because her mother always expected her to stay alone too long without satisfying her. Such lack of interaction meant that Eileen, and every child in her situation, had no resources with which to fill the gaps between moments of care and attention. Hence there could be no transitional space and no playful development of satisfying experiences of being alone in the reliable presence of the mother, as in Lynn's case. Instead of transitional space, Eileen only experienced emptiness.

Interaction forms in terms of structural formations based on good memories are lacking. However, this lack has its own way of leaving its mark as Margaret Mahler has pointed out:

> Beyond a certain level which, however, has as yet to be defined, the immature organism is not able to achieve homeostasis by itself. Whenever during this early phase, 'organismic distress' – that forerunner of

anxiety proper – appears, the mothering partner is called upon to contribute a particularly large portion of symbiotic help toward the maintenance of the infant's homeostasis. Otherwise, the neurobiological patterning processes are thrown out of kilter. Somatic memory traces are set at this time which amalgamate with later experiences and may thereby increase later psychological pressures.[12]

If such situations happen too frequently, as was the case with Eileen, then these destructive somatic memory traces have a handicapping effect on development in as much as they undermine even further the minimum conditions of basic trust.

In spite of all the privation Eileen suffered, she nonetheless managed to find certain ways – even if very damaged ones – by which she could accomplish something in her environment. She learnt to walk and this independence of locomotion meant she could look for the 'symbolic part-object' that she had so often had to do without. She was not looking for a particular person in the way that a more fortunate baby soon learns to distinguish between his mother and others, but anyone who happened to cross her path. She learnt (one of her few life-giving modes of interaction) that by holding tight, clinging, hugging, she could to some extent prolong the fleeting moments of care and thereby obtain some sort of social contact. So as soon as she had learned to walk, she would cling to her mother and to her siblings whenever possible. In this way she finally found a means of asserting her unlimited neediness in the environment. However, while it is possible for a less deprived child at this age to accept a 'no', to respect himself, and, when he hugs people, to sense whether the other person is willing to be hugged, her hugging was determined by privations and unlimited neediness. In this case, as with a hungry infant, the possibilities and limitations of the environment do not enter into it. (Later this was called 'lacking a sense of distance' and was regarded as a symptom of her suspected brain damage.) With this clinging behaviour which was the result of her basic experience of being pushed away and got rid of, she repeatedly provoked this pattern instead of being able to defend herself effectively against it. She was brushed off, pushed away and 'got rid of' because her mother had to cope with a heavy work-load (another child had now been born who could stand up for herself better than Eileen was able to as a baby) and because her siblings were preoccupied with their own concerns and neediness. As soon as she was put in a home Eileen's clinging behaviour resumed and even intensified. I understand Eileen's clinging as symptomatic behaviour for it seems to be meaningless and dysfunctional like a symptom and, of all people, Eileen had the least idea of what it meant when she was thrusting herself on everyone like that. If we look closely and try to understand, this symptomatic behaviour is evidence of a need which Eileen had never learnt to formulate; it is evidence of her unlimited neediness and deprivation. As she could not express symbolically in any other way what she needed, she was condemned to enact her needs and deprivation over and over again with any number of people.

Symptomatic behaviour is not a symbolic expression of needs (this is also valid for those needs which do not arise from pure privation) but a re-enactment of their non-fulfilment. If the child is lacking space in which to work over experiences into sensuous-symbolic modes of interaction and to free them from direct dependence on the two-person relationship, then they always remain stimulus–response patterns. The child then has no inde-pendent idea of what he needs or of his capacity to get what he needs from his environment. Furthermore, he lacks the distance with which to evaluate the appropriateness of his reflex responses. In particular, it is those modes of interaction that cannot be separated from destructive memory traces which, as a rule, cannot be developed further in a creative way. Similarly most of the care given to a child who grows up in deprived conditions is inextricably bound up with the destructive experience of lack. Whenever this occurs, the child remains stuck at the level behaviourists call condi-tioning which is practised methodically in behaviour therapy. However, there is no room here for creative play and autonomy based on a child's curiosity and pleasure in physical and intellectual functioning.

Spitz's observations throw light on the shocking formation and handi-capping effect of symptoms in situations of deprivation. When there is a 'partial withdrawal of affection', he writes, 'anaclitic depression sets in. Next, shortly after losing their caretaker, babies start to cry and cling to anyone within reach; then they begin to withdraw more and more, screaming a lot and finally they just whine and become lethargic.' The consequences of a complete withdrawal of emotional contact are commonly called hospitalism. With many children damaged by hospitalism Spitz observed:

> . . . bizarre finger movements reminiscent of decerebrate or athetotic movements. These children went through progressive stages of deteri-oration and by the end of the second year the average of their developmental quotients stands at 45% of the normal. This would be the level of the idiot. We continued to observe these children at longer intervals up to the age of four years. [. . .] By that time, with a few exceptions, these children cannot sit, stand, walk or talk . . . . Increased infection liability, on the one hand, and progressive deterioration, on the other, led to an extremely high rate of depression and mortality in these children.[13]

The lack of loving care and attention gives rise to serious symptoms:

> Clinically, these infants become incapable of assimilating food; they become insomniac, later they may actively attack themselves, banging

their heads against the side of the cot, hitting their heads with their fists, tearing their hair out by the fistful.[14]

Perhaps Eileen obtained from her mother more attention than the children in the foundling home who were the subjects of Spitz's shocking observations but what her mother was able to give her was in any case not enough. And so along with a generally severe retardation, she developed a string of symptoms resembling those of the children Spitz observed: clinging, making strange, complicated twiddling movements with her fingers and hitting herself in the face. In addition, she developed a form of echolalia which was pure repetition without any trace of a perceptible understanding of language. She would repeat certain sentences, mostly greetings and instructions, over and over again, without there being any recognisable connection with the actual situation: 'Oh, Eileen', 'come on, Eileen', 'come here', 'leave that alone', 'stand up' etc. The intonation and pronunciation were amazingly well imitated and yet her words sounded meaningless and empty.

As bizarre and shocking as such symptoms may seem and although they appear initially to have little meaning, it is incumbent on us to try and understand how they have come about and what their meaning is. In attempting to do this I am simply offering an outline for an understanding which will need to be re-evaluated anew with each person with learning disabilities.

Eileen had not been able to fill the transitional space with positive memories. There was no protective cushion of interaction forms, ideas, phantasies to protect her from the constant void and loneliness, from being invaded by the powerful feelings of discomfort in her organism, from being bombarded by sense impressions from without. So each time reality intruded, her inner equilibrium was inevitably shaken. She tried to recover her balance by means of 'stereotypes': rocking her upper body, making complicated twiddling movements in front of her eyes and mouth, making endless circling movements with ribbons in front of her face, repeating her parroted sentences endlessly and hitting herself monotonously in the face.

Rocking is an endless movement in search of equilibrium – and equilibrium, homeostasis, was Eileen's only lifeline. By rocking she was endeavouring to shut out the unreliable and threatening environment and to make everything fuse into boundlessness and limitlessness. Body-rocking induces dizziness, contours become hazy and everything becomes discontinuous. The environment becomes blurred, inducing the boundless state of Eileen's rocking. Like this she could avoid becoming aware of the reality of her loneliness and unsatisfied needs.

It was the same with her twiddling and playing with ribbons: the continuous movement in front of her eyes produced the enveloping feeling of dizziness. In his example of the finger twiddling of an autistic girl, Marcia, Bruno Bettelheim gives a detailed analysis of this symptom:

Twiddling as a symptom (to which should probably be added rocking, head rolling and head banging) is highly over-determined, has many roots and serves many purposes. Among its uses, we have little doubt that it creates a 'deep screen' on which the child projects his own private reality. For example, while autistic children show an apparent inattentiveness to sensory stimuli from the outside, some actually produce this lack of receptivity by the excessive, unvaried self-stimulation that arises from their strange motor behaviour. In this way, outer stimuli are blotted out by and 'lost' in the sensations the child stirs in himself. [. . .]

The twiddled fingers, as they move in front of the face, have the effect of blurring the vision of reality. The result is that whatever the twiddling child sees, he sees as if through a self-created screen. Reality, if seen at all, flickers by in a discontinuous manner but a discontinuity that the child himself creates. [. . .] In lieu of an unbearable reality he creates a private one whose visual appearance he controls through the speed of his twiddling. To some degree it is thus an effort to reshape reality and make it bearable.[15]

Furthermore, Bettelheim makes a connection between Marcia's twiddling and early severe experiences of deprivation:

Only Marcia did not find such relief [thumb sucking; D.N.]. Her hand had no opportunity to grasp the breast and so to support the grasping mouth in its sucking. [. . .] And while it did come to stand for the breast [which in reality had been missing; D.N.], it was a breast Marcia reached for but which nevertheless remained inaccessible. She shook or twiddled only the forefinger, supported often by the third finger; but though she was constantly moving the finger or fingers toward her mouth, they never touched it, and much less entered the oral cavity.[16] [. . .] This twiddling seems the opposite of thumb (or finger) sucking. Far from satisfying the desire to suck, it symbolises the desire for, and total absence of, this pleasure.[17]

Eileen is not an autistic girl and yet her twiddling as well as the game with the ribbons circling in front of her face can be understood in the same way. The symptomatic behaviour represents the attempt to master an unbearable experience of reality through repetition. A great deal of energy is required in such attempts at gaining control. As in Bettelheim's descriptions of Marcia, Eileen's twiddling was so complicated that no one could copy it, although attempts were often made to do so, because the movements had the beauty and elegance of a kind of finger ballet. Through her efforts to survive this girl, who had severe learning disabilities, developed an inimitable, masterly skill.

Symptomatic forms of behaviour are thus in no way meaningless 'stereotypes' as traditional teaching on learning disability often implies. They are survival techniques in which a large part of the vital energies of people with learning disabilities are tied up.

Eileen's attempts to extend her autistic shell with her fingers and ribbons were insufficient. There was always stimulation from the outer world or from her own body which was stronger, traumatically interrupting the continuity of the inner absence, as I would call her permanent condition. I trace her echolalia, her parroting of instructions back to this. Without the necessary potential space she could not learn to speak but she could repeat mechanically. If you said something to her, for example, if you asked her to 'stand up' or 'come here', what you said did not meet with an under-standing that would allow her to decide whether she wanted to respond to it; instead, it interrupted her state of forlornness and the lack of awareness of herself and the environment around her. It forced something from her; it was stronger than her self-created boundlessness. It invaded her continuum and threatened to destroy it. Her amazing capacity to mechanically repeat instructions derived from this and she could do it at any time, not only after she had just heard them.

In this way she endeavoured to integrate the repeated impingements on her continuum into this boundless monotony and to render the trauma harmless by means of such repetition. Just as she tried to create the con-tinuum with her rocking, so she tried to make the instructions merge with this rocking: 'Eileen no – nononono . . .'.

Rocking occurs even with words and sentences: baby Lynn could already perceive and sense this swinging of the pendulum outside herself. In the game with the mobile she got an idea of how hunger comes and goes and of how her mother is able to satisfy it. This is an interaction based on an exchange, first, of signals (Lynn's crying, the mother's voice signalling her availability) and, later, of symbols (when the child can call out with names instead of screaming). Lynn's world gradually evolved from a narrow two-person relationship in which she felt cared for and held to one filled with third parties: objects, other people and symbols. Eileen's world did not extend in this way to the three-dimensional: symbols, words with meaning had no place in it. Unlike in Lynn's game with the mobile, her rocking, even with words, was not based on an emerging sense of boundaries and objects in the external world which are good and helpful. 'Rocking' with her voice, with mechanically repeated words, blurred the threatening contours, integrating them into her state of boundlessness.

Such parroting is by no means always void of meaning. Echolalia is present in the most varied forms. For some people – mostly those with autism or infantile psychosis – this parroting definitely has meaning. It represents a compromise between the attempt to let the reality of a threateningly structured world be submerged in this continuum and the contrary desire to have some influence over it.

Brigitte is also the daughter of an unskilled working-class family with a large number of children. She is a very disturbed and unhappy young woman who frequently pulls her hair and berates herself angrily: 'Haven't I told you, you shouldn't . . .' and so on. The rest of the self-scolding dies away into an incomprehensible angry muttering. This is also an attempt to amalgamate the abuse into a continuum. At the same time, however, it seems to me that Brigitte is nonetheless trying to make contact with the environment (she is clearly less retarded than Eileen and has learnt in some areas to acknowledge a world of objects) and wants to show how unspeakably bad, evil, and worthless she feels.

In one of Brigitte's music therapy sessions that I was able to take part in as a guest student, I observed the formation of an echolalic sentence. The music therapist was sitting on a blanket stroking and caressing Brigitte's baby doll. Brigitte was standing back a little, looking on with yearning. She was berating herself harshly as if her longing to get involved in this symbiotic situation and to take the doll's place were a terrible crime and she did not trust herself enough to do it. Finally, the music therapist stood up and held out her hands to Brigitte who took hold of them and pinched them very hard. Taken aback by the sudden pain the therapist reacted by reproaching her: 'Ow, that really hurt!' Brigitte flinched and took a step backwards. She began rocking from one foot to the other and then, in synchronisation with her rocking, said, 'Ow, that really hurt, that really hurt . . .'. This sounded so unbearably desperate and forlorn that I was moved to tears in the corner from where I was looking on. The music therapist understood the situation, went over to the piano and played two notes alternately, two screeching, painful, dissonant notes, in rhythm with Brigitte's rocking and speaking. Brigitte went on rocking like this for a long time, contained by the therapist's understanding. She kept on repeating the sentence which had disturbed and hurt her so much, and which was further proof of her badness. Slowly, with the empathic musical accompaniment, the pain lessened, her rocking slowed and she spoke more softly. The therapist went on playing with her until she had rocked her fright away and regained her equilibrium.

What was happening here? The therapist offered a symbiotic relationship; she enacted with the doll what Brigitte herself was dearly longing for. Brigitte could not put herself in the doll's place because some experience or other told her that her longing to be held and cuddled was something bad and forbidden. I do not know much about Brigitte's history apart from her social background; however, observations from her therapy – understood as re-enactments of her early life experiences – allow us to make certain assumptions. When I asked Brigitte's music therapist if I could sit in on a few therapy sessions, she suggested I should attend Brigitte's sessions because she wanted to speak with me about her work with this young woman. She simply was not making any progress with her – Brigitte would not take part in any of the games she proposed. She had bought the baby doll for her because babies fascinated her, but this had not brought about any changes in the therapy.

In the first observation session I could see how the therapist was very caring towards Brigitte, proposing, in vain, many forms of play. However, I was alarmed by the way she treated the baby doll, that is, hurriedly, carelessly and roughly, scarcely paying any attention to it during the session. The doll is Brigitte, I thought to myself. Together with my colleague, we set up a role-play in which the therapist was supposed to hold and cuddle the doll so that Brigitte could feel that she was accepted. The therapist's hurried and careless handling of the doll seemed to be an unconscious aspect of her counter-transference towards Brigitte, a partial re-enactment of Brigitte's childhood during which she had probably been hastily and roughly treated by an overworked mother. At the same time, the environment – like the therapist offering to play games – was driving her into a corner by stimulating her with sense-impressions and demands. It was as if the prohibitions and persecuting injunctions which Brigitte tortured herself with, while staring with yearning at the symbiotic scene between the therapist and the doll, represented her mother's voice. The latter may have tried in this way to ward off her child's symbiotic needs, for she was overworked just as the therapist was also overstrained in her work with Brigitte. This was finding expression in her careless handling of the doll.

When Brigitte pinched the therapist's extended hand and she over-reacted, the hypothetical original trauma was re-enacted. Perhaps as a baby Brigitte had sometimes bitten her mother, as babies do when they are experimenting with separation and autonomy and, just like the music therapist, she had reacted with shock and withdrawal (but without being able to comfort Brigitte). So what this experience probably meant for Brigitte was this: by saying 'I', I am asserting myself against the symbiotic partner and am beginning to feel my own desires for symbiosis and separation; I am destroying the other person and so I must be unspeakably bad. Brigitte's capacity to say 'I' was clearly so fragile that after the trauma she again gave up the capacity she had already developed for a symbiotic relationship (later expressed in her predilection for babies), and regressed to rocking, to a continuum, void of desire. With the unspeakable despair, however, which she expressed in her echolalic sentences, she nonetheless maintained a certain contact with the environment. It filled her parroting with meaning whereas Eileen's sounded only empty for she had never reached the point from which Brigitte regressed so disastrously.

Where there is no possibility for elaboration through symbolic play, imperious realities are expressed as traumas. They cannot become meaningful experiences but are like pebbles that have been thrown into a lake causing ripples that can be seen as attempts to regain an equilibrium disturbed by the stone or the trauma. Initially, this is the only form of integrating experience that is available to infants. It has its origin in the rocking by means of which the first experiences of vibration in the womb are absorbed. We know from experience that the ripples in a lake get wider and wider and that once a pendulum is set in motion it goes on endlessly unless there are external forces opposing its motion so that it finds its point of equilibrium again. For Eileen, Brigitte or anyone else who develops deficient interaction forms and who is denied the space they need to grow in, these containing forces – to stay with the image – are too weak. So their ripples, their self-rocking, their endless repeating of the trauma in an attempt to restore balance has to go on for ever.

Eileen discovered one form of play, one interactional game: throwing a ball. She would throw it and sometimes it came back; that is, when her carers caught the ball and saw that Eileen wanted to throw the ball back and forth to them. But this 'back and forth' experience was not one that Eileen was familiar with. Eileen played just as a baby does when it throws things away and forgets them if no one gives them back, enjoying it when what has 'gone out of sight and out of mind' re-appears again and again. This was her attempt to work over her unchanging experience through play: the experience that the people she abandoned herself to, whom she tried to hold in her arms, could really accept her because 'really accepting her' would mean staying with her until she was satisfied. That was impossible. Eileen could never get enough. She was insatiable because she did not have the confidence of knowing that the separation was not final. In the ball game she was actively trying to control the experience of being abandoned and thrown away which she repeatedly provoked by her clinging. Unfortunately, her carers did not understand that it was important for Eileen that the balls she seemed to throw away heedlessly came back to her again. Only in this way could she learn that relationships are not irrevocably destroyed by each and every separation. She thus experienced herself as being destructive when she threw herself away, for even with the best will in the world those caring for her sooner or later stopped taking her in their arms which meant for Eileen that she had destroyed them with her insatiability. And now the same thing was being repeated in the ball game: when she just threw the ball away in any direction she liked and it did not come back, then she felt she had 'destroyed' it. Her ball game also acquired a traumatic character. Once again Eileen had to try to come to grips with her trauma. Her search for a response and mirroring and her dissipated vital energies now had to be turned against herself in the form of self-aggression in order somehow or other to have the experience of an indestructible partner. So she would hit herself in the face unrelentingly and monotonously and this at last obtained a reliable response: reliable and indestructible, always a dull pain. Sometimes she pretended she was crying but she was not really: there was no one there to hear her.

People with learning disabilities who come from a less disadvantageous social background than Eileen also develop symptomatic behaviour like this. An infant may be particularly needy without its mother sensing it or it may be that she simply finds no way to meet its neediness and, discouraged and oppressed by guilt feelings, gives up. Children who are born deaf and blind mostly develop symptoms analogous to the ones I have described. Their capacity for sensorial perception and thus for the formation of sensory-symbolic interaction forms is so severely limited that even the most loving and empathic care can scarcely save them from severe disability. However, unlike mothers from marginal families, whose only means of defence when a child like Eileen cannot manage with what they have to offer is to act with indifference, mothers from a better social background respond to the sense or perception of their child's special neediness with anxiety and guilt feelings. They do not act with indifference towards their child but rather are driven by these feelings which produce different effects in the child. Outwardly, the symptoms may be the same – general retardation, finger dangling, echolalia, head-banging, etc. – but such forms of behaviour not only trigger guilt feelings in the mother but also release analogous counter-transference feelings in caregivers and therapists. They are provocative. Eileen's hitting herself was calm in comparison, it did not provoke or make anyone angry or anxious; it simply had a quality of being desolate, meaningless, completely inconsolable. The environment shrugged its shoulders with lame indifference and hopelessness: nothing could be done about it. I felt the same way when I first got to know her. To begin with I could not see any space there for therapy at all. The way she hit herself, it seemed to me, symbolised the infinite hopelessness of someone who had experienced nothing but privation. She had learnt in the most merciless manner what it means to be weak in a society where opportunity is only given to those from whom profit can be made. This society has already pushed her parents to its fringes but, as the weakest among the weak, she has absolutely no place in it at all. She no longer has access to that which, according to the logic of productivity and profitability, is considered as a *lebenswertes Leben*.

Potential space demolished and the invasion of phantasms

The space that is essential for a child's development is frequently not merely lacking, but destroyed or undermined by active interference in the mother–child relationship. This is apt to unsettle the mother's confidence or sense of competence and to plunge her into feelings of guilt and panic which dominate her relationship to her child thereafter. Fears of failure and guilt feelings play a destructive role not only in the middle class but also in the working class, unless the privation is so great that there is no room left for anything but indifference. Mothers frequently react with guilt feelings when they are forced to pass on their own lack of space to their needy child. For Eileen's mother, indifference was her means of survival and did not just affect Eileen. Parents, whose social conditions are not quite so desolate, sometimes ward off their guilt feelings with an indifference that nevertheless reveals their feelings of despair. Once I saw Inge's (see Chapter 7, 'A child without behavioural difficulties') mother crying because she had to put her six-year-old daughter in a home because she (the mother) was paralysed and living alone in impoverished social circumstances – as if she herself was to blame for her deprived situation. She had probably always resorted to indifference as a defence against guilt feelings. When she could see that Inge needed her help but that she could not get to her in her wheelchair, and so had to leave her alone for hours, indifference was her main line of defence against guilt. This defence had a different meaning for Inge's development than the indifference of Eileen's parents. In Eileen's life there was simply a lack of transitional space because her mother's activity, feelings and actions were completely preoccupied with surviving deprivation, and so she had 'nothing to spare' for Eileen. On the other hand Inge's mother, whose phantasies were usurped by guilt feelings, was totally fixated on her child. Inge's neediness took up a lot of space in her feelings and thoughts but it was space that was entirely invested or filled by the mother's needs and guilty anxiety and therefore was not available for the child.

It is not just a matter of real space, of real time. These are just preconditions for the space for phantasy needed by the mother if she is to be able to give her child the opportunity of creating his or her own space through play. She creates the transitional space for the child insofar as she is free in her own phantasies to empathise with the child's needs when he or she needs her, and to attend to her own desires when the child is able to be alone.

A mother like Inge's is not free in her phantasies: when she looks after her child she is always afraid of 'having too little to give' and so she cannot relax and be playful. When she leaves the child alone, it is not because she has her own life to live but because she cannot do otherwise, and her despair about this is communicated to the child in the form of tension. Inge breathes in the tense atmosphere like a poison spoiling the space she needs for breathing and playing in.

In the relationship between Inge and her mother the space for phantasy is restricted by privation; it is cathected with the mother's sense of guilt. In middle-class families privation seldom plays a role. Here, the space is not lacking but is destroyed or buried under anxiety.

When Lynn was nine months old – by which time she was already a happy, energetic and curious little girl – a threatening crisis erupted in the mother–child relationship which hitherto had been fairly harmonious. During a routine check-up, their doctor noticed that Lynn was unable to make movements lying on her tummy and showed no inclination for crawling. He told the mother it was time Lynn was learning to do this and asked her if she would consider taking Lynn to see a physiotherapist. When he saw that the mother was alarmed, he tried to appease and reassure her, saying there was no need to worry. However, from then on, the mother could not help watching her child's attempts to move with unease and mistrust and Lynn made no further progress, simply crying when her mother tried to talk her into doing something. After giving the matter a lot of thought – she did not want to harm her child, wondered if she already had and also noticed that Lynn did not like 'practising' – and after speaking with friends who supported her decision, she decided against the prescribed physiotherapy sessions. Lynn would learn to crawl in her own time. This was a hard struggle for the mother to go through. Only when she felt a bit more secure about her decision against physiotherapy and, particularly, when she was finally able to stop staring obsessively at Lynn's movements, did Lynn show signs of making new attempts at locomotion. At this juncture, there was another visit to the doctor. He asked the mother what Lynn had learnt in the meantime and wanted Lynn to demonstrate her new acquisitions. Lynn, however, was 'unable' to do anything and just screamed pitifully. Only when the doctor stopped observing her in order to talk with the mother was she able to pull herself up into the standing position by herself.

Later, the mother told me how during this period of crisis she had gradually become aware that since this traumatic visit to the doctor she had been unable to accept Lynn as she was, and was always preoccupied in her phantasies with the 'defect', with anxieties, and guilt feelings. Lynn was no longer able to play by herself but was under pressure because the mother needed to see specific games and movements to prove that she had nothing to reproach herself with. Lynn's strength (which her mother was only able to recognise retrospectively) had been to resist so steadfastly. Only when the connection became clear for the mother was she able to gradually recover her former relaxed attitude towards her child (soon after, Lynn was able to walk). After the doctor's intervention* the space between mother and child was too taken up with anxiety, mistrust and guilt feelings. The mother loved her child no less than before; she gave her just as much attention as before but her devotion and her confidence had been undermined and her

---

* I would like to comment here that the doctor cannot be held responsible. His intervention, which, as the mother told me later, was made with all due caution and with the intention of strengthening the mother, unfortunately triggered the latent guilty anxiety of the mother whose role in bringing her child up alone was particularly precarious.

child could sense this: the mother's anxiety and guilty phantasies deprived Lynn of space to play and grow in. Her development was retarded. Mother and child could only overcome the crisis when the mother was able to free herself of her anxious phantasies and to see her child's retardation no longer as a threatening disability but as a helpless protest.

A crisis can occur when a doctor's well-meaning intervention triggers the mother's latent guilty anxiety and she wonders: 'Have I somehow damaged my child?' When she looks at her child her expression is no longer one of joy and pride but of doubt. She is constantly watching him anxiously, looking for some sign of the child's achievements to confirm that she has in fact not damaged him. The potential space is no longer free as in the game with the mobile; on the contrary, it is undermined and cathected with worries and doubts. When a child develops learning disabilities, a similar situation prevails but in most cases it is much more extreme and less easy for the mother to see through. External interventions – diagnoses or personal observations and events that are likely to plunge the mother into anxiety and doubt – are more massive and more incisive. Whether due to organic impairment or some other cause, the child's vulnerability is greater and the mother–child relationship, often already fragile, is less protected and generally more endangered.

Sarah was a wanted child. Her parents' joy over her birth was certainly marred by the fact that she was born with a cleft palate and so for a long time had to be fed with a tube. The mother had intended to breast-feed her but now she decided that she would give her own milk. She bottled her milk and drove to the hospital every morning so that her child could be fed with it. One morning when she went to deliver her milk and visit her young daughter she was told, 'Sarah . . . Sarah . . . but she is not here any more!' She then learnt – her whole body was trembling with shock – that the child had been moved to another hospital. When, still numbed from shock, she asked why, she was told that Sarah could be looked after better in the other hospital (why this had happened so suddenly and without her being informed she was not told). When she got there she learnt that her child was in an oxygen tent. The reason given was that Sarah had turned blue and the decision had been taken as a precautionary measure.

Later, a young foreign doctor said to her several times with a note of urgency, 'You must ask them to tell you exactly what happened; question them closely about it!' She could hardly take in what the doctor was saying as she was in such a state of confusion and anxiety. First, she tried to get them to let her take her child home because she wanted to keep control over what happened to her. To do this she would have to learn how to feed Sarah with a tube. A sister on the ward showed her what to do explaining, 'You must make sure the tube is introduced into the oesophagus and not the trachea. If the child is gasping for air and turns blue, that means you have not done it properly!'

Furnished with these instructions and warnings she finally took Sarah home with her. Feeding her soon became an ordeal, however. She was constantly anxious about doing something wrong and of endangering her child's life. She could never feel relaxed and so the life-giving mother–child interaction with which everything begins could never develop into the cosy, relaxed togetherness which is so important for building a mother–child relationship based on trust. On one occasion her worst fears materialised. During a feed, the child began gasping for air as if the tube had been introduced into her windpipe. Feeling completely at the end of her tether she got the child into the car, drove her to the hospital and asked that she be taken into care again; she simply could not cope any longer. Her request was refused and she was told that she would have to manage on her own from then on.

Meanwhile, what the foreign doctor had said to her kept going round and round in her head: 'You should question them closely . . .'. What had he meant? This was really troubling her so she began to make inquiries at the hospital, but no one could answer her questions. When she asked to see the medical file she was told it had 'disappeared'. She asked about the young doctor and was told he had moved to an unknown address.

Why had Sarah developed learning disabilities? There is reason to suspect that when she was put in an oxygen tent due to a lack of oxygen intake, she suffered brain damage. The mother was naturally afraid of this too. The diagnosis of organic brain damage thus seemed obvious. And yet it seemed to me too easy to assert that Sarah's severe learning disabilities were a direct consequence of brain damage.

> What the constitution or the diagnosis of brain damage means exactly is almost impossible to say. We only know, for instance, that abnormal electro-encephalogram results are statistically more frequent in people with psychopathological personality traits. We shall have to make do for the time being with the statement that diffuse brain damage in infancy is an unfavourable biological basis for the development of personality. The chances of compensating and offsetting unfavourable developmental conditions, traumas and so on, are certainly more restricted, which means such individuals are more at the mercy of their environment than others. At any rate, in this respect, it is important to consider the fact of brain damage as the basis of psychopathological developments and as indicating certain limitations in the capacity for development.[18]

Let us go along with these remarks and suppose for the time being that Sarah really did suffer brain damage from oxygen starvation. It follows that the unfavourable conditions in which she found herself would have been extremely difficult for any infant. Her mother had to cope with a baby who was not only difficult to feed but was also particularly sensitive and in need of protection. She thus suspected and feared brain damage and in her more or less conscious phantasies imagined all sorts of consequences without having any precise information.

Sarah's early life situation made it particularly difficult for Sarah to achieve compensatory capacities. On the contrary, she learnt very early on that the life-giving situation of feeding signified danger. On at least two occasions she had the experience of nearly choking during feeding. These bad experiences could only have been offset by a sufficient number of compensatory good experiences. However, she had no experience of the satisfaction of suckling and swallowing; the only thing she had ever swallowed was a tube. Worse still, probably, was the fact that at every feed (when she was finally at home with her mother) she could sense her mother's rising anxiety. While she wanted to do Sarah good by giving her milk, she knew there was a risk that she might cause her to choke to death.

Suckling and swallowing are usually the first active experiences a child has. The earliest forms of interaction a child acquires are based on these early experiences and when they are lacking it must be very difficult to compensate for them. With Sarah, however, they were not simply lacking; in their place she experienced time and again what was probably a rather unpleasant or even painful procedure which she could take little part in actively. While one of the first interaction forms of more fortunate children is being able to signal what they need by crying, not only did Sarah not have this experience but, in addition, when she cried because of hunger pains she was also signalling her fears of dying. It is not surprising under the circumstances that Sarah turned out to be a rather quiet child. It is also understandable that she did not learn to look at her mother with joy or later on to reach out to her with her arms.

So the potential space between mother and child and the trust on which it is based were undermined by nameless anxiety, that is, the mother's fear of killing her child, her fear of the nameless something which the young doctor may have been referring to, the child's anxiety which cannot really be called anxiety as yet because she had not even had the opportunity of developing such a structured feeling. She had only experienced the 'organismic distress' which Mahler calls the 'real precursor of anxiety', and which Sarah experienced not only when she was hungry but also during breast-feeding. So she had no other choice but to feel, hear and see nothing.

I wonder what it must be like for a mother who has to bring up her child under such dreadful conditions, who is left alone with her anxieties, and who is caught up in a kind of crime-story until she is told that in future she will have to cope on her own.

For Sarah, in any case, there was hardly any 'space for growth'. Her first important interaction forms were inseparably fused with her mother's anxious phantasies and her own fears of death and suffering; her mother's lively, loving phantasies had been destroyed and the potential space which they could have created together was usurped by the mother's anxiety.

Sarah and her mother's story may seem like a dreadful isolated case, but it is in no way so. It is not infrequent to find similar dreadful stories lurking behind the facade of entirely normal life circumstances.

The other extreme can also be found. Case histories where everything was apparently normal have evolved towards learning disability. There were no obvious traumatic events or family constellations to give cause for doubt and frequently the fact that behaviour was entirely normal resulted in no questions being asked.

Helmut, the only child of a married couple living in comfortable circumstances, has learning disabilities. When he was two years old he had an infection with a high fever and from that point on his parents noticed a clearly retarded development, suspecting that he had suffered encephalitis during the infection. From early on, both parents, but particularly the mother, tried to compensate for the suspected organic defect as much as possible by intensive practising. The young boy is very co-operative and often asks, 'Mummy, when are we going to practise again?' He is still very dependent as a teenager on his mother's constant care. When he is asked a question, he frequently gives seemingly meaningless answers and he himself asks the same more or less silly questions for hours on end which his parents patiently answer. All of this can easily be 'explained' by his learning disabilities.

Sarah became autistic; Helmut developed into one of those friendly compliant simpletons who time and again lead us into believing that their disability is due to a purely organic cause.

'Oh, là, là, why do you ask me to read? Don't you know that I can't' – this was how a ten-year-old girl who was brought to a consultation with Maud Mannoni[19] saw her situation. Everyone knows that there is an organic defect and consequently it is clear that the child 'can't'. Helmut saw himself like this too and his parents also believed that he was unable to do anything. When he was sixteen, he started music therapy. His first mark of success was to be able to get to therapy alone using public transport. His mother told the therapist, 'At last I have got him to the point where he can get here by himself!' It was *her* success, *she* got him to do it. His only achievement was that at long last he had successfully carried out a task in accordance with his mother's wishes.

In the context of these interactions his seemingly meaningless questions and answers do not sound so senseless. 'Did I destroy Mrs M's (his music therapist's) bell?' he asked his parents over and over again, always receiving the same answer which was that they did not know. Of course, they were right, and yet so was his question. If his parents always 'knew everything', if he always had to be shown by them what was best for him, if they knew and he did not, if they had to 'make' him do everything, then logically his parents ought to know this too.

Both examples have one point in common with Lynn's lateness in learning to walk: the mothers each had reason to fear their children had a disability. Clearly, in both Lynn's and Sarah's cases the mothers even feared that they might damage or had already damaged their child. The mothers, I repeat, no longer have the freedom for playful phantasy; they are filled with anxiety and stare at what they fear to be signs of their child's disability. The mother's relaxed presence and capacity to be alone, which enabled Lynn to have her first experience of playing with the mobile, becomes difficult, if not impossible, if the mother can no longer have confidence that the child's autonomous activities are important and good and helpful for its development. By talking about the bell that he was afraid he had destroyed, Helmut was probably trying to tell his parents something about the destructive effect of his mother's anxiety-dominated phantasies in which she imagined she had to decide everything for him since he could no longer take care of himself owing to his disability. Maud Mannoni, the only psychoanalytic author to date who has seriously tackled the issues of learning disability, speaks of the 'mother's phantasms', and describes how she was led 'to search for the meaning that a feebleminded child may have for his family, above all for the mother, and to understand that unconsciously the child gives a meaning to the feeblemindedness that is governed by the meaning his parents give to it.'[20] Such phantasms, she writes, are derivatives of the phantasies that every mother has about her child which have their roots in unconscious memories of her own childhood.

> What does the birth of a child mean to the mother? Insofar as what she wants during pregnancy is above all revenge for a repetition of her own childhood, the arrival of a child will take its place among her vanished dreams: a dream that must fill the void left in her own past, a phantasy image superimposed upon the 'real' person of the child. The mission of this dream child is to restore, to make up for what in the mother's history was regarded as deficient, what was felt to be lacking, or to prolong what she was forced to give up. So what will become of this child if, burdened with all his mother's vanished dreams, he arrives disabled? The irruption into reality of an image of the disabled body will be a shock for the mother: at the very moment when, on the phantasy plane, a void is filled by an Imaginary child, she is confronted by the real being who, because of his disability [. . .] will awaken earlier traumas and disappointments.[21]

The child with a disability and, I would like to add, with a disability that is feared or phantasised by the mother, compels the mother to adjust her phantasies to him anew. Unlike a healthy child who can make up for a deficiency by himself, he requires the mother, so it seems to her at least, to act and decide for him. The child thus acquires in her phantasies the status of an object and cannot learn to recognise himself as a person with his own desires that seem different to those other people have. When Mannoni speaks of the 'meaning' the mother bestows in her phantasies on her child's retardedness, I feel it is important to emphasise once again that, in order to feel empathy, she has to have recourse, in the context of her motherly regression, to phantasies that are rooted in her own early infantile experiences. These phantasies do not only stem from the mother's own privations and negative experiences and, as long as she can play freely with them, they do not 'overlay' the child's 'real personality' but to a certain extent facilitate his development. Only when the mother is compelled to fixate her phantasies in the unconscious and to use societal phantasms as a defence does the child become an object of them. Such fixations arise when something has shaken the mother up in such a way that she can no longer trust her mimetic ability. The phantasies stemming from the mother's own childhood which form the basis of her capacity for empathy can no longer function when she feels that her child has something 'completely different' about him, something dreadful or monstrous. When the mother–child relationship begins to 'derail' or go awry phantasmatically, there is always a sense of dread, be it conscious or unconscious – a 'nameless dread' or, to use the words of one mother, 'a primitive and private anxiety isolating me from other people', i.e. anxiety which makes her feel lonely because it cannot be expressed. It is the anxiety that arises when one can no longer trust one's own perceptions, feelings and impulses, when something has undermined or destroyed this trust. This was what happened to Helmut's parents. After their child's infection, they could no longer believe in his own capacity for self-development. Similarly Sarah's mother found herself alone with her child and lost her capacity for spontaneous empathy. The mother's anxiety and dread should be seen as the starting-point of the phantasmatic 'derailment', rather like the feeling we would have if, when riding a roller coaster, we suddenly lost confidence in the rails or thought they were faulty in some way. A mother who finds herself in such a threatening situation will then try in panic – to stay with the metaphor – to bring the racing train to a halt, or to struggle against it, and, in so doing, will clutch at the shortest straw which seems to offer something to hold on to.

This means anything that can replace the disoriented mother's broken trust in her own perceptions and confidence in her own actions. By casting aspersions of guilt and doubt on mothers' competence, the environment, instead of giving mothers who are in such a desperate situation the support and the relief from responsibility (as well as from guilt) they need, allowing them to recover their inner equilibrium and a spontaneous relationship to their child, actually drives them into even deeper anxiety, that is to say, into the arms of the phantasm which they then clutch on to like a straw.

Diagnostic pronouncements, treatment prescriptions and omnipresent prejudices give the mother a false sense of security in institutional procedures
by telling her 'it's biological' and not psychological.

The phantasm organises the disintegrated structures of her world into a
new system of stability but at the price of her own perceptions and capacity
for self-determination, fostering a deep unconscious dependency on what I
referred to in the last chapter as the 'diagnosis-making instance'. Feelings
of disappointment, anxiety, death wishes, scorn, feelings of helplessness,
omnipotent phantasies and so on, which are provoked by the monster child
who is apparently completely different and unpredictable, are now bound
by the phantasm. It may look something like this: 'If I behave myself
properly (according to the rules) then I can take the decisions relative to the
life (and death) of my child'. In so far as this phantasm binds the anxiety-
provoking feelings and keeps them unconscious, it brings a certain relief
and stability. It is clear what is happening: the breakdown of mimetic
competence is compensated by a stable system of explanations and instructions on what to do, in which the bad feelings are given expression without
having to become conscious.

The phantasms are not always individual phantasy products but have a
universal social character. This is even true in the extreme case in which a
severely mentally disturbed mother makes her clearly organically healthy
child carry her anxiety. Jean M. Hundley recounts in her book *Der kleine
Außenseiter*[22] how an extremely ambivalent pregnancy drove her to the
edge of a psychotic breakdown and how she could only save herself by
projecting her anxiety onto her unborn child:

> I longed to give my husband a son, but my age worried me. When Ellen
> (who was twenty months old when David was born) was born, I was
> thirty-eight and knew that women in this age group were increasingly
> likely to have mongoloid children. And yet here I was again: forty years
> old, very tired, and was facing another childbirth. I often had attacks of
> migraine and my arms and legs were grotesquely swollen. I felt dizzy
> and now and then suffered from breathlessness. Furthermore, I was
> anaemic and felt a constriction in my throat that was worrying me.[23]

The feelings of constriction in her throat indicate that her anxiety was
expressing itself in bodily symptoms, just as the child was also still a part of
her body. She was clearly ambivalent about the pregnancy Actually she felt
too old and weak to have another child but she wanted 'to give' her
husband a child. But why, when she herself did not want any more children? Apparently her little daughter was not good enough for her husband
and she had to make up for this deficiency with a son. It is the same old
story: only by giving birth to a son can the wife compensate for what she
has learnt to see as a deficiency: that she was once a girl herself and is now a

woman. So Mrs Hundley wants to 'prove' her worth to her husband by giving him a son. At the same time, however, she does not want a child. Why should she want a son who, by compensating for the phantasmatic deficiency, simply confirms its existence? She thus has no choice but to hate the child she is carrying who is causing her such a distressing pregnancy.

During the entire pregnancy she thought she could sense 'that David was not normal, that even before his birth, there was no hope for him'.[24]

> I was worried about the health of the child in my womb and had a nagging fear that things were not as they should be. The doctor had turned the baby twice during the sixth month and during the whole pregnancy I felt restless and ill-at-ease. Something was different about this child. To me it seemed to be lethargic: too discontented to be able to be quiet.[25]

She describes her depression and she has already begun to ward it off by projecting it onto the child inside her: 'like me' it is both discontented and restless. After the birth her anxiety about her strong and clearly healthy baby intensified.

> When I was lying in the dark ward, I could feel how I was sinking more and more deeply into a lonely well full of worries. I was surrounded by a constricting emptiness. My anxiety was intense and at the same time suppressed – a primitive, private anxiety, cutting me off from other people. None of the other mothers experienced this anxiety. I could have told them about it, but they wouldn't have understood. For them there was no difference between my baby and theirs and I should have been very happy.
>
> My anxiety was nameless. I was pursued by the shadow of a suspicion, a cloud of unpredictable size, which one day, I felt, would burst and pour out something horrific that would flood and drown me. But I didn't want to drown.[26]

People often express anxieties of being flooded and of drowning when they feel so threatened by unconscious phantasies that they fear becoming psychotic. Through the projection onto her son of her own threatening feelings triggered by the unwanted pregnancy, Mrs Hundley tried to ward off her phantasies and to keep her anxiety in check. She attributed her projections to the difficulties she experienced in breast-feeding her newborn child. 'He doesn't let me breast-feed him easily,' she told the doctor, 'and he behaves in a rather rejecting way. But mainly, I think, it is the way he looks at you. When I look at him, he doesn't look back at me like a normal child. He gives the impression he has no idea I am there.'[27]

The projection is obvious: you cannot expect a newborn baby to look back at you, to show interest rather than rejection, to 'know' its mother is there. She expects David, her newborn son and the 'proof' that she is a real woman, to look at her, to recognise her as a whole person; he is supposed to make up for her earlier, now unconscious, experience of being rejected as a girl, of having no value, of not being recognised (just as her daughter is now of no value to her).

Even before David's birth, the mother found a way to organise her defensive anxiety in line with the phantasm:

> There were other anxieties as well. When I was about five months pregnant, the Justice Department of the State of Victoria decided against the conversion of the death penalty for a certain Peter Tait who had been found guilty of murder. The entire State was in uproar over this crime. [. . .] When I saw the doctor for a routine check-up, he said: 'Tell your husband, that we don't want any undisciplined people like Tait running around in a respectable community. I only hope that he is hanged.' [. . .]
>
> I didn't want to discuss it. I had too many worries. I loved my husband, who was so understanding and had a high degree of respect for human life and, due to his position, had to help with the preparations for the hanging. [. . .] I felt compassion for the murderer, for the victim and for the victim's family. I couldn't sleep well, and when I did sleep, I was disturbed by nightmares. My limbs ached. My days were linked together by ghastly thoughts, meaningless and aimless thoughts. I was so worn out that life became a real strain.
>
> I functioned like a robot. I wasn't living spontaneously any more, I felt I was like a machine. I existed as a means to an end – to keep the baby alive – but I couldn't shake off the nagging anxiety that something was wrong with this child. I felt as if I was swimming in a void and the world was rushing past me too quickly. Too many things were oppressing me, and whenever I allowed myself to think at all, I thought about the execution.
>
> Finally the government psychiatrist ruled that Peter Tait was suffering from 'mental disorder' as defined by the law[28] and there was no hanging. I will never forget the feeling of relief that spread through our house [. . .].[29]

In her unconscious phantasies the child in her womb was associated with the murderer Peter Tait, who suffered from mental disorder as defined by the law – in this way she could project her own death wishes onto the child who had forced the ordeal of giving birth on her:

> Under the dreadful, yellow light (of the lamp), this was a long drawn-out night of endless nebulous torments, hour after hour of indistinct suffering. [. . .] Images crossed my mind, thronging scenes from the

past. I saw myself as a child falling off a horse. [. . .] There was a storm over a gloomy cemetery. Lightning flashed and I saw my grandfather's grave. Bombs fell from the sky and I was lying in a ditch. Colourful streaks crossed in front of my eyes. Then I saw my mother's face. She had tears in her eyes just as when my brother went away to war. Such a long war . . . what would happen if I died tonight?[30]

The child's birth is experienced here as a war: she goes to war herself taking over her brother's, the man's prerogative. She experiences the mother's farewell tears that only the man-hero deserved – the phantasy could easily be pursued further. Dying, suffering the hero's death in war – with the child as the enemy: can this make up for the deficiency of being a woman?

Hundley's account makes emphatically clear the basic conditions under which every mother–child relationship inevitably develops in a patriarchally structured society. I mean that women are devalued, which means that the mother–child relationship always develops within a precarious equilibrium. Admittedly, both the relationship and the child are particularly endangered if the mother is very disturbed – but the mother's personal disturbance is in no way (as was sometimes assumed to be the case for autistic children) the most important factor. Whenever the precarious equilibrium of the relationship is threatened, whether it is due to the announcement of the diagnosis or to real perceptions (especially to unconfirmed perceptions from the environment) of a weakness in the child or to external visible restrictions, it seems that a 'derailment' – a loss of mimetic competence – is unavoidable.

Underlying such an interactional 'derailment' are nameless anxieties. In the attempt to bind these anxieties, the mother's phantasies become attached to that which has no name and therefore is terribly threatening, that is, hate. The mother believes she has no right to hate her damaged child, particularly as she knows how much the child is exposed to the hate of the outside world. It is already difficult for mothers to find a way of giving expression to negative feelings towards their child, feelings that are generated by a situation that demands so many sacrifices from them for the child's sake. So it is especially difficult when the mother sees herself confronted with a situation in which she has to protect her child from the animosity of an environment which is hostile towards people with learning disabilities.

Every mother is probably more or less aware of fleeting phantasies in which she wishes that her extremely demanding and unthankful infant would 'go to the devil'. If she feels confident in her relationship with the child, she will be able to admit such phantasies without anxiety. However, if she knows or believes her child is disabled, she is dragged down into a threatening vortex of ambivalent feelings. 'On days when medical and psychiatric findings, on the one hand, and one's own opinion, on the other, leave no doubt that one's child is feebleminded, one's world collapses. [. . .]

Only someone who has faced the desperate question of "death or life" at the bedside of his own anomalous child knows how awful the temptation is.' When hate and despair become so powerful and the mother cannot rely on support from her environment, when she is driven into a corner by subtle or overt allusions to euthanasia and by attributions of guilt, it is barely possible for her to consciously tolerate these feelings. Her fear of the 'dreadful temptation' is too great.

Although Sarah's mother has more than one reason for having ambivalent feelings and latent death wishes, she also knows how easily the slightest slip may destroy the difference between such wishes and reality. When, in addition, she knows, or has a sense of how repressed wishes often find expression in bungled actions – which may not be dangerous for a 'normal' child but for Sarah they might well be life-threatening – then her own potential space for phantasy, which is essential if her child is to acquire its own space, is dangerously restricted. How can she differentiate between her phantasies – her extremely difficult child really should go to the devil (just for a while, until she has recovered) – and reality where, if she makes only a small mistake while feeding her, the child really might 'go to the devil' and, what's more, for ever?

When it is no longer possible to differentiate between aggressive phantasies and reality, where the child is really in danger, then the space for phantasy is undermined or destroyed. The mother is then unable to 'name' her aggression towards the child and, consequently, the child cannot discover through identification with her a form, a name, for his own aggression and autonomous strivings. On top of that, the mother's anxieties about her own phantasies make it impossible for her to recognise her child's aggression for she can only experience it as blame. So the aggression remains unsymbolised, fixated in the unconscious, and can only be enacted unconsciously and destructively between them. It then seems inevitable that things will go awry. It is inevitable that, because of her anxiety about the unnameable aggression and her guilt feelings, the mother will become fixated on the diagnosis-phantasm as a crutch to sustain her in her task.

However, such a 'derailment' is not unavoidable. It can be avoided if, instead of being oppressed by subliminal feelings of blame and being forced to phantasise, the mother can find solidarity in her environment; and if, instead of focusing on what the mother does wrong or on what is wrong with the child, the environment gives meaning to her task by actively providing, when necessary, the space the troubled mother–child relationship is so much in need of if it is to succeed under such difficult conditions. In the literature I know two descriptions of situations where, at the point when things started to go wrong, the environment intervened in a supportive way so that a negative evolution was avoided and a completely 'normal' development was possible. In one case severe epilepsy was avoided and, in the other, a probable autistic, psychotic development in infancy.

As these examples are so encouraging I will cite them in full. The first comes from Winnicott's paper 'Hate in the counter-transference' in *Through Paediatrics to Psychoanalysis*:

> This was the case of a baby girl who had attended from six to eight months on account of feeding disturbance, presumably initiated by infective gastro-enteritis. The emotional development of the child was upset by this illness and the infant remained irritable, unsatisfied and liable to be sick after food. All play ceased and by nine months not only was the infant's relation to people entirely unsatisfactory, but also she began to have fits. At eleven months fits were frequent.
>
> At twelve months the baby was having major fits followed by sleepiness. At this stage I started seeing her every few days and giving her twenty minutes' personal attention [. . .].
>
> At one consultation I had the child on my knee observing her. She made a furtive attempt to bite my knuckle. Three days later I had her again on my knee, and waited to see what she would do. She bit my knuckle three times so severely that the skin was nearly torn. She then played at throwing spatulas on the floor incessantly for fifteen minutes. All the time she cried as if really unhappy. Two days later I had her on my knee for half-an-hour. She had had four convulsions in the previous two days. At first she cried as usual. She again bit my knuckle very severely, this time without showing guilt feelings, and then she played the game of biting and throwing away spatulas. While on my knee she became able to enjoy play. After a time she began to finger her toes.
>
> Later the mother came and said that since the last consultation the baby had been 'a different child'. She had not only had no fits, but had been sleeping well at night – happy all day, taking no bromide. Eleven days later the improvement had been maintained, without medicine; there had been no fits for fourteen days, and the mother asked to be discharged.
>
> I visited the child one year later and found that since the last consultation she had had no symptom whatever. I found an entirely healthy, happy, intelligent and friendly child, fond of play, and free from the common anxieties.[31]

Winnicott does not say explicitly why the child resorted to the self-destructive symptom of epileptic fits. However, we can infer that on account of an infection at five years of age the child must have developed a phantasy of poisoned food – after all, food really had been poisonous for her for quite a while. Similarly her feelings of anxiety and rage towards her mother must have been marked by this experience. The mother must have sensed the aggression; perhaps the child bit her breast and this may have aroused latent guilt feelings in her so that, instead of accepting the child's aggression with understanding, she had to repudiate it in panic. After that, the only outlets for the child's aggression were depressive withdrawal and, later, epileptic fits. Only when the paediatrician tolerated, 'survived', her biting and throwing away and, in spite of her aggression, offered further security, was the child able to develop a playful way of expressing her aggression and then the fits and depression disappeared.

The second example is of a 'psychotherapy with an infant' reported by the therapist F. Pedrina.

In the first consultation with the parents I learnt that Andreas had suffered his first outbreak of eczema when he was two months old. This was a major crisis for the mother who had only just recovered from a very difficult experience of breast-feeding him. She remembered he had shown signs early on of being very strong-willed. Sometimes he cried so much that he became all red and fluid would appear on his facial skin, which then dried and became encrusted. She thought this was an early stage of eczema.

Various dermatological treatments were tried. Andreas' mother experienced his illness as a reproach, as a sign of her inadequate care. Fearing comments from passers-by, they stopped going out for walks. [. . .] Andreas was her first child. The pregnancy and birth went smoothly without any complications and was a satisfying experience for the parents except for some agitation over the obstetrician's treatment at the end of the pregnancy. During a check-up he feared that the child was too small which resulted in further investigations and a period of bed rest was prescribed.

In his mother's arms Andreas cut a striking figure: a completely immobile form, withdrawn inside a shell. He made big eyes at me – as if he consisted only of eyes – and had a blank, sad expression. He didn't smile.

For me, the diagnostic picture was one of anaclitic depression: an apathetic infant with a blank expression with whom it was difficult to make contact; any attempts to do so upset him. Developmentally speaking, he seemed to me somewhat retarded and his mother reported that he had not put on any weight for two months. [. . .] The parents, especially the mother, were under considerable strain.

I [. . .] decided to start psychotherapy with Andreas and the mother. Over a period of two months [. . .] they came to me twice a week. As there was a quick improvement, the sessions were reduced, at the mother's request and after a short holiday break, to once a week (until he was ten months old). Thereafter, we had occasional meetings. [. . .] I tried to put myself in his position and to see a meaning in his behaviour. [. . .] We tried together to find a position which would be more comfortable for him, where he would have his hands free to fiddle a bit. He tugged on my clothes a lot which I saw as a sign of co-operation.

The mother noticed that it was good to have to come to see me: otherwise she would hardly have gone out of the house any more. I gave her support with the feelings of shame she felt about bringing me this disturbing spectacle of a child.

[. . .] Sometimes, when I looked into his calm eyes with their increasingly blank expression, I could only see madness or endless falling – where was he going? [. . .] During a moment of quietness, I asked the mother to talk about Andreas. I learnt that the false alarm caused by the obstetric investigation had triggered great anxiety in her about her child's well being so that she had fallen ill psychosomatically and only felt reassured and well again when she saw her newborn son. But this only lasted for a short time as other worries soon followed.

It was time for this child to have some better experiences. Andreas began to take part more often in little games and showed interest in objects which he would keep in his mouth for a long time. Now and then there was a smile, a gurgle, a mumble or mumbled exchange with his mother. She took part in this play without turning away as she had at the beginning [when she always tried to stop him from scratching his eczema, D.N.].

Then there was a relapse. The mother arrived at the session in despair: Andreas, she said, was unbearably nervous and she had been unable to do anything else before the session than hold his hands away from his face.

Andreas was very disturbed when he was with me too and it was impossible to do anything with him. I put some music on which calmed him down a bit. However, we decided to have a shorter session. While she was dressing Andreas, the mother talked slowly, quietly and in a controlled way about the feelings of despair which once again had overwhelmed her during the night. She had been thinking about her impossible life, about how others had an easier time of it than her and how she could not stand it any more. In fact, when she got up in the morning she was very nervous and perhaps Andreas had sensed her mood. Now, she felt calm, she said. Andreas had fallen asleep in her arms.

After this striking episode, the therapy developed quickly. From then on the mother felt better, more competent and self-sufficient, and was clearly withdrawing from the relationship with me. Andreas, too, made fast progress; he was more lively and open to contact, he was more active in exploring the world around him and in play. His eczema had disappeared.

He only let his mother take him in her arms when he was very tired. She remembered that as a small infant Andreas had never allowed her to hold him in her arms like this; he had always withdrawn. Gradually Andreas wanted his mother's closeness more, letting himself snuggle up to her and be fondled by her (he was one year old). He developed a new kind of interest for different things and activities. [. . .] When I visit him now, which is not very often, he expresses a wide range of feelings when he greets me.

What happened in the therapy?

The mother went through a process during which she became conscious of, and could reach, her post-natal depression. First, she clung to the hope she found when someone came along who was prepared to help her. She saw how I accepted the dreadful, withdrawn infant, although she had imagined everyone would reject both him and her. She began to identify a bit more with me and accepted the idea that I could help her understand her child: on one occasion she said she would play with him like I did. On the basis of this small bridge of trust, she told me about the difficult time she had had at the time of her son's birth; she relived her anxieties and despair and shared them with me. In this decisive hour, she saw how Andreas, who previously could not be hushed, now fell asleep in her arms because she herself was calmer. She realised how remarkably close and linked both their psychic states were. On the one hand, she experienced that she was able to soothe him and that this brought both of them satisfaction. On the other hand, this was proof that Andreas' illness had something to do with her, whereas up till then she had sworn that the blame lay in her husband's family history. In any case, after this she recovered. She could devote herself to the child without difficulty and assume her motherly role and responsibilities.

During those times when the mother was reflecting about herself, I fulfilled a classical therapeutic role. Before, during the period of crisis when the mother had remained silent, I perhaps offered her the holding that she had never been able to accept from her environment.[32]

There is nothing further that needs to be added to this.

Chapter 4

The enactment of soul murder

There is an old children's game where one child says to the other: 'I'll repeat everything you say'. That is the challenge and the 'attacking', mimicking child thereby gains complete power over the child who is 'being attacked' or mimicked.

This game seems to me to be an exact representation of the desperate situation in which the partners of an interaction that has 'derailed', on a phantasmatic level, find themselves. It is quite simple. All the ways in which the partner expresses himself, including laughing, crying, coughing or sighing, are copied without concern for meaning. In this way the partner who is being attacked is put in an apparently hopeless situation and usually quickly loses his composure. Running away from the situation is hardly the answer because it is now, above all, that he really needs listening to. Furthermore, allowing the aggressor to triumph would be an admission of impotence. Defending oneself against the attack with words is impossible because the rules of verbal confrontation are not operative in this game. Frequently, the game ends with the child who is under attack bursting into tears at some point or seeking to silence his tyrant with a desperate physical assault.

The game is like a vortex. Once under way, it holds both children in its inexorable grip. It has power over them both: the attacking, mimicking child cannot turn back either; he does not want to let the other child enjoy the crushing triumph which he himself is now celebrating, even if he is unable to enjoy it because he also is locked into the situation.

Slavishly tied to his partner's utterances from which he may not deviate in the slightest way – for that would mean surrendering – he asserts his ego in this destructive relationship by means of mimicking: *I'll* repeat everything you say. Nothing remains of the ego but this slavish repetition. Such dependency further intensifies the hate, the driving energy and the torture to such an extreme that the mimicked child's ego, which the attacking child can no longer free himself from, breaks down.

However, the other child, who is being mimicked – who, in fact, is in a dominating position insofar as he is the one who dictates what happens –

finds himself in an even more desperate situation. He is heard and yet not heard. The message gets lost in the process of being heard. Soon, the only thing he wants is to get his message across to his partner. He can only express this wish, however, in one way, which puts him even more at his tormentor's mercy. What he says is taken from him, rather than accepted. The other child accepts what he says but only on the perceptive surface; he listens, it is true, but does not take in what is said. By signalling that he is listening, he ties the other child down with his insatiable need to be listened to. In this way the mimicked child is dispossessed of his own most funda-mental desire. Worse still, not only is he dispossessed of his desire, but the other child derives power from it, putting his own interpretation on it, reversing the intended meaning into its opposite. In this way the utterance becomes estranged from the mimicked child and, emptied of meaning, it is used as a weapon by his tyrannical opponent.

Under the destructive spell of this interaction form, the mimicked child's unstable ego can no longer assert itself and collapses. It is gripped by impotent archaic rage and forced into regression. Dispossessed of language and its capacity for self-assertion, and consequently the capacity to say 'I', it can no longer control its aggression and is overwhelmed by it. It either turns it against itself in depressive withdrawal or it is driven to physical attack. Both signify defeat, a falling back on an earlier stage of the conflict that has already been overcome, that is, a loss of ego control and autonomy and a collapse of the capacity for symbolic expression.

This is the attacking child's triumph, albeit an empty triumph over an opponent who had no chance. When his opponent breaks down, the mimicking child loses the object of his persecution and hate, because it was only in the context of this interaction with his opponent that he was able to affirm himself. This slavish conformity had become the basis of his self-affirmation. But now he is thrown back on his own resources; he is assailed by all the feelings which, as long as the 'game' worked, he had projected onto the other child – helplessness, abandonment, and anxiety about losing the very basis of his identity because the opponent's ego no longer lends itself to being mimicked.

For children who have got entangled in this cruel structure, the 'game' seems in most cases to lead inexorably to breakdown. Nevertheless, the attacked, mimicked child has one possibility of extricating himself: he must say something that the other child can no longer simply repeat because it would tell him something about himself or because he might, in retro-spect, begin thinking about what he was doing. A teacher, who was being mimicked by an entire class simply said: 'I wonder who has treated you so badly that you now have to treat me like this?' Saying this broke the spell of the game. It is only those who have escaped the reality of such situations who can *play* such dreadful games. But when there is a learning disability or an autistic or psychotic development this can really become inescapable for the child and his mother. Not in the form of parroting, of course; the interaction form of this game already shows, however cruel and pitiless the spell of the game may be, that even if it is not really integrated, it has been survived. The game takes place on a verbal level but, by annulling the basic elements of verbal communication, it shows that its origin is pre-verbal. Its interaction form stems from the area I have described as coenaesthetic perception and mimetic behaviour.

The game demonstrates the hopelessness and violence of an interaction reduced to two dimensions: the symbolic dimension is annulled; speech and gestures are robbed of their sensuous meaning. Instead of becoming involved mimetically in the meaning of what the other says, there is a mime, i.e. mimicking, emptied of meaning and sensuousness. What keeps the game going is the anxiety of losing control of the situation. When the mother–child relationship 'derails' or goes awry there is a similar anxiety: the unconscious anxiety of inflicting severe and irreparable damage on the child with the feelings that have been made unconscious in the phantasm. This anxiety means those who are caught in the phantasm are slavishly bound to it, just as the mimicking child is bound by the rules of the game to which he is hopelessly enslaved without being aware of it.

Interpreting the partner's gestural and symbolic behaviour in a manner that is governed by the phantasm and deprived of spontaneous perception and empathy is what mimicking is; miming, robbed of its sensuousness. Let us return to the example from the chapter on diagnosis. When Gabi's mother realised she had a severe phobia but did not recognise the connection it had with her own, recently actualised murderous intentions and her reaction to the diagnosis, and, in conformity with the phantasm, saw this symptom as a sign that her daughter was 'mongol', her behaviour was not very different from the echolalic repetition in this 'game'. What has been seen and experienced is acknowledged (in the case of Gabi's mother one cannot speak of a general lack of empathy – though this shows how powerful the phantasm is) but the dimension of meaning is excluded, made unconscious and repressed, due to anxiety arising from death wishes.

The phantasm makes everything seem as if it is inevitable, self-evident, meaningless, purely biological, unalterable and unquestionable fate. When the mother clutches in panic at the phantasmatic 'that's exactly how it is with my child', this 'that's how it is' impairs her empathy. The phantasm suggests to her what she should understand replacing her own feelings and perceptions. The symbiotic relationship thus loses its basis and the paradoxical effect of the phantasm is that it binds the mother and child to each other precisely for this reason – just as the paradoxical effect in the mimicking game is that mimicking is a disguise for not listening to the mimicked child's wish to be understood, binding him even more hopelessly to the other child. When, in the void of the destroyed potential space, the mother is already clutching in panic at the straw of the phantasm, then the phantasm constantly creates a new vacuum in which it robs the mother of her own empathy, her mimetic competence, and thus pre-programs her to grasp at the phantasm in all situations requiring empathy. The vacuum of empathy produces the vortex of the phantasm just as in the game, vacuum and vortex arise because the mimicking child merely hears without really understanding. The meaning of what is perceived is destroyed and is therefore emptied of meaning both in 'the game' and in the mother–child interaction which has 'derailed' phantasmatically. The mother's perceptions of herself and her child have no meaning any more, no sensuous meaning apart from that which is suggested by the phantasm. However, in this situation the mother only has her defenceless child as a visible and tangible partner. This makes her situation much more desperate, and the 'game' deadly serious.

Of course – and this is already suggested by the allusion to the 'game's' echolalic character – it is by no means easy, in the real context of the 'derailed' mother–child relationship, to differentiate between the one who is mimicking and the one who is being mimicked. It is not only the mother who 'mimics' the child, letting the sensuousness of their common experience get lost in the void of the societal unconscious by taking refuge in the pseudo-security of the phantasmatic diagnosis 'it is biological'. The child also mimics the mother, her anxiety, attempting through mimicry to live up to the phantasm, because the phantasm is the guarantee of his mother's security. He behaves just as the mother fears and needs him to behave, i.e. in ways that are characteristic of a person with learning disabilities. At the same time, she herself needs him to behave like this to provide reassuring confirmation of those fears. In so doing he makes it difficult for her to assert her perceptions over and against the devouring power of the societal unconscious.

Susanna, a nine-month-old girl with Down's syndrome, had received an official disabled person's ID card testifying that she had difficulty in walking. At the same time the parents were thinking of getting therapy for Susanna and having her examined. The doctor noticed that Susanna was not crawling as much as she should have been. So the parents now began watching all their daughter's attempts at locomotion with anxious mis-givings. But Susanna was suddenly unable to do as much as she had been able to do before; she just lay on her tummy 'flat as a flounder' (as her mother put it). At night, when she was sleeping, her mother sometimes found her on all fours, an initial stage of crawling which she had not yet attempted during the day. This defensive pattern – not being able to do exactly what the parents were anxiously expecting – has now become an observable characteristic in Susanna. Quite clearly, she felt paralysed when the confident parental attitude that things would develop naturally in their own time, an attitude underlying the developmental stages of more fortun-ate children, was not there. She was living up to her parents' phantasies of her; she was trying to force her parents to give her what they could never give her, i.e. trusting acceptance. So she assimilated her parents' anxiety, mimicking it, thereby increasing the panic and creating a vicious circle.

Mimicking is mimesis emptied of meaning, lacking intentionality. Far from being a gestural expression of coenaesthetic recognition of the other – as mimesis in an undisturbed mother–child relationship would be – mimicking interferes with self-perception and the perception of others. Without the participants in the interaction being aware of it, the phantasm, as a panic defence, slips between the partners of an interaction that is going awry, filling the potential space with its non-perceptibility. By eluding sensuous recognition, it is the negative of the third party, the negative of the symbolic dimension. Under the spell of phantasy, everything that has been perceived becomes a sign for something that is still only seen as being outside the relationship, i.e. the sign of an organic impairment, of the doctor's error, of the mother's guilt or innocence.

Of course, this is not only true for the relationship between a child who is developing a learning disability and his mother. Phantasms dominate interactions of every sort: our activity, beliefs and actions are based on powerful unconscious attitudes. Phantasms are the psychical configurations by means of which societies ensure that their hierarchical systems are unconsciously internalised by individuals so that they then appear to be natural and immutable. They are organised in institutions giving them their aura of being indispensable realities. Erdheim has provided evidence of this, taking school as an example. A typical societal structure is reproduced in 'the game'. The unerring accuracy and precision of children's play eluci- dates the powerful mechanisms of the enactment of soul murder; moreover, it shows how they are rooted in the long and dreadful history of human self-destruction. The way the game works is the very model of interactions that have gone awry phantasmatically. A subtle form of exercising power is expressed in it which is so omnipresent and taken for granted that adults accept it as natural. Play can elucidate the effect of the mimetic taboo that determines everything we think and feel, as well as the dominant structures and institutions of our culture down to the last detail. Adorno and Horkheimer, whose aphorism on stupidity I cited at the beginning of the last chapter, have traced the domination of the mimetic taboo from the beginnings of history to the present day and have inferred that there is a self-destructive tendency in collective human activity.

The mimetic taboo is a cultural defence making anxiety-provoking perceptions unconscious. It keeps drives and regressive impulses to yield to inner and outer nature from conscious awareness. Such impulses are dangerous when controlling and exploiting nature is the main objective since they undermine self-control and the control of outer nature. The mimetic taboo thus distances us from instinctual drives, from nature within us, and creates a split between nature and man, body and mind, man and woman, impotence and omnipotence. In their interpretation of the Circe in Homer's *Odyssey*, Adorno and Horkheimer have shown how mastering nature was accompanied by the patriarchal domination of women by men.

As the mimetic taboo became more entrenched during the Enlightenment this split increasingly affected people with learning disabilities by singling them out for special treatment in that they were the ones who were left behind by the progress of enlightenment. While there was still a place for them in feudalistic-agrarian based cultures which had not yet subjected them to an institutionalised special treatment, with the growth of the bourgeoisie and capitalism they were increasingly brought together and managed within institutions, becoming 'objects of treatment' and the concern of women. The institution 'Learning Disability' originated as a counterbalance to an increasingly totalitarian enlightenment.[1]

In our achievement-oriented culture, the mimetic taboo is particularly present when the ability of one of its members to perform, especially on a cognitive level, is put in doubt and his natural dependency cannot be denied. It is organised in all the various institutions whose purpose is to stabilise relationships that have 'derailed' phantasmatically. In addition to their overt task of providing care, they also have the function of organising and protecting 'learning disability' as an institution, understood in terms of the phantasm I have described. The phantasm makes its effects felt in institutions in the form of a lack of empathy and selective blindness on the part of workers.

In a staff-group discussion on the case of a girl who not only had severe learning disabilities but was also ill, and for whom there seemed to be little hope, I took the risk – although I was new in the institution and full of naive enthusiasm – of speaking about my own dreams and wishful phantasies about treating the child as well as about painful feelings involved in my work with her. A psychologist took me up on this: 'Does working with this girl really affect you so much? It doesn't affect me at all; I just take her as she is.' Somewhat shocked, I asked the others in the group if they could understand the way I felt: some supported the psychologist and others observed an awkward silence.

Here is another example from the same institution. I had just returned from my holidays and a carer told me in passing that the girl had been very sad in recent weeks, that she had hardly smiled at all and had been almost totally unapproachable. The child's principal carer, who had taken care of her intensively for more than a year, had left the institution at the beginning of my holiday. I said that the girl certainly had good reason to be sad on account of this loss. I did not say that I also related her sadness to my holiday absence, having in the mean time grown more cautious. However, the defensive reaction was not long in coming. I was told that the child simply went through phases like this and she had a tendency to have epileptic fits that I should not overlook (as if I had done so).

This was a lesson about the stereotypical lack of empathy encountered particularly in large institutions, about mimicking as mimesis emptied of meaning. But it was true that the girl suffered from frequent fits. It is also probable that during the weeks when I was on holiday, and after losing her carer, she suffered badly from fits and so was even less responsive than usual. But the reason for all this still remained unexplained. Why was she in this phase now; why was there an increase in the attacks at this juncture? And why did the carer say she had had a 'sad' time rather than that she had had 'several fits'? These were questions one was not supposed to ask. Acknowledging the attacks and her ill humour without asking about meaning is like the mimicking in 'I will repeat everything you say'.

However, I also found I was reluctant to empathise. I might have realised how badly the psychologist and the carer needed to appear so unmoved and unempathic, to hide their feelings, outwardly at least, instead of which I put them in the sadistic role of being 'institutional people' and masochistically took on the role of victim. In so doing, I also warded off my own feelings of hopelessness – only I repeated my old mistake (the mistake of one who has deserted institutional counter-transference) by projecting my defensiveness onto the others.

The mimetic taboo determines and organises the phantasm of 'learning disability' as a reluctance to empathise. It is thus enacted as a ghastly caricature of a failure to keep nature under control, i.e. those with learning disabilities who, so it seems to us, are helplessly left to the mercy of nature, their damaged nature, according to the diagnosis. What's more, they 'are' nature – pure, untamed instinctual nature – and so they represent the all-powerful drives in ourselves which we have to struggle so hard against.

The phantasm is enacted in a scenario in which impotence and omni-potence are personified in two ways: on the one hand people with learning disabilities are seen as being stupidly adapted and extremely humiliated, in need of stimulation from others who feel omnipotent and, on the other, as behaviourally disturbed, extremely depersonalised, drive-embodied, threat-eningly fascinating people whose omnipotence needs neutralising by behavioural therapy. This contrast between two types of learning disability can frequently be found in the literature, however little specific individuals may fit the picture. Often they are labelled with the diagnoses of Down's syndrome or autism. An anthroposophical doctor told me once that he believed that 'Mongols' represent a sort of earlier, more natural, purer and immediate human being, while autists exhibit the extreme of human depersonalisation. There is no denying this observation. But what he saw as nature's vengeance for the human hubris of wanting to control nature, I would prefer to describe as different positions in the scenario of society's enactment of psychic murder: 'these people' are embodied by the contempt of adjusted people and the mystification of resistance and, in addition, seem determined by their nature and past history.

'Little Mongols', 'Down's children' or: the contempt of adjusted people

> — Mummy, 'handicapped' is bad, isn't it?
> — What makes you say that, Gabi?
> — Because people often look at me in such a strange way; and then you always look so sad. I do notice it![2]

Because of its racist connotations, the nasty word 'Mongol' has long been banned from teaching manuals on learning disability. Nevertheless, I use it between inverted commas because, to my way of thinking, the otherwise commonly used terms 'Down's syndrome' and 'Down's children' are no better. Such formulations seem to me to be stigmatising. Who does not have vague memories of hearing about 'Mongols' in history lessons at school, a wild, barbaric, Asian race who invaded European culture in the Middle Ages, pillaging, murdering and plundering? A race pictured as inferior and uncivilised, rather like those of Sinti and Rome in my chain of associations, who, not long ago, in the midst of our European culture, along with people with learning difficulties and other undesirable people, whose lives were considered to be *lebensunwertes Leben*, were murdered with industrial efficiency. It is understandable that this fascist-like term has been replaced by the label 'Down's syndrome', introduced into medical practice by Langdon Down, the first person to have comprehensively described a definite group of symptoms as the syndrome of 'Mongol idiocy'. It makes me feel uneasy already when I think that Langdon Down is not well-known, however common the English word 'down' may be: down, down with them! – this association, whether consciously or not, comes quickly to mind.

Clearly, from the first stages of life onwards, it is written on their faces that 'handicapped is bad' and everywhere they go they are have to put up with 'looks', 'being looked at strangely'. The saying 'if looks could kill . . .' has a particular reality for 'Mongols'.

From numerous play-situations with 'Mongols', I am familiar with the gesture of shooting dead with an outstretched forefinger. This gesture, common amongst children, was especially striking for me in the play of 'Mongols' because it often has a central meaning. It is used very often, at times quite literally with the forefinger, but more frequently with looks or words: 'Just look at this! Such children shouldn't be raised; they shouldn't be allowed to live.'[3]

The eleven-year-old 'Mongol' girl M. had made sense of these looks of pity, furtive curiosity, disparagement, contempt, loathing and hate in her play. I now want to quote from a report that Rezia Bücklers has written about her play sessions with M., which she did as part of her training as a teacher for children with special needs.[4]

M. said the baby was sick. I was to play the doctor who gave the baby injections. Then I was the mummy who consoled the baby. M. asked me to shoot it. I was appalled. I didn't know now whether I was doctor or mummy. I refused. M. screamed at me to do it. I said it would be dreadful to shoot the baby. Now she wanted me to be the sick baby. I lay down, cried like a baby, and was shot by M. Now M. was again the baby and I had to shoot it and did so.

In the following session M. was strolling through the shops. [. . .] She stayed for a particularly long time in the pet shop to look at the cages. I told her that she had seen cages like that at home and how awful it was for the birds that were locked up not to be able to fly. M. gave me a puzzled look and then we left. As we were leaving she flapped her arms like a lame bird. Once we were home she immediately wanted to play being mummy and baby in hospital again. Again the baby had to be given injections or be shot. This time it was clear that the doctor had to shoot the baby. I asked her if the mother was watching and protecting the baby? M. said no and began to cry. Then she urged me again to shoot it; this time, however, I said, 'Mummy is taking care of you and protecting you'.

In a later play session M. played out this scene again and now it was even clearer which experience she was trying to work through.

M. placed her head between my legs and said that she was a baby. I asked if it had just been born and M. nodded her head. She said the baby was dead. I said: 'How awful, was the baby shot because no one wanted it as it was?' M. nodded and I felt very sad. M. sat on my lap, lay her head on my shoulder and cried a lot.

The doctor announced the diagnosis to M.'s parents with an expression on his face that said: a child like this should be put in a home immediately (a suggestion which often accompanies a diagnosis of 'Mongolism'). The girl associates the initial despair and rejection in the parent's eyes all the looks she has been met with in her environment since this traumatic first encounter; the looks of the environment which her parents seek to protect her from, in as much as they encourage her to make herself as inconspicuous as possible in public. It is these looks, she pretends, that have turned her into a little bird whose wings are broken or which has to sit in a cage (in the context of her experience, her parents' desire that she should be as inconspicuous as possible can only be understood as a request to feign death, to let herself be 'shot' by the looks) which it cannot fly away from.

After M. had played this game for a while in her play sessions, until the student had found a way to understand and to get out of the shooting role, her mother observed at home how she was pretending in her play that her doll was a 'still-born child'. Feeling very shocked by this, she wanted to talk about it with the student – until a short time before she had stated confidently that M. did not know what 'death' was: 'such children' surely could not understand something so abstract as this. 'Inevitably, the subject of the mother's phantasies following M.'s birth came up in our discussion. She said that she could not remember wishing M. was dead or having murderous phantasies towards her. M.'s father was now smoking very nervously. She went on to say that she could remember that her brother had told her once how she had admitted having such phantasies to him after M.'s birth. I sensed from the acute tension within myself (I was beginning to tremble inwardly) how threatening the conversation was getting. Together we then managed to get back to the subject of social defamation and the conversation became less threatening.'

We did not talk about this theme again in later conversations. M.'s parents pointed out again and again how M. was successful at school. As they had already said once before, M. did not know what 'dead' was, they now said several times that M. could not cry and that, consequently, she would probably even have to have an operation on her lachrymal sacs.

What is going on here? The baby was born and immediately 'shot' by pointing forefingers, the diagnosis and dismayed looks. 'Children like this should be put in a home.' But the parents decided, against the doctor's well-meaning suggestion, not to do that; they decided they wanted to keep 'such a child'. Soul-murder . . . they tried to undo what they had done by using the doctor's suggestion as an outlet for their death wishes, forgetting them and restricting their perception in order not to have to recognise that their child could not forget. They said M. did not know what 'dead' meant, that she could not cry and needed an operation. Above all, however, M. had to be protected from the 'killing' looks of the outside world. She should look as inconspicuous as possible (she had already had a few operations, apparently stemming from this phantasm of the inconspicuous girl, which were only partly indicated medically); in any case she should behave inconspicuously. And M. understood all this in the light of her initial experience. She could not undo what had happened, this was no longer possible; rather, in spite of her parents' conscious efforts, the socially delegated murder was being enacted over and over again. The parents could not acknowledge that she was afraid of dying and accept her despair; she had to stay like a lame little bird in 'the cage' of the phantasm, feign death in the street and really let herself be psychically murdered by other people's looks. Her parents were unconsciously enforcing society's judgement by trying to protect M. from it; and this was so intolerable that they were left with no other option than to deny this knowledge, to magically talk themselves out of it, to take refuge whenever possible in M.'s achievements when they came up in conversation while M. was playing, as if this were proof of what they believed they had to demonstrate, i.e. their innocence.

Only with an outsider, her play teacher (and with me, her supervisor), was it possible for M. to gradually overcome the barriers of non-understanding and to begin again to flutter her 'broken wings'.

Just as the parents reacted with shock to the announcement of the diagnosis, so the student also reacted with shock to the child's phantasy of this scene. Like the parents, she too could initially only react defensively with denial: no, she did not want to shoot 'the baby', and when M. insisted on the truth of this enacted scene, she had no choice but to comply with it and 'shoot'. It was either–or. The phantasm has so much power that it not only overwhelmed the shocked parents but even the student who was less involved, dragging them into the splitting mechanism of either–or. Only in her supervision, where she looked for an 'uninvolved' third party, could she approach an understanding, and even for her the pain was almost unbearable. However, only when she herself had felt something of this pain which M. had to live with constantly did she discover how to respond: the child wanted to be protected not by denial but by having the dreadful reality recognised. And it was only when she had completely understood this that M. no longer had to enact the scene of the baby's murder in her play sessions and could even try, in a somewhat mitigated form – 'still-born child' – to communicate something of this to her mother. The latter, however, was still under too much strain.

M.'s parents denied what I call society's 'delegated murder', or rather their compliance with it, and the failure of their defence. The news of the diagnosis put them in a position where initially they could only fend off the unbearable news with their backs to the wall. The proposal 'children like this should be put in homes' means, for most parents of newborn 'Mongol' children, anything but the helpful, exonerating support which it is no doubt intended to be, consciously at least. For parents it means: 'Something terrible has happened to you which you had better undo and keep quiet about'. 'So they might just as well have said to us straight away, let the child starve. I think that putting a child in a home is soul murder!' said Susanna's mother. Unfortunately, the proposal echoes the deep shock which the news of the diagnosis certainly causes parents initially and very few are able to react with as much presence of mind as Susanna's mother who replied to the doctor by saying: 'You must be out of your mind! That's completely out of the question!' And not many are so sure of what they feel in the initial stages of shock. At first, the impulse of most parents is to wish their child had not been born or was dead. On top of this wish comes the friendly-tolerant sounding suggestion to perpetrate the soul murder that Susanna's mother speaks of with the sanction and even direct backing of society.

Most parents, however, only decide to keep their child at home after major inner conflicts. Thereafter they have to struggle with guilt feelings for a long time for having let themselves be enticed by the suggestion of soul murder while they were in a state of shock. 'Why did no one help us to accept the child, why did everyone only talk about putting him in a home?' asks Hermann's mother. She and her husband had been told at the time that he was not 'fit for being cared for at home', so putting him into a home was unavoidable. Why? Why is it taken for granted that the birth of a Mongoloid child *is necessarily* a calamity for the parents?

Just as it seems unquestionable that the birth of 'such a child' signifies a disaster, it is also taken for granted that it is possible to avoid this disaster by testing the amniotic fluid and then, when necessary, by carrying out an abortion in the fifth month of pregnancy. That such an intervention and the entire procedure of undergoing an amniotic fluid test is a severe psychological burden for the mother, not to mention the risk involved, apparently counts for little in face of such weighty arguments.*

Ingo was two and a half years old when he was brought to me for the first time. He was a lovely, bright 'Mongoloid' boy. His mother told me about the difficulties she had had with the child at the beginning: 'Oh, I had this child, I didn't want him, I prayed to God to let him die; I left him alone on the diapering table and hoped he would fall off and be dead!' Ingo had been a long-hoped-for first child but, when he was born 'Mongoloid', relatives blamed the mother for not having had an amniotic fluid test done. Now she had brought 'shame' on the whole family. At least her husband had accepted and loved the child from the outset and that had been a great help.

A little later in the conversation Ingo's mother told me that she was pregnant again and that very soon they were going to have an amniotic fluid test done. It was dreadful living with the uncertainty: should she have an abortion or not? She and her husband could hardly speak together any more about the pregnancy and often they even avoided looking at each other. It was completely impossible to be happy about this pregnancy. And when she then looked at Ingo, she felt absolutely awful. 'I certainly do not want to abort Ingo!', she said, in great despair.

'No one had the slightest idea that the amniotic fluid test might be unnecessary or, in the event of it turning out to be negative, that an abortion was something to be discussed. [. . .] The reactions of other people, however, make one thing clear: having a child with learning disabilities is something to be avoided if at all possible, he has no right to live, he only embodies the negative possibility. Personally, I feel that this is euthanasia. If handicap is the sole reason for questioning a person's right to live, why does it occur only before the birth?', writes Hanni Holthaus in 'Letter from a Mother'.[5] 'The others', society, think that a 'Mongol' child is something

---

* I would like to note here that I do not in any way condemn the *possibility* of having such an examination and an abortion.

that can be avoided and leaves it up to the mother herself to do what is necessary. How she feels about this is her problem. Ingo's mother, too, was under pressure from 'others', the relatives, who had talked of 'shame'. She could not tolerate this again. However, this social pressure for abortion signified a new catastrophe in her relationship with Ingo who, after lengthy struggles, had finally turned into the lively and curious little boy whom I now knew. Both mother and child had a series of illnesses that were manifestly partly psychosomatic in origin.

While she was waiting for the results of the test (which took three weeks), Ingo fell ill with a serious infection. His mother caught it and, while she was still struggling through her illness, Ingo caught scarlet fever and needed looking after for weeks on end. Meanwhile the mother learnt she would not 'have to' interrupt her pregnancy. After he got better she herself came down with an infection which laid her up in bed. During this time the mother became deeply depressed, while Ingo became nagging and demanding and often tormented her. She was unable to climb out of her depression until after the birth of the second child. Ingo reacted to his little brother jealously and made his mother's life difficult with strong outbursts of anger. 'I keep trying to explain to him,' said the mother (when later, she got in contact with me again to arrange music therapy for Ingo), 'and he simply doesn't understand it because he is handicapped!'

What did this mean? What was he supposed to understand? That his parents loved him just as much as before, his mother said. But for Ingo things were not as they were before: he clearly sensed that if his brother had been 'Mongol' like him, he would never have been born. And also that his mother's amniotic fluid test had remobilised the death phantasies that she had almost overcome. She was not able to admit it to herself consciously and so to work through them to some extent, as she had been able to do when we first got to know each other. She would have had to be prepared to kill a child like Ingo if necessary – this was how she put it to me – and by becoming depressed she succumbed to the power of society's delegated murder. She had struggled for so long and had managed to gain a lot of space for herself and Ingo. During the severe ordeal that the amniotic fluid test had been for her, this space had broken down and was filled with the phantasm: 'he doesn't understand because he is handicapped'. Can he really not understand? Was Ingo not reacting like this, with outbursts of despair and anger, precisely *because* he understood what had happened, what this uninterrupted pregnancy and the birth of this 'healthy' little brother meant for him as a 'Mongoloid' child?

Although the mother insisted that it was good to forget sometimes that Ingo had learning disabilities, now she had to use the idea that he really was handicapped as an explanation for what she could not face: if she knew how well Ingo understood in his own infantile way, how could she possibly stand it? So the only thing this mother, who was a lively and sensitive woman, could do, was to retreat into depression and the solid ground of society's phantasm: Ingo can *not* understand, because he has a learning disability.

What are the consequences of such a disastrous relationship? The phantasm helps to ward off feelings of guilt; these are unconscious, of course, because they are so unbearable. Guilt feelings for having subsequently made up her mind to kill a child like Ingo; feelings that were strengthened by her anger towards her difficult little son, who she now had more than enough reason to want out of the way, although she could no longer admit having such feelings. Because of her guilt feelings, this anger also had to be repressed and used on an unconscious phantasmatic level as well as in depression.

The phantasm can now be formulated in the following way: 'such children' (they should be prevented, aborted, in time, before it can be called euthanasia and murder) are so handicapped that, by definition, they simply *cannot* understand that the words above in brackets have no meaning for them. M. cannot cry about it; Ingo's anger comes from the fact that he does *not* understand.

Society's delegated murder is lurking everywhere. It is particularly present when the parents are at a loss for arguments to deal with the new situation that has brought them into conflict with all the old prejudices, which until recently they had shared without needing to question them. Since they have decided to combat the idea that 'such a child should be put straight into a home' and to accept their child, they now want to do their best to protect the child from such prejudices. M. must not cry, must not despair about her situation; Ingo must not understand what for us is inconceivable about his intolerable situation. M. should make herself as inconspicuous as possible so that the 'killing looks' do not affect her too often. All these are desperate protective measures adopted by parents in their state of helplessness. These are measures suggested by the phantasm and, without realising it and without wanting to, they entangle their child in it even further.

This mechanism works down to the last detail. Even the 'Mongol's' tongue has to be controlled. It is said that it has a tendency to hang out because it is too long. A mother remembers from her first consultation with a recognised female specialist the macabre congratulations: 'Children like this can turn out to be very sweet. In fact, we had one just recently; we cut a piece of his tongue out. Now he looks very sweet!' More human methods do exist, such as the plate which is fixed to the infant's or toddler's upper jaw designed to train the tongue's muscular tonus by the movements it requires.

Hermann was six months old when he was prescribed one of these plates. At times he would play on his lips with his tongue, especially when he was hungry. The doctor thought the sooner he had one the better, and that it was the best thing for the child, etc. The mother also wanted the best for her child, but when Hermann cried and struggled against the thing in his mouth, she despaired; she did not want to bother him. In this state of conflict she decided to follow her feelings: she gave up with the plate. 'Err, it looks awful, the way he lets his tongue hang out!' the doctor said to her at the next consultation. Where was this mother going to find the strength from now on to stand up to the doctor's opinion?

Almost a year later – Hermann no longer let his tongue hang out as the doctor had predicted he would but, as children of his age like to do, he still played with it sometimes – the mother talked to me about the dreadful experience she had gone through at the time. She told me that when the doctor had prescribed a plate, she had warned her that she had to be careful that Hermann did not swallow the plate as it could be dangerous for him . . . – Society's delegated murder: give your child a plate; if he swallows it, society is rid of an unwanted member. Of course, the doctor had not meant it like that, but is this not what was implied?

Only now is it clear to me that this is what Hermann's mother had resisted so desperately. (There is no doubt that little 'Mongoloid' children play with their tongues more often and more extensively than other children – in fact it is really bigger and so it is more important in the child's experience. But playing with the tongue and letting it hang out are two quite different things.)

The fuss that is made about the long tongues 'Mongoloids' have is also significant from another point of view, and not only because of the symbolic significance: 'cutting out the tongue' is also what it is called when someone is silenced. It is once again the fact that it is commonly taken for granted that the tongues of 'Mongoloids' have the tendency to hang out which sets me thinking. The tongue, not the child who lets it hang out, does something which may also have meaning. Letting one's tongue hang out does not have any meaning, it cannot have any since it is natural: that is how the phantasy works. It is simply not part of the phantasm that no human being – even a 'Mongol' – who likes and respects himself, and who does not want to degrade himself in the eyes of others, simply lets his tongue hang out (even when it is unusually long), since it will invite ridicule and scorn. Of course not; in their friendly state of adaptation, 'Mongols', by definition, do not possess so much self-awareness and self-confidence.

Susanna, who is just over one year old, always begins to cry when she feels she is not being taken seriously or is being laughed at: does she really need the unpleasantness of a plate and an operation to make her keep her tongue inside her mouth and use it as the rest of us do? Admittedly, Susanna already has much more self-respect than many 'Mongoloids' will ever develop – but when they really let their tongues hang out in a heedless, self-despising manner, then it is certainly not because they are too long.

Where are 'Mongoloids' supposed to get self-respect and self-confidence from if their own questions about their identity and situation in our world are subject to a taboo, if M. 'cannot cry' and 'does not know what being dead means'? When, as a small boy, Nigel Hunt, author of *The World of Nigel Hunt – Diary of a Mongoloid Youth*[6] asked his grandmother what a Mongoloid was, he received – according to his father – the 'truthful' answer: 'an inhabitant of Mongolia'. Is there any more effective way of deflecting and placing a taboo on the first tentative question: 'Who am I in this world?' And surely there is no better way of destroying a child's waking intelligence than absurdly countering his question in this 'truthful' way (it thus becomes unquestionable for the child)? In the 'game' the mimicking child counters his partner's utterances by imitating them and, through such pseudo-replies, imperceptibly undermines the other's self-respect and self-assurance. Similarly this boy, in the void of his lack of self-awareness which he is struggling to free himself from by being curious, is knocked backwards by such as-if answers, without being able to defend himself. Being so young, how is he supposed to know that his vague sense of dissatisfaction is justifiable, that this apparently grown-up answer does not take his question seriously at all? Language is always controlled by grown-ups, the others, who in such interactions rob the child of control over the key dimension of self-reflection.

This is pinning a person down to the concrete level. Someone who is not allowed to inquire into his own place in our world – or rather whose inquiry is met with an answer that in fact is a non-answer – stands no chance. The capacity for abstraction depends on one's place in the world. When I say about myself: I am white, German, a woman, a member of the middle class, I am speaking abstractly; I differentiate myself through these attributes from blacks, Senegalese, men, and my place in society is thereby defined. The place of 'Mongoloids', however, is essentially defined by what they are prevented from knowing, i.e. that they are 'Mongoloid'. They do not count; we do not take them into account; they 'simply embody the negative possibility'. How are they supposed to learn to count, to calculate, to have mathematical control over the 'positive possibility'? I do not wish to dispute the fact that constitutional factors may play a part in the weakness 'Mongoloids' have in arithmetic (as well as other compliant people with learning disabilities – my observations suggest that friendly-stupid compliance and a weakness in arithmetic often go together); however, as far as I am concerned, this can no longer be taken for granted.

The answer 'an inhabitant of Mongolia' does not suppress the question itself but rather its meaning. This nevertheless allows for a specific way of speaking, i.e. imitating, repeating. 'Mongoloids' are famous for their marked readiness and capacity for imitating. Imitating, mimicking is what is left when someone does not own or know himself. In this way a 'part of the tongue of the sweet and lovely little Mongoloid is also cut out'.

Just how difficult it is not to collude in 'silencing someone' I know from my own experience of therapies conducted with children with Down's syndrome. Susanna's parents – still shocked by the diagnosis – courageously decided to keep their little daughter, but in spite of this Susanna could not fail to be aware of her 'fate'. Even though I had worked with her regularly since she was fourteen months old at her parents request, in addition to having visited her sporadically from an early stage, she could not be spared this experience. It is true that she was now able to say a few words and knew a few names, including her own; but she only used these words in situations where she was really taken by surprise, as if she first had to be thrown off balance in order to show what she could do. The parents now began to be more attentive – as their little girl could not walk yet she should at least have been showing signs of positive development by speaking. Her parents' wishful phantasies that Susanna might one day wake up to find she no longer had Down's syndrome came out clearly in our discussions. These phantasies are not only difficult to work through because of the parents themselves; I must admit that I also indulged in them. In my phantasies too, the fact that Susanna had Down's syndrome was an attribute to be denied and got rid of by therapy. Why Susanna was not showing that she could speak, why she completely gave up speaking again when she was one and a half was difficult for me to understand. First I had to see how the way I was caught up in the phantasy myself was contributing to this. She stopped speaking when both the parents and I took her early, almost 'normal' language learning, as a sign that Susanna was 'not so Mongoloid after all', i.e. that Susanna in fact was not who she seemed to be. The last word that Susanna continued to utter for a while, very frequently, and with a lot of emphasis, before she eventually completely gave it up, was her name. It was as if she wanted to say: 'Here I am, me, "Mongoloid" Sanna.' When I understood – and it was not easy for me – I played Kasperl doll scenes for her with the characters 'Mummy-witch',* 'Susanna-princess' and 'Little Mongoloid'. Mummy-witch only wanted the princess and disapproved of 'Little Mongoloid', but Susanna-princess could only live together with 'Little Mongoloid'. So the princess and 'Little Mongoloid' defended each other with the active support of Susanna who watched my scenes with great interest. I had to play these games over and over again; sometimes Susanna would then cry, grinding her teeth and I had to stop and comfort her. It was all too close to the bone for her.

It also becomes more difficult for children with Down's syndrome to acquire a self-image because the environment offers them no possibility of identification. To begin with, their features are not represented by dolls or picture-book illustrations. A colleague once asked me when a Down's

---

* She calls me 'Mummy' like her mother.

syndrome child normally learns to look at picture books. 'Why should they want to learn this when they cannot recognise themselves in them anywhere', was my reply. Then she remembered that a two-year-old girl who had Down's syndrome, and was coming to her for therapy, had once shown interest briefly in a picture representing a Chinese girl. (Once I understood this I had a 'Mongoloid' doll made specially for my work.) But it becomes even more difficult for such a child to recognise himself because he can sense how other people only see, reject, or do not want to accept his 'difference'. Everyone is afraid of identifying with 'this person' – ultimately no one wants to face in himself the attributes which are collectively projected onto Down's children: stupid-compliant, defenceless and helpless, but 'sweet'. We cannot identify with such a contemptuous person, we can only reject him; and so the Down's syndrome child can find nothing in himself which can give him a reason to be proud and to say: this is who I am. It is particularly unfortunate that parents cannot narcissistically invest a child with Down's syndrome, cannot be proud of him. Instead they sometimes succeed in taking a certain pride in the results of their educational efforts. This secondary narcissistic investment is no longer directed at the child's genuine self-expression, but complies with his inevitable attempt to undo his own existence. Yet, even if this secondary narcissistic investment enables a Down's child to imitate, perform, show friendly interest, and, at times, smartness, it does not give him autonomy and self-awareness.

It seems to me that the most appalling thing about the scene between Nigel Hunt and his grandmother is that, unlike in the 'game' of the mimicking child, the grandmother's meaningless reply was not meant as an aggression or an attack. Indeed, she wanted to protect her grandchild from the negative meaning of the word 'Mongoloid'. Since she was no more free of the phantasm than the rest of us are, she could only achieve this by being an instrument of the phantasm: by placing a taboo on the symbol 'Mongoloid' and disguising the inability to speak by her as-if answer. Even the most gifted and intelligent child could not defend himself against such loving care which he is so much in need of – it finally scares away the outstretched feeler, letting the child become shy and stupid like the snail Adorno and Horkheimer speak of in their simile. The child senses the love and needs it all the more in that the answer, which is no answer, deprives him of his basic sense of self. He experiences that the language which adults master is the unavoidable evil causing him subterranean, nameless anxiety, so that he has to feign death inwardly – renouncing what is inaccessible for him. As a substitute, he has to cling onto those who seem to understand the answer 'an inhabitant of Mongolia'. Insofar as they appear to master what for him is a source of anxiety, he tries to ward off the unbearable anxiety of not knowing himself by imitating exactly what they expect of him, but which he does not understand.

This brings us to what are supposed to be the natural characteristics of Down's children, that is, their marked readiness to imitate, and their 'unassertive, friendly-compliant manner'. 'These children can be very sweet and good'; 'these children often become the sunshine of the family'. Many mothers still hear such doubtful words of consolation when they are under the shock of the diagnosis. It goes without saying that they do not always turn out to have such a 'sweet and good' nature and so at times a helping hand is necessary. Ingo's mother was warned several times in a well-known child care centre that she should put a swift end to Ingo's signs of defiance and resistance to prevent him from turning into a little tyrant. The cliché flips over so easily: a brazen 'normal' child, especially a boy, is intelligent, but a brazen maladjusted 'Mongoloid' child becomes a little tyrant whose tyranny must be eradicated by education. In the back of our minds there is an anxious phantasy which the cliché serves to protect us from, that is, the phantasy of a barbaric-wild Mongolian living out his aggressive drives without restraint. The scornful phantasm of the well-adjusted person is based on the projection of this fear of the overwhelming power of the drives and their reversal into the opposite in the cliché (to be preserved at any cost) of 'sweet little compliant "Mongoloids"'.

They are pinned down by such disdain and seen as the frightening spectre of what we refuse to believe about ourselves and despise. This pinning down may at times be quite explicit – more often, however, it operates in a more subtle way, disguised by loving devotion and care for bodily and mental well-being. It is scarcely noticeable, even when we try not to be taken in by the phantasm.

Here is a scene from a visit by Susanna's family: Susanna and I were sitting on the floor and had been playing with soap-bubbles; I was now blowing them in her face, onto her neck and her hands. She was enjoying herself; was she trying to blow bubbles too? It looked like it, I was not sure. Her father was rustling the cake packet and she went to get herself a cake. Her mother laughed: 'When she sees cakes, you can't interest her in anything else!' I was shocked, taken aback, and at first reacted with denial: I didn't want to interest her in anything at all and did not have any 'learning goals' . . . but perhaps it was true, in fact, that with a part of my attention I was not just blowing bubbles with Susanna but trying to interest her in 'blowing' as a learning aim? If I am honest, though, in our happy togetherness there was a tinge of this mistrust, of poisonous contempt: 'If I don't show her how to do it, she'll never learn by herself!' Only a touch of this poison, admittedly, but enough to make our playing so unenjoyable for her that it was difficult for her to share with me her own efforts at blowing. Why not? Probably for the same reasons that Lynn would resist crawling as long as her mother needed her to learn to crawl as a proof of her own innocence. Performing the required activity would mean being dispossessed: blowing would no longer be a sign of Susanna's autonomous and curious exploration of the environment, but rather a sign of my success as a facilitator, proof of my omnipotence.

This was Susanna's (and Lynn's) way of defending herself: when she feels we do not have confidence in her own spontaneous childlike explorations, in her own learning through experience ('He always has to be motivated; he has to be encouraged to look, to listen, to react at all.'[7]) she resists and keeps it for herself. She does not let herself be dispossessed.

Here is another scene: Susanna's mother told me that even when she tried to coax Susanna with cakes, Susanna did not want to pull herself up to objects. She could, but only did so when she believed she was alone or when her mother was pretending to sleep. Just at this point the father came in. Susanna crawled eagerly towards him, beaming; he held out his hands towards her so that she could pull herself up. She started to do so but then suddenly buckled at the knees and crawled away. I had the impression that she was refusing to do what was expected of her, what others did not believe she could do. I said this to the parents and they reacted just as I had in the previous scene – they were taken aback and were unwilling to accept it. I do not think it is a coincidence that from that day on Susanna no longer had to hide the fact that she was capable of standing up.

In play situations with children with Down's syndrome I have often seen that, contrary to what we think, they are very aware of what is happening to them in the world and that most of them have no words with which to communicate this awareness meaningfully to those around them. They symbolise the lack of self-awareness which has been forced on them, e.g. the stairs between the cellar and the attic have been destroyed; or the room is dark because no one has put in the wiring for the light overhead; or, in M.'s case, the doctor who carried out cosmetic surgery on her, repeatedly gave her anaesthetics to make her unconscious:

> The child repeatedly came into the hospital and was given anaesthetics. M. insisted that it was as a punishment. The other children could go to the children's birthday party. So one child came into hospital (I usually had to play this part), because she had to have an operation or to have her teeth pulled out. The child was repeatedly given anaesthetics . . . I said that it was awful always to be made unconscious, they always want to change her body because the parents do not like it. And the child was very anxious, yet no one listened to her. She was completely alone and the anaesthetics made her mute. I said that it was unbearable. Then M. wanted to dictate something to me. She wanted me to fetch some paper and something to write with. Then she dictated:
> 'The child is in hospital.
> The doctor gives the child anaesthetics.
> The child is given anaesthetics for one hour.
> The child cries and screams, because she is given an injection.

Now the child is bleeding.
The child is very afraid.'
She dictated my name and asked me to write down my telephone number. She continued dictating:
'The child cries for help. Song-book.'
A little later there was the following game:
M. laid the table in the kitchen for all the children, because there was going to be a birthday party. I was the child who was having a birthday party. I had to help M., the mother, lay the table and fetch the dolls (the other children). When M. took the tablecloth off the table, she discovered a large burn mark on the tabletop. M. had once made such a mark on her parents' dining-room table. I had to think about this. She wanted to know how the mark had got there, and while I was explaining this to her, she bawled at me telling me how naughty I was. I had to go to the dentist straight away and to the hospital and could not take part in the birthday party or eat with the other children. M. sent me out of the kitchen and locked me in another room where I was given an injection. She went and I told her I was afraid of the dentist; that I wanted to accompany her and so on. M. was sugar-sweet, but I had to stay there. I cried and M. went back into the kitchen. After a while I went into the kitchen but she sent me off to the doctor again. This happened once again and, finally, I said: 'I have finished with the dentist'. M. asked me to tell her what it was like at the dentist's. After I had described this in detail she sent me out of the kitchen again and lit the candles. She had really made a lovely table for a party, yet I was not allowed to be there. She said she hoped everyone (her and the dolls) would enjoy their meal and started eating. I stood outside the kitchen, M. had pulled the curtain in the passageway to, and I was only allowed to watch through a crack but could not be present. I grew really very sad. I said: 'The poor child is not allowed to be present. They do not want her to be present because she is different. She is so sad and alone. No one listens to the child . . .' and so on. While I said this, M. and the dolls wished me a good meal after every sentence I said. She forbade me to speak. Once she shouted loudly: 'Yeah, yeah!' After that she began to cry but wiped away her tears quickly with a napkin. I cried too. M. looked behind the curtain and saw that I was crying too. It was just as distressing for me to cry as it was for her and I wiped away my tears [. . .]. When the father came to collect M. she hid under the kitchen table. I would very much have liked to hide too as I was so embarrassed by the idea that he might notice how sad I was or that I had been crying.

I would like to let these play-scenes speak for themselves and only comment on a few aspects of them. The child is given 'anaesthetics' as a punishment because she had made a burn mark on her birthday – the burn mark of her

parents' pain about his being 'Mongoloid'. This was how M. had experienced her parents' attempts to protect her from knowing that she was the
cause of this pain and still is (the frequent periods in hospital and operations have not freed her from the stigmatisation, from her 'Mongoloid'
appearance which make people look at her). She now lets the student feel
just how difficult it is for her to tolerate becoming aware of her situation
(after she has patiently overcome barriers of understanding with the student
for more than a year already and has sought new ways of expressing her
painful experiences) now that she is beginning to refuse the anaesthetics
(when she asked the student, as they were playing, what it had been like at
the dentist's, she probably would have liked to hear that from now on 'the
child' would refuse to let her teeth – her means of self-defence – be pulled
out). The student's tears help her to bear what she is in the process of
understanding. As the father is too deeply involved in the situation, he must
not be told anything about it yet. 'The child cries for help. Song-book.'
Once again she tries to dissimulate her cry for help, it's only a 'song', what
she has dictated is not so true then . . . . And quickly she hides herself and
her tears under the table (lets them fall under the table), so that the father
does not see them. For her, he is guardian of the phantasm to which she
owes the unconsciousness, the 'anaesthetics'; in this way he is exonerated
from guilt feelings.

Susanna also hid 'under the table', refusing to confirm my omnipotence
(her impotence) by blowing bubbles back. She was right; but she shamed
me with her resistance and, consequently, it was difficult for me to see her
refusal as an achievement. How much easier it would have been to tell
myself – in line with the phantasm – 'she cannot do it, because she has
learning disabilities', and thereby to despise her for my failure.

> No science has yet explored the inferno in which were forged the
> deformations that later emerge to daylight as cheerfulness, openness,
> sociability, successful adaptation to the inevitable, an equable, practical
> frame of mind. There is reason to suppose that these characteristics are
> laid down at even earlier phases of childhood development than are
> neuroses: if the latter result from a conflict in which instinct is defeated,
> the former condition, as normal as the damaged society it resembles,
> stems from what might be called a prehistoric surgical intervention,
> which incapacitates the opposing forces before they have come to grips
> with each other.[8]

Adorno certainly did not have Down's children in mind when he wrote this.
But the fact that their 'successful adaptation to the inevitable', their
'equable, practical frame of mind' is the result of a massive and very early
intervention, is demonstrated by M. The stigma of her birth, the 'killing
looks' in the first few days of her life, have already dealt her a blow which is

bound to undermine her strength permanently. As a newborn child she had no possibility of defending herself and so her first experience was: it is bad to be alive at all. 'Having learning disabilities is bad.' Feigning death, merging with the environment, are the most primitive reactions in the animal world in extreme situations of danger. It seems to me that the much-praised distinctive readiness of Down's children to imitate finds its essential roots here. With newborn babies we can already observe the death-feigning reflex, the mimetic self-adjusting to environmental death phantasies. These infants are said to show a general lack of vitality and some of them do not take in the food they are offered.

> When Johannes was born and I first saw him, I immediately had the impression that somehow he looked different. During the first day I suppressed this. [. . .] He did not cry, he did not cry at all as a baby usually cries; he was completely withdrawn and showed no signs of wanting to drink anything. [. . .] For me he was not there at all, was not born. (interview printed in *Tageszeitung*)

Was this 'withdrawnness' really only a sign of a weak constitution? Or was Johannes not already reacting to the repressive reaction of his mother, who had most probably noticed what was wrong with him and felt that he 'was not there at all, that he had not been born?' Susanna would not have anything to drink as long as she remained in the hospital where her parents had been advised that the best thing would be to put the child in a home straight away. 'Then one may as well let the child starve' said Susanna's mother later, still furious about this suggestion. As soon as Susanna was at home – immediately after the diagnosis had been declared, the mother had asked for her to be discharged 'at her own risk' – where no one wanted to put her in a home, she developed a healthy appetite that very same evening.

This process of breaking the infant's will to live or its vital forces from the moment it is born (even when the diagnosis is withheld from the parents the infant is aware of the 'killing' looks) determines its entire future development. Susanna's capacity to play has been undermined by mistrust and anxiety and so she is reluctant to show what she is capable of, which I see as a sign that the death-feigning reflex is at work. In this way she fulfils the phantasm. So the child is already weakened by the time he is at the stage of tentatively beginning to explore his identity. He does not have enough strength to resist the meaningless pseudo-answer or refusal to answer his question, and the unexpected rejection of the question must, I assume, be wholly destructive for his autonomy.

It is an acknowledged fact that 'these people' are particularly gifted for rhythm. In fact I have known 'Mongoloid' people with severe learning disabilities who could not speak but could clap to a complicated rhythm which many 'normal' adults would first have to practise at length. All their remaining vital energies seemed to be concentrated in the effort to adapt to the present situation, totally sacrificing any autonomy they possessed to this end.

Most 'Mongoloids' certainly make progress by means of their capacity for adaptation, often to an astounding extent in the light of the drastic undermining of their psychic space so early on. This seems to occur on the pattern of a false self-organisation (Winnicott). The original will to live, which has been broken, now finds expression in the fear of dying which can be sensed all too clearly behind their friendly compliance; and, this fear of dying is the motor that drives the child to behave as well as he can, as he is expected to behave. Instead of developing his own desires, he appropriates the desires of his environment; and, in this roundabout way, he may still manage to find a way forward which amounts to something more than bare subsistence.

It seems almost impossible to free oneself from the phantasm; in my work I can feel it pulling at me over and over again, even if I am gradually becoming more conscious of it and able to resist it. When I see how Susanna's mother strives to defend herself, when I see how she repeatedly tells me particular scenes she has experienced with 'Mongoloid' adults in public in order to learn to love the clumsy, unloved, scorned aspects of them so that she can love Susanna as someone who will also become a 'Mongoloid' adult, then I can sense how difficult it must be to live with one's own child in face of the omnipotence of the phantasm in both the inner and external world. However, it is not completely impossible, as the following example shows.

Nina is a twelve-year-old girl with Down's syndrome. Initially, her mother had rejected her outright and wanted to put her in a home, but then came to terms consciously with her death phantasies and decided to keep her. Meanwhile Nina had joined an integrated school class (she was by no means the weakest student; at times she practised fractions by herself enthusiastically). The following scene occurred: the class was watching a film together that depicted the children a few years before. Afterwards, a boy said to Nina, 'Nina, in the film I found you so ugly, with your glasses and your eyes and so on, I could have puked'. As it was time for a break, Nina went out with the other children. After the break it was obvious she had been crying. She came into the class and wanted to have a group discussion. When the class had sat down in a discussion circle, Nina said to the boy, 'It was so nasty of you to say that to me earlier. You really hurt me. You really shouldn't say things like that!'

Here is another scene: a classmate was teasing Nina because she was always doing mathematics and never wrote essays. Nina replied, 'I can write essays but maths is difficult for me so I have to practise a lot!'

A third situation: during a lesson, foreign words were being discussed. The teacher asked if anyone knew what 'chromosome' meant. A child explained that 'chromosomes' were there to make sure that nothing went wrong in the body cells. Nina jumped up and said furiously: 'And you are trying to say that with me they didn't, is that it?' Irrespective of the results she obtains at school, can it be said that this girl really is 'mentally handicapped'?

Autistic perceptive disorder and the mystification of resistance

Autism, autistic child – these are emotive words which are guaranteed to provide every seminar meeting, every book, a public. Similarly, publications, autobiographical reports, scientific studies on the subject are numerous and the theme 'autism' is a money-maker amongst the diploma and seminar studies of some faculties. Quite often, when someone speaks of a child who is 'severely autistic', the gleam in their eyes as they utter these words betrays an element of pride about knowing such a 'special' child – as if one somehow shared in this 'specialness' by knowing the child.

Book titles reflect this fascination and play on it. Take, for example, *The Empty Fortress, The Siege, Sonrise/A New Day – How We Healed Our Special Child, Can Autism Be Cured? The Little Outsider*, and so on. According to the phantasy 'these children' are beautiful and possibly hidden geniuses, in any case – that is how the mother of the autistic child Elly[9] put it – 'not a usual backward child'. Einstein and Mozart were said to be autistic as children, and the specialised literature does little to contradict this myth of autistic genius. Sometimes the myth is even nourished: for example, there is the book *Nadia*,[10] a volume of pictures with the drawings of a 4- to 6-year-old autistic girl whose achievements in drawing are in fact quite astounding. It is not only outsiders, who have little to do with the often very difficult reality of day-to-day life with autistic people, who share this fascination. Even in their environment, autistic children are frequently seen as 'special' children and an unusual amount of attention is bestowed on them. I have repeatedly observed that in a group of children with learning disabilities the only autistic child (or the child with 'autistic traits') is given much more intensive attention, care and therapy than the others are.

The parents of autistic children tend to be more familiar with the suffering they have to go through with their child – and yet they also are often caught up in the myth of 'special children'. I have often had parents tell me, almost imploringly, that their child who has been diagnosed as 'having learning disabilities with autistic traits' is 'genuinely autistic' as if the other diagnosis were degrading, a narcissistic illness, as if it were somehow better to have a 'genuinely autistic child'. Some parents derive a narcissistic satisfaction from having a child with this 'special' illness, as do educators and therapists who speak of their autistic pupils with a gleam in their eyes.

Clara C. Park writes that she explained to Elly's siblings, 'our common task [is; DN] not to see this as a burden but as a privilege'.[11] 'I even made use of intellectual snobbism and explained to the children, [. . .] Elly is no ordinary backward child, but suffers from a rare and interesting illness that has only recently been discovered.' She feels this thought can at least provide some 'small satisfaction'.

In the book *Ein neuer Tag*[12] a clear description is given of the narcissistic significance that the autistic boy Raun Kahlil has for his parents. The book was first published under the title *Sonrise*, which is so blatantly grandiose that the father-author and the publisher apparently did not hesitate to change the title in a later edition. The father B. N. Kaufmann describes how he himself discovered what was wrong with his son:

> I wanted him to help me understand more about his condition. Deaf ears . . . dumb, apparently inattentive. But was this unresponsiveness really the most striking aspect? He kept on looking at me, through me. His eyes didn't seem to take in my image; they simply mirrored me. I asked him once again, but it was as if I was talking to the wind. And every time I looked at my son, I was confronted with myself again. I was searching for the answer within myself.
>
> [. . .] Fair curls, like Shirley Temple used to have, big brown eyes that were looking somewhere else as they reflected my image.
>
> One word suddenly emerged from my thoughts like a neon light. A bewildering, frightening and strange term. I tried to focus on it more closely. Then I shrank back and tried to shake it off. I looked at Raun again. His gentleness encouraged me. I focused more intensely on the word. It was circling in my head like a vulture, waiting, until I relinquished. Undeniably I had reached an extreme point, a vision, which was mine alone, and I had the choice of letting it develop into madness. The word could no longer be disavowed and I pronounced it. Autism. Infantile autism.[13]

The book *Sonrise* almost strikes one as being like the celebration of a holy cult. But even though, generally speaking, the specialised literature is more sober and this report does not represent the typical attitude of parents of autistic children, which is generally determined much more by the nightmare of day-to-day life with their child, a trace of the myth can nearly always be found. I myself am thoroughly familiar with this fascination.

A colleague once asked me whether she could introduce Brian to me because she wanted to speak with me about his music therapy. She took me to his ward after telling me a bit about him. There we were immediately surrounded by a group of toddlers.

Even before my colleague had introduced him to me, I had seen Brian in a corner of the room. I went over to him immediately, regardless of the fact that the other children were clamouring for attention. He was sitting in his corner, rocking, taking no notice of me, and just looked up briefly, almost imperceptibly, when his music therapist entered. The educator, who was looking after the children, laughed and said, 'Brian's the only one that everyone loves'.

I found the neediness of the fleeting, imploring expressions on the faces of the many children who had surrounded Janice and I as we came through the door threatening; but I only understood this later as I reflected on this scene, feeling harassed and overstrained. I had gone over to Brian for the simple reason that Janice had asked me to; but, behind this was my strong need to avoid the needy solicitation of the other children; to withdraw, just as Brian withdrew into the corner and rocked himself out of reach.

'Actually, I think it's perfectly all right to spend the whole day rocking in a corner.' – 'Somehow I also often feel like an autistic child.' – 'I can't let myself express my anger so openly.' – 'I would also like to be able to be so uncompromising.' – I have often heard such phantasies. Who would not like just once to be able to shut oneself off like this, not to get involved in anything, to reject everything, to be able to scream without restraint? Autistic children are thus surrounded by the aura of 'refusal', of 'uncompromising resistance', children who have the aura of being special, untouchable, indeed holy.

This idolisation can, however, quickly turn into disappointment, hate, and scornful devaluation, for instance, when one is obliged to realise that the child's behaviour, which at first seemed like resolute refusal, does not change in spite of one's fascination and admiration (which is easily mistaken for understanding), and that he continually frustrates, overtaxes and bothers us with his withdrawal or rage. If, in the scene with Brian, I had not sensed that, far from understanding him, I was simply copying his withdrawal and thereby trying to absorb something of his untouchable aura (overtaxed as I was by the other children's overwhelming neediness) and if I had not sensed that I needed him, I would probably have been very offended and disappointed that he did not look up to greet me happily as someone who at last was able to understand his 'uncompromising refusal'. And such an offence could very easily have turned my initial fascination into disappointment and rejection. The perception of the child as a fascinating 'stranger' easily switches imperceptibly into that of a hated and 'sinister' troublemaker; and, it is not uncommon for autistic people and their relatives to be confronted in public by nasty outpourings of hate.

Mirjam, an autistic girl in puberty, went shopping in a store with her mother. The store was full of customers one of whom was a dwarf. Mirjam saw her, pointed at her, and said: 'Look, there is a really small woman!' The people standing around reacted indignantly, taking up position in a semi-circle around Mirjam and her mother and insulting them: what a cheek – no education – and this is the Year for the Disabled! – This sort of thing

should be punished . . . . The small woman was crying. Only after a while
was Mirjam's mother able to make herself heard. 'You should think for a
minute, before you pass judgement', she said, and then apologised to the
crying woman before explaining: 'This child is severely disabled.
Unfortunately I have left her disabled person's identity card at home.'
'Anyone can say that', 'badly brought up', 'what a nerve!' they went on;
Mirjam's mother simply took flight with her daughter and once they had
got home she burst into tears.

Here is a stoning scene from the 'Year for the Disabled'.

Mirjam was no longer a toddler when this scene took place. Perhaps
things would have been different if she had been smaller. Generally speaking, toddlers are allowed to be much more uninhibited and freer than older
children; this is particularly true for 'autistic children', even if such awful
scenes in public are an everyday experience for some parents of autistic
toddlers. The aura of 'being special' only attaches itself to the toddlers;
adolescents and adults lose this fascinating aura, are scarcely spoken about,
and when they do not succeed in extricating themselves from autism, they
are pushed aside and forgotten along with all the other people with learning
difficulties in society. It is only in the small child, apparently, that the myth
of refusal, madness and genius, of beauty and obsession, works for us. I
have sometimes observed how fascination for an autistic child topples over
into rejection and shoulder-shrugging indifference when he reaches puberty.
In a state of resignation, parents then often give up wanting to go on
helping their child who has disappointed their hopes for long enough
already. 'He is like a dog,' fifteen-year-old Christian's father said to me, 'if
you don't train him, he has no idea how to behave.' (It is not so much, as
one might think, the renowned 'coldness' of parents of autistic children that
I am hearing here but rather the distressed indifference of a father after
almost fourteen years of pointless suffering.) Even Christian's educators
who, when Christian was still a good-looking eleven-year-old, had moved
heaven and earth to try and integrate him into a home, and had found him
a place in varied forms of therapy, now spoke of the pimple-faced fifteen-
year-old, who was becoming unmanageable because of his growing physical
strength, in terms full of hate and rejection. They felt it was a waste of time
making any further effort for him.

Idolisation and stoning are two sides of the same coin: 'I could do that
too!' switches – when it can no longer be affirmed – into 'I would never do
that!' 'Autists are like mirrors' says Mirjam's mother, reflecting on the
stoning scene. 'They reflect what everyone in society would like to do but
do not allow themselves to do because it is not the done thing.' And then
she adds: 'Often, in situations like this, when we were being insulted Mirjam
would simply begin screaming loudly. And Mirjam can scream very loudly!
I always stood by wishing I could scream out so uninhibitedly too. Sometimes I have thought that I should have screamed like that in my childhood

and youth when I was treated unfairly and meanly. I did not do it; on the contrary, I had to put up with everything because I was so dependent.' The resistance which we cannot muster in ourselves, the unselfconscious curiosity that we deny ourselves (because it too easily smacks of 'look, such a person should not be allowed to live', the curse of our history), the unrestrained anger that we do not give way to – our impression is that is autistic people who let themselves do such taboo things openly and thoughtlessly. By idolising them we secretly collude in this; by stoning them we repeat what was done to our own impulses and what we continue to do to them. They act as a mirror for us. When we look at them and see ourselves, our forbidden ideal-self, projective identification is at work. What we are searching for in our meaningless world is meaningful drama and at the same time protection from the 'tyranny of intimacy' – Richard Sennett has described this need people have today[14] – and autistic people show us what we are lacking.

But who are they to hold a mirror up before us so that we can no longer see them? As I am trying to write about this question it strikes me that this mirroring process is reoccurring in my text: my intention is to write about 'autistic people' and my thoughts and perceptions are concerned with discovering what the phenomenon of autism says about us and our society. The attempt to get beyond this mirroring barrier and to say something about autistic people, their experience and suffering, meets with considerable difficulties. This is clear from the different theories on the origins of autism which are often in acute conflict with each other. There are those who hold that an organic defect is responsible for autistic development, and others for whom autism is a psychical disorder. Between these two positions there seems to be so little room for agreement that the advocates of one camp are often barely able to listen to the ideas of the other. One side warns that 'therapeutic efforts' based on psychogenetic theory 'not only do not help the child but make the overall situation worse in that they increase the parents' fears and guilt feelings',[15] without even referring in the literature index to Bettelheim's book *The Empty Fortress* (1974), which, at the very least, casts considerable doubt on such a categorical statement. According to Cornell there is 'no evidence that psychoanalysis or a psychoanalytically oriented form of therapy has any specific effect on autistic children'.[16] Bettelheim's statistics of success, his detailed case histories reporting successful treatment or considerable improvement, are clearly not considered to be convincing.

The hypotheses of organic defect theorists are studied no more carefully by the advocates of the other camp either. Niko Tinbergen and Elisabeth A. Tinbergen,[17] who have recently made a new study of the psychogenetic theory (equally, however, leaving Bettelheim out of the picture), cite Ricks and Wing: 'Even in mild cases of autism the central problem seems to reside in the fact that those affected have special difficulties dealing with symbols which affects language, non-verbal contacts, and many other aspects of cognitive or social behaviour patterns'. On this score they add the comment, 'We believe [. . .] that this statement is not very fruitful and should be rejected'. By way of justification they offer the observation that 'many autistic children, if not the majority, occasionally show that they possess considerable cognitive and linguistic capacities'. To what extent this is meant to contradict the thesis of Ricks and Wing remains unclear.

The argument most often advanced against Bettelheim is that his theory increases the 'parents' anxiety and guilt feelings'. Indeed many parents of autistic children feel attacked and destabilised by Bettelheim. 'His view of the causes that gave rise to this illness contains [. . .] a reproach directed at the parents. So much of what he said was judgmental.'[18] Here too, difficulties in communication need to be clarified. Bettelheim speaks of an 'autistic *Anlage*' rooted 'in the conviction that one's own (i.e. the child's; D.N.) efforts have no influence over the world because of the earlier conviction that the world is insensitive to one's own reactions'.[19] But it should be borne in mind that he is speaking of the child's conviction and not of immediate reality. Bettelheim is perfectly aware that these need distinguishing and, with regard to possible underlying organic causes, he leaves it open as to whether the parents' behaviour, which seems to the child (and then perhaps also the environment) to be rejecting, was not also determined by the 'child's unusual reactions to his parents'.[20] Bettelheim is deeply concerned with the autistic child's experiential world; he takes it seriously as the child's psychical reality and tries to help him through it without attributing blame.

However, parents, and others who, out of solidarity with them favour an organic hypothesis, are not the only ones to react defensively towards the psychogenetic theory. Bettelheim also rejects the arguments of the organicists and does not enter into controversy with them. With respect to Rimland he says: 'I can only wonder why he decries what he calls "the all too common practice of blatantly assuming that psychogenic etiology can exist or does exist", and that to do so "is not only unwarranted but actively pernicious".' Further on, Bettelheim says: 'Nevertheless, it is one thing not to wish to make parents feel guilty because it makes them miserable and gains nothing for the child. It is another thing not to wish to find out what experiences may have caused or contributed to infantile autism because to do so is "pernicious".'[21] One can agree to this but why does Bettelheim not ask himself why Rimland, and he is not the only one, rejects the psychogenetic theory in such a wholehearted and emotional way?

If one reads Bettelheim carefully, from whatever theoretical point of view, one cannot fail to notice the know-all and judgemental tone (his book *Gespräche mit Müttern* is a notable case in point). Further, it is one thing to say 'that it is senseless and inexpedient to give the parents of autistic children the feeling that they are responsible for the whole illness' (without reflecting on the fact that the expression 'inexpedient' is tell-tale) and another thing not to want to accept that this is precisely the effect of Bettelheim's work. Here the theorists from the other camp are reacting to a perception of Bettelheim's unconscious motivations and confuse them with his theory; however, Bettelheim himself reveals that his self-perception is distorted.

This is a puzzling situation: distorted perceptions of each other on both sides are represented with verve. The situation is dominated not by conscious controversy with each other but by denial, and a refusal to come to terms with mutual perceptions. Thus there is a distortion of the working over of perceptions being enacted between scientists themselves, and this is widely regarded today as the central problem of autistic people.

This perplexing theoretical situation does not of course help me to get any nearer to the experience of autistic people – on the contrary, I have drifted off into the empty abstractness of theories. There is a noticeable difference here with 'Mongoloidism' where hardly any attempt is made to study the 'Mongoloid' syndrome theoretically because everything seems clear; the disability can be traced directly to a chromosomal abnormality, abstract reflection is superfluous, and one can immediately concern oneself with concrete measures. With autism nothing is clear: medical findings vary from traumatic brain damage to indications of various illnesses to the complete lack of verifiable organic findings. Any attempt to identify a uniform organic basis or even the purely psychogenetic basis fails for lack of evidence or because counter-evidence can easily be found.

Perplexity and drifting into empty abstractness: this is a counter-transference experience I have had in music therapy with autistic patients. A few weeks before I was due to leave the institution, thereby interrupting the music therapy, Wilfried (an autistic man whom I will speak about at greater length in due course) began wetting himself during his sessions. He had never done this before. As he stood there in his trousers that were all wet through, he was moaning quite pitifully, obviously finding the wetness on his legs very unpleasant. The first time this happened, the care-person on his ward wondered whether she had forgotten to take him to the toilet on time. But when it occurred repeatedly, one of the carers asked me whether this wetting might not be a consequence of the therapy. I was taken aback and initially rejected the idea out of hand. Wilfried and I had always got on so well and nothing had changed where that was concerned!

But the thought stuck in my mind. At first I struggled to defend myself against uncomfortable feelings: it simply could not have anything to do with me. I felt unfairly blamed – had I not always done my best? So I looked for some other explanation for the wetting. It was only slowly and painfully that it became clear to me that the carer, whom I knew and thought highly of, had not said this to me as a reproach. Only then did I see that he was right. For there was indeed something different in my relationship with Wilfried: in view of the forthcoming separation, I had already begun inwardly to take leave of him. Initially, he reacted by expressing rage, in ways we were both familiar with from our previous work. This time, however, I did not understand and responded by withdrawing. The symbiotic feeling of being linked, which we had enjoyed for so long, gradually gave way, without my noticing it, to a situation in which I was drifting away from Wilfried, losing contact with him. As I now began to reflect on these connections, the feeling of drifting away turned into leaden fatigue. Wilfried sensed this closely, moaning painfully and wet himself again. Eventually, after a long while, he was almost on the point of having a fit of rage again.

It was very difficult for me to understand that Wilfried was not whining with self-pity but angrily, because I was leaving him. True, I could talk myself into thinking that I was not leaving Wilfried out of malice but because I had no other choice – but my feelings told me I was responsible; after all, I was the one who was leaving him. The carer's suspicion had touched on these self-accusations; for me his remark had sounded like 'I find you guilty' even if he had not meant it like that.

The drifting away, the leaden fatigue, were thus defences against the reproach that I could hear in Wilfried's angry moaning and in the carer's remark. I lost myself in unreality in order not to have to recognise what my eyes and ears told me and what I unconsciously understood very well: this whining or moaning had previously always preceded and accompanied Wilfried's phases of rage. Insofar as I only wanted to hear the pitiful, infant-like whining about wet diapers, I deprived Wilfried of vital understanding by not mirroring his anger; instead I mirrored a distorted image; that is, of the small, impotent, helpless Wilfried and not the strong Wilfried who in his fits of rage had been able to wrench steel doors off their hinges. I was now afraid of him as I noticed how close to the surface his rage was. As I did not understand and perceive his anger, in my phantasy it became demonic, omnipotent, and was in complete contrast with the impotence and helplessness which I had reduced Wilfried to through splitting. My fear of his rage was in fact fear that the part of my perception of Wilfried that I had split off and denied might violently break through my barrier of denial and stir up my guilt feelings.

But for Wilfried, my drifting away, my perceptive splitting, and the denial of his anger in which all his strength was bound, undoubtedly had devastating consequences. The distorted mirror deprived him of the possibility of expressing his anger. To the extent that I was trying to comfort him like a small infant, I simply mimicked his helplessness. Instead of understanding, phantasy took hold, mystifying Wilfried's strength and his despair into something demonic, inhuman; while, at the same time, and dissociated from this, he still came across to me as small and impotent. And by wetting himself and threatening to have an outburst of rage he was already beginning to measure up to this phantasy.

When I think about this therapy situation, I really see something 'destructive' in my guilt feelings: by confusing Wilfried's anger with blame, I was endangering our relationship. If the carer had spoken with the same know-all undertones which drown Bettelheim's conscious intentions, he would have wrecked my chances of understanding and our therapeutic relationship might well have ended in catastrophe. The reports of mothers of autistic children clearly show what a difficult situation they find themselves in due to the blame they incur from those around. It is so easy, so tempting, to blame them: a mother whose child's behaviour is clearly impossible, but who does not appear to be handicapped – on the contrary often even looks pretty, sweet and quite intelligent – must be guilty. The more the child demonstrates his lack of containment through his often panicky way of acting, the more controlled and 'colder' the mother becomes (and in this way she conforms to the phantasm of the autismogenic mother): Mirjam's mother's only resource – in one of the many stoning scenes which she has already been through – is showing her daughter's disabled person's identity card, certifying that Mirjam suffers from 'mental disorder as defined by the law', thereby officially sanctioning the phantasm. The effect of the disabled person's ID card is that society banishes the autistic person as 'murderer Peter Gait, suffering from mental disorder as defined by the law' and the projection of guilt and responsibility can thus be deflected onto the weakest.

It is indeed a question of projecting responsibility and guilt feelings: a colleague recounted how in one year of therapy she had 'brought an autistic child so far' that he could cry. This, however, was of no interest to the parents: all they wanted was to see that the child was learning to dress himself independently and so on. Naturally, the parents did not want to understand: how could they have tolerated it when their child's tears were evidence for the therapist of their guilt? This is also true when therapeutic projections are kept hidden: as a result of bad experience the parents of autistic children are seismographically sensitive; they sense what is hidden and react unconsciously to it, and it is then perhaps that they become completely 'cold, inaccessible and controlled'. It is understandable that my colleague had guilt feelings about this therapy that had been interrupted and that these were readily passed on to the parents who had broken off the therapy. But now I am the one who is in danger of projecting: by considering my colleague to be self-righteous, I am quickly forgetting how difficult it was for me myself to have to recognise the part I played in the broken off therapies of Inge and Filippa (see below). My colleague's anger was after all justified. It is indeed really a fine thing and an important therapeutic success when a child can at last cry and it is also terrible when such work is broken off; only, in this case, it is not the parents who should be held to blame. On the contrary, it is the phantasm that imposes itself unconsciously in such unbearable scenarios and we all collude in its perpetuation.

Cathi's mother told me that her daughter often knocked toddlers over. She was clearly fascinated by intense expressions of emotions, whether laughing or crying, and when she knocked a child over, it was probably because she wanted to see him crying. I suspected that Cathi was passing on something she had experienced herself. When I said so I touched a sensitive spot: whereas previously the mother was openly and strongly emotionally involved in our conversations, now her expression became impenetrable. It was as if a tiny danger signal had made a hermit crab withdraw like lightning into its shell. 'You mean, Cathi is passing on what she has suffered from me?' she asked warily – and now it was my turn to be taken aback. This is how the 'coldness and excessive control' of the mothers of autistic children may present itself. I would probably have been subjected to this coldness more intensely if I had tried to discuss with the mother the possibility that, because of helplessness and exhaustion, she may at times have damaged her child. But this was not my concern – every child has to cope with the fact that his mother cannot always be patient and full of understanding. This will enable him to develop 'normally', and not autistically.

I explained to Cathi's mother what I wanted to say: that I could imagine how Cathi, who was often so overwhelmed by her feelings that she had to fly into a tantrum, might look at a crying child with fascination, even rapture. What might it be like to have such an intense feeling without being completely overwhelmed by it? – to be desperate and angry but not to such an uncontained extent as she experiences? Now the mother relaxed and the relationship between us improved again. She then told me a story that was very instructive. Her daughter was born at six months and had spent a long time in an incubator on the ward for prematurely born babies; today, she herself worked on a research project on such a ward. She had noticed how, as soon as they are able to move, the tiny human beings, in their inhuman apparatuses, manoeuvre themselves in such a way that they are touching one of the sides of the apparatus, even if it is only with the head, in order to feel in some way contained, held, and secure. This longing can easily be recognised since the explorations cease as soon the babies have a cover over them. What a miserable substitute they have to put up with compared with the warmth of the enveloping womb! Cathi obviously still suffers from not being held, and her mother too. Now I see this as coldness, the coldness of society. Incubators have existed for many years and this mother, who herself has had to watch on impotently as her child was suffering in one of these machines, has been led – paid as a temporary worker – to do research into how this machine can be made more human and warmer. This is a mother who, according to the myth, is cold and restrained . . . . Admittedly this myth, like so many myths, has long been banned from official phraseology – but banning the word does not mean the myth has been dispensed with any more than is true of the word 'Mongoloid': its power is even greater when it is taboo.

In her book *Kein Kind zum Vorzeigen*[22] Ingrid Häusler shows in fright-ening detail how history, as well as environmental blame, make mother and child feel out in the cold without sufficient holding. The book is a barely tolerable statement of plaint and indictment. However, even though some details are perhaps portrayed in an exaggerated and one-sided manner, involving too much projection, what is intolerable is that the indictment is justified.

> When my parents took me back to the clinic (having visited me shortly after I had given birth in hospital where Frank, who was just a few days old, had to remain in an incubator because of an infection), my father said out loud what we were all trying to suppress: 'And even if he dies, it is still better than having to raise a problem-child . . .'. I felt a stab in the heart and I thought: that's my punishment for not having wanted the child in the first place![23]

In this small episode the impending catastrophe is already in sight: the father who said this to his daughter, who had just become a mother, was himself the father of a 'problem-child' (the author's younger brother had had meningitis as a small infant). He probably had little idea of the effect his words would have on his daughter who, because of this brother (by the same token it would have been better if he had died too) had suffered considerable privation in her childhood and had felt very deprived. Now, following the traumatic experiences during and shortly after the birth, and in view of the danger her baby was in, she had no energy left to resist this condemnation to death, the delegated murder.

'That is the punishment for . . . .' This anxious response marks the beginning of the phantasmatic 'derailment' of the mother–child relation-ship. It is the basis for the unfurling of the destructive effects of the phantasm. The initial trauma was made worse by several other experiences. After being discharged from hospital Frank was a fairly restless infant and like most restless infants he had three-month colic pains. No one who has experienced how unsettling an infant's crying from colic pain can be easily forgets it. For Frank's already seriously destabilised mother, however, these colic pains must have been particularly threatening: perhaps the 'problem-child' was already showing symptoms of 'the expected punishment'? On top of this there was a competitive situation with the mother-in-law in whose house the young family was living.

> Once when he was again having trouble with his bowel movements and did not want to let me comfort him, I was beginning to get quite desperate when my mother-in-law came over and comforted him – and Frank calmed down!' Unlike Lynn's mother she was unable to grate-fully accept the mother-in-law's help (probably given with a hidden,

unexpressed note of reproach) because it played on her self-doubts, undermining further her self-confidence as a mother. I felt humiliated; I was inwardly extremely angry but swallowed it all. I asked myself, 'what am I doing wrong, why am I not able to cope with my child? I really am doing everything I can!'[24] At three months the baby refused the mash the doctor had prescribed. Frank 'had gone hungry the whole day in order to avoid the necessary carrot mash; then, when he was clearly having tummy pains because he was hungry, he still refused to eat but he was not aware of the connection.[25]

Aware? A three-month-old infant? Retrospectively, and in view of the diagnosis, the mother saw this as a perceptual disorder, already at this tender age. To me, at any rate, it seemed that there was a perceptual disorder between mother and child. This was a mother who was lacking in confidence and who was told that the right thing to do (and there is nothing she wants to do more, she is doing everything she can!) was to give the baby carrot mash immediately. She thought it was necessary so that the baby would not develop into the 'problem child', the 'punishment'. The fact that Frank did not like the mash was already a symptom. In her state of uncertainty and anxiety the mother had to cling to authority and could not trust her own feelings and the baby's need for milk. Thus her anxious reaction and the drastic rearing method of letting the baby go hungry simply give the child the message: your feelings are wrong, they are the symptoms of a 'problem-child'.*

As she was writing this down the mother had a close sense of the connection between this hunger-scene and the child's severe disturbance which later became apparent. She adds to her account the description of a symptom arising at a later stage which is easily recognisable as an attempt to elaborate the trauma: Frank was hitting himself repeatedly and compulsively on the mouth with a spoon or a doll. The connection was certainly not one she was conscious of and was prevented from becoming so by guilty anxiety. So she grasped at the phantasmatic crutches she had at hand in order to explain what worried her most about Frank's reluctance to eat the mash: 'We had the feeling that Frank's relationship to his own bodily needs was not right'.[26] How could it be when she herself trusted more in authority than in her own feelings and in her child's own signs of vitality?

Here too, a socially delegated murder is at the origin of the 'derailment'. Nothing unequivocal of course; not a clear judgement such as 'this child

---

* Starving the infant was formerly a common child-rearing method; by itself it would never have had such catastrophic consequences. The danger in such methods lies much less in the actual damage caused to the infant's integrity than in the phantasmatic significance they have between the parents and their child.

was born with learning disabilities, and is thus *lebensunwertes Leben*)'. It is much more of an 'if': 'If it dies then it is much better than if . . .'. Whether it must inevitably turn out to be a 'problem-child' remains an open question. Hope and fear in face of the unknown and unavoidable exist side by side and remain unexpressed, as was the case in the theoretical conflict between the psychogenetic and organic hypotheses. The mother certainly immediately links up this 'if' with feelings of guilt-ridden anxiety. She was afraid she had already damaged her child with ambivalent and rejecting feelings and that she was now being punished. So the ground was prepared making her vulnerable to invasion by the phantasm. From now on the whole history of the relationship between mother and child became a struggle to prove her innocence – while the child's indications of organic damage (a microcephalus and a mild locomotion disorder were diagnosed) and disturbed development seemed to provide early evidence of her 'guilt'.

But the mother did not only feel destabilised and torn between hope and fear; she also had feelings of revolt and anger. Anger towards her father, himself the father of a 'problem-child', for putting a curse on her child in this way; anger against parental authorities who 'pass on their own neuroses to their children [. . .] by misusing their child day-in day-out for their own purposes'.[27] She felt anger towards 'fathers and institutions that do not provide the mother with the help she needed'. If a mother dares 'to think of herself sometimes' (e.g. by asking questions about an unplanned pregnancy, as she herself did) she will be plagued with 'guilt feelings'.[28] She was conscious that she wanted to do things differently, better, and that she did not want to use her child to 'realise herself vicariously', as she criticised her mother and mother-in-law for doing.[29] Yet in other places she writes, without noticing the contradiction, that without Frank she 'probably would never have had the idea of exploring her own needs'.[30]

Anger, fear, guilt feelings, grandiose phantasies (of being able to do things better, in spite of extremely difficult circumstances, than her parents and parents-in-law who seem to her to be condemning authorities) dominated her feelings and phantasies about being a mother. 'I wanted to bring Frank up "with as little repression as possible"; that is, in spite of all the difficulties, I wanted to maintain a basically positive attitude towards him, not demanding "absolute obedience" from him, to give him time to gain confidence in me and, above all, not to force him into doing anything. In contrast, my parents-in-law regarded obedience as important and, to my dismay, even had some success by insisting on it!'[31] Although it looks as if the authoritarian structuring which the parents-in-law imposed on the child, along with their refusal to accept 'that Frank was quite different from other children',[32] offered him a form of holding he seemed in need of, she was unable to learn from this (which would not necessarily mean forcing Frank to adapt); it dismayed her, driving her even deeper into her fears of guilt and failure. To counter this she could only hold onto a rigid principle that theoretically sounds right: 'a non-repressive upbringing'. Of course this remains an empty principle: her fear of blame compelled her to demand absolute obedience in an authoritarian way, if authority deemed it necessary.

What is being enacted here is a dissociation between stoning and idealising: the respect for the child's autonomy, which principle requires, is denied on medical grounds when she lets him go hungry because of the carrot mash; but it reappears in the form of idolisation in the wording she uses. 'In order to avoid the necessary mash', the three-month-old child goes hungry, acting very wilfully; 'when he refuses food he is being wilful in a way I would never have imagined possible'.[33] He is wilful and is already her 'tyrant'. When Frank was one year old, she writes, 'he would sabotage such attempts to get him to imitate'. The little saboteur who does not adapt, does not do what she wants him to by adapting guiltily to authority. Unlike her, when she was a child, he does not react to the pressure to conform 'by withdrawing (timidity)', but with 'uninhibited defiance'.[34] 'It is Frank, with his behaviour, who turns our shabby norms of achievement and good behaviour upside down',[35] not her: her resistance, her self-assertion, her narcissism as a mother who wants to raise her child without repression is broken. And while she lets Frank go hungry on the instructions of those in authority, she feeds him with idolisation, the fragments of her own wounded narcissism. But although in the hungry child's state of distress, idolisation is the only thing he can get, he clings on to it in spite of being hopelessly overstrained; and so the helpless baby 'triumphs' while the mother suffers from her 'defeats' and 'humiliations'. Soon the 'resistance', the 'defiance', the refusal to conform, and incapacity to imitate become part of the little saboteur's defensive character armour.

'Our feeling was that Frank's relationship to his bodily needs was not right at all':[36] an organically caused perceptual disorder then. Or, he was a little saboteur: two contradictory concepts existing side by side in the mother's phantasies, just as they led to an unbridgeable gulf between the theoreticians. Is the child naturally incapable or is he resisting? This dissociation crops up everywhere. One finds it in the conflict over whether autistic people suffer from learning disabilities or not; in the contention that there is a circumscribed, common defect, which so far has not been proved; in the behaviour of autistic people who, alongside what is often severe retardation, frequently show themselves capable of individual accomplishments of a striking nature – accomplishments, however, that often seem to have little significance – and, finally, in the fact that they can often appear to be blind or deaf, but then prove to have an unusually fine hearing or visual perceptive faculty.

In the review *Autism* a mother recounts a conversation that she had with her son Detlef after he had found his way out of his autism through years of patient exercising with her. 'Detlef, why weren't you able to look at me when you were younger?' Detlef: 'Because I saw too much'. [. . .] 'When I look at you for any length of time, then I see every wrinkle. Then you are ugly. Your nose is crooked; it is always like that. When I look at the doll (it was lying in his field of vision) for long, then it is not good any more.' The mother comments on this: 'If what Detlef says is right [. . .], then we have struggled against disturbances of perception in the areas of seeing and hearing. As a toddler he experienced his environment as chaotic. It seems that he saw more than he was able to work through.'[37] Certainly, the elaboration of these perceptions is disturbed if the mother can no longer tolerate this 'no good any more', as well having her weaknesses subjected to close scrutiny because she inevitably experiences this as a verdict of guilt. Ambivalence: the ability to perceive a good mother, and simultaneously, a 'no longer good, an ugly', disappointing, limited mother has become impossible because of the phantasm making the mother anxious that she is guilty, absolutely, irrevocably evil and bad. Thus the child's correct perception results in chaos for him since he sees how he destroys the mother with it. Anxiety – and whatever made it so intense (generally the awareness or apprehension of an organic impairment plays an important role) – has driven the autistic child's mother, just as it drove me, as Wilfried's therapist, to splitting: she had to be omnipotent so as not to have to disappoint her child or to hurt him under the difficult conditions of this mother–child relationship. The perceptive-elaboration disorder stems from the fact that the child senses only too well his mother's fears of being stoned when he says 'so you are no good any more'. He experiences how his disappointed, angry looks, make the mother, whom he needs so much, virtually disappear. He then has the option of ignoring this or, through compulsive acting out, of provoking a response from her as proof that she has survived.

By remaining blind and deaf in the leaving-situation with Wilfried, I was also clinging to the fantasy of omnipotence: I was the omnipotent one who remained 'only good' under impossible conditions. However, I could not take responsibility for the real sense of impotence that had driven me to give up and so I projected this onto Wilfried as the 'person with learning disabilities'. But I also unloaded my anger onto him through projective identification and feared the demonic-omnipotent fighter in him. Only when I had succeeded in differentiating between the 'damage' that I was doing to Wilfried by leaving him, and my reasons for this decision, which were not 'wrong' but signified an admission of impotence, and only when the reality that had pushed me to such a bad decision could be integrated in my self-awareness and self-criticism, could I manage to empathise with Wilfried, to share his anger and desperation about this 'bad experience'. He did not have a fit of rage and could preserve the gains he had made in the music therapy in spite of the bad separation.

Unlike children with Down's syndrome, autists experience an interaction form in which their autonomy is not encroached upon, but where narcissistic omnipotent projections of the environment propel them into an 'autonomy', an absolute egocentricity, a resistant attitude, and refusal to imitate that is empty, without any basis. Of course, it was not an autonomous decision that led the starving three-month-old Frank to refuse the mash. The basis of resistance is also lacking because – reinforced as it is by narcissistic projections – it has no object: resisting, being angry at the object means destroying it. It was precisely what made me succumb to leaden tiredness and exposed Frank's mother to intolerable self-reproaches. But without an opponent the resistance remains an abstraction. Autistic people feel compelled to assert themselves against a nothingness; they find themselves faced with the vacuum of the maternal (or therapeutic) anxiety, a vacuum which threatens to engulf them, which they must therefore resist with all their strength (intensified by the narcissistic projections of the environment). The fear of change stems from the fear of perceptions that cannot be controlled omnipotently. In a rather absurd way autistic people often conjure up omnipotent phantasies in us: wrenching steel doors off their hinges, climbing up trees and onto roofs with unbelievable agility, an ability to repeat long conversations word for word, imitating voices exactly. We marvel at such abilities, but they rarely have a communicative quality about them. They are empty, abstract, without an interlocutor. Included here are the 'cognitive and verbal capacities' Tinbergen and Tinbergen mention, which they see as an argument against the observation that autistic people suffer from a weakness in their capacity to use symbols. But it is precisely this capacity which highlights, often to a frightening extent, such a weakness. For example, a young autistic man I know possesses an unbelievable skill in handling electrical wiring. He can establish connections, contacts, resistance and never creates a short-circuit, even in the most complicated situations, yet he is far from being able to put this ability to use in a real work context in his environment. This capacity functions as a symptom whenever there is a need to avoid contact; if someone gets too close to him, then a human short-circuit might occur. An autistic girl, classified as having severe learning disabilities, has discovered perspective in drawing much earlier than other children and masters the principles perfectly, but she draws in a way which shows that this capacity is abstract and that the girl does not understand her drawings as a representation of real space.

These skills are only meaningless, however, if we are unable to see that the young man is trying to re-establish the resistance that makes the connection between the positive and negative electric pole possible, in other words, the human contact which is missing in his relationship to the environment; and, that the girl, in her inner emptiness, is trying to represent the space she is lacking because she cannot find anyone who can understand her peculiar way of expressing herself and tolerate her feelings.

Nourished with idolisation and wounded omnipotent phantasies, 'autists' provoke the hate which is often directed at idols when they disappoint the exaggerated expectations people have of them. In order to save them from stoning we declare them to suffer from 'mental disturbance as it is defined by the law'. But this way of protecting ourselves is stultifying and signifies hopelessness. And yet there is still hope. The omnipotent phantasy often gives rise to a completely rigid and distorted structure, but it also nourishes fascination which time and again serves as a platform for parents, carers and therapists – sometimes successfully – to take up the struggle against fate.

Chapter 5

From anxiety to technological treatment strategies

Andrea has an idiosyncratic habit which is regarded as inappropriate and needing to be brought under control. Her idiosyncrasy is that she prefers to go over to the house opposite to fetch the building blocks for her game from there rather than choosing the building blocks in the day room. Andrea is also required to practise day-in day-out how to fit a pre-cut piece of jigsaw puzzle into a ready-made hole making the same old picture over and over again.

If we are honest with ourselves, we all quite often catch ourselves turning our lack of understanding, and hence our anxiety, impotence, and anger against those whose behaviour repeatedly frustrates our efforts to understand them, for instance, against Andrea when she bothers us daily by insisting on fetching the building blocks from the neighbouring building – which in fact we are not supposed to have access to – even though there are plenty of them here. Or against the boy, whose despairing eyes belie his smiling face, giving us no opportunity to understand his despair. Or against a child on whose account parents or carers have to put up with reproaches and insults from relatives and acquaintances, in institutions and in the presence of superiors. The sense of unjustness is all the more hurtful to the extent that we do not allow ourselves to put the blame on the child.

We find many reasons for disliking and fearing people with learning disabilities, but such reactions towards those who are weaker than us arouse guilt feelings, and the methods we use to protect ourselves from anxiety, hate and guilt feelings reflect the distressing situation we have got ourselves into. Admittedly, there is a difference between protecting ourselves against something that is intolerable for us which we react to because we feel hurt – but here we are giving way to our own weaknesses and accepting the way the institution 'Learning Disability' dominates our feelings, even the sadness and guilt feelings – and not recognising the defensive methods for what they are, i.e. measures of self-protection, giving them instead the label of 'rigorous education' or 'therapy'. This is how defence turns into complicity.

There is no shortage of methods that lead to complicity. I cannot investigate all of them here so I will only discuss two of the most important: behavioural therapy and special re-education, and these only in their negative extremes. For a critique of physiotherapeutic methods as well as medicinal epileptic therapy I would refer readers to the book *Kopfkorrektur*.[1]

Impotence, the taboo of hate and conditioning

The basic principle of behavioural psychotherapy which is so much in vogue in 'teaching on learning disability' seems quite straightforward: a child is rewarded when he does something good; the reward is withdrawn, or he is punished, when he does something bad. The following citation is taken from *Verhaltenstherapie bei geistig behinderten Kindern* by Gottwald and Redlin:

> The basics of operant conditioning. Successful learning, as the name suggests, is controlled by the consequences of actions. [. . .]
> 1. The action has a pleasant consequence: this action occurs more frequently in the future, so it is reinforced. The pleasant consequence of the action is described as a stimulus, the increased frequency as (positive) reinforcement. When a stimulus clearly belongs to a primary drive system (hunger, thirst, and so on) as is the case, for instance, with food and fluids, then it is described as a primary stimulus. [. . .]
> 2. The action has an unpleasant consequence: this action will occur less often in the future. In this case one is referring to punishment, Type I. Through unpleasant consequences such as noise, heat, blasts of air, electric shocks and so on, behaviour patterns can be suppressed.
> 3. The action puts an end to a pleasant situation. The cessation of a pleasant situation also has the effect of a punishment, Type II; i.e. the action will occur less often in future. [. . .] In the technical literature, when a pleasant situation is interrupted for a while, it is referred to as 'time-out'.
> 4. The action puts an end to an unpleasant situation. If an unpleasant situation stops as a result of an action, then this action will be repeated when the unpleasant situation reoccurs; the behaviour is also reinforced here and this is called negative reinforcement.[2]

How is a therapeutic approach that is organised around such principles experienced and elaborated by those receiving therapy, by parents who have to carry it out, and by the therapists themselves? Here is an example from my own experience.

When I first began working with Christian, I did not know how fragile he was and how much he needed a reliable and stable environment. Once I found that I was asking too much of him during a session. He began shouting in frenzied rage and panic, banging his head against the stone floor. I was shaken and appalled and reacted emotionally, i.e. not very meaningfully from the point of view of behaviour therapy, where head-banging is regarded as a common symptom. Experiments have been conducted showing how such maladjusted behaviour can be extinguished:

> Bucher and Lovaas [. . .] have investigated closely the effect of pure extinguishing strategies on the frequency of self-destructive behaviour. Their patient was severely retarded [. . .]; for one year he had to be strapped to his bed twenty-four hours a day; otherwise he would continually bang his head against the bed and pummel himself in the face with his fists etc. The child's head was disfigured with scars. In the experimental situation the child was freed, left by himself and observed unnoticed. The banging no longer had any social consequences. In the first hour the patient hit or banged himself 2500 times, in the fourth hour 1600 times and in the eighth hour only five times. This effect did not, however, generalise itself to other environmental situations where presumably the extinguishing conditions could not be rigorously maintained.
>
> In view of these results, the following therapeutic process can be outlined for such cases of auto-aggression: punishment through isolation, extinguishing social reinforcement, and encouraging desirable behaviour patterns which are not compatible with self-destructive behaviour. However, this extinguishing strategy is time-consuming and since it has to be taken into account that children seriously mutilate and blind themselves or incur skull fractures, it cannot be justified on a regular basis. Lovaas et al. [. . .] made use of an incidental observation and began punishing self-destructive behaviour in two schizophrenic children with short, medically harmless, but painful electric shocks.
>
> Within a few minutes, and after only a few shocks, the self-destructive behaviour of Lovaas' patients disappeared and did not occur again for eleven months without need for further punishment.[3]

[One wonders what the sense is of watching a child hurting itself for hours on end and even of counting the blows 'in the interests of science'?]

Compared with such scientific methods, my reaction to Christian was thoroughly 'inappropriate': I tried to calm him down by holding his head, because I could not tolerate watching him inflict such pain on himself. Christian struggled for ages to get free from my hands which were holding him while a storm of anxiety and guilt feelings, as well as understanding and empathy, was raging within me. He felt so overwhelmed, so threatened with annihilation by the demands I was making on him. I talked to him – what I said exactly, I can no longer remember – but basically I tried to tell him how much his distress and anger were affecting me. Gradually, Christian calmed down and eventually said 'thank you' to me very clearly, which was remarkable for a boy who, at the very most, usually only uttered a barely comprehensible word if he absolutely had to. Now that he had regained control of himself I was able to let go of him.

A psychologist I spoke to about this saw things somewhat differently from me. She felt Christian had started behaving badly in order to avoid unpleasant stress, to provoke me, to make me feel guilty and to get attention. An appropriate response to this would simply have been to extinguish it. A calculating little blackmailer, inconsiderate, only concerned with his own advantage and comfort – if I had seen Christian this way, then I probably would have been able to summon up enough anger and hate to be able to punish him with contempt while he was banging his forehead. He was a kind of powerful opponent in contrast with whom I would have felt small and helpless. This is how inferior one feels as a therapist or as a mother if one needs affirmation but does not get it. It seems, however, that it was important for Christian that I could sense that things were too much for him and that I could recognise my own error. Holding him was for me rather like apologising to him: 'Christian, I am sorry I have been so threatening for you, I didn't mean to be. This sort of thing cannot always be avoided; I am not perfect but in any case I am ready to help you cope with your anger and fears in such situations.' By saying 'thank you' Christian accepted my apology and my promise and since then he has never hit himself again in my presence.*

In their book Gottwald and Redlin describe another experiment using people as test cases:

> Furthermore, two consequences of the self-destructive behaviour were studied experimentally. These consequences were examined in random order on different days:
> Friendly attention with the words: 'You are a lovely child, I know; you aren't bad at all'. Under this condition the frequency of banging rose fivefold. The sharp increase showed that such comments, which were recommended by the psychoanalytically oriented hypothesis of 'hostile introjection' or 'guilt feelings', had the effect of reinforcing abnormal behaviour.
> 2. If the banging was completely ignored (extinguishing of social reinforcement), then it gradually decreased in frequency.[4]

---

* I do not see holding as a panacea – as holding therapy (cf. Tinbergen and Tinbergen, 1984) seems to do – but rather as the appropriate reaction in this situation to my counter-transference and to the boy's uncontained behaviour which, moreover, does not necessarily always meet so quickly with success.

Very much in the style of operant conditioning, it is assumed that, on the basis of psychoanalytic assumptions about hitting oneself, a technique of manipulation can be derived and used arbitrarily. The same 'interpretation' is repeated to all the 'test persons' without taking into account that this phrase does not get to the main problem or could be completely wrong. Had I said something of the sort to Christian on the basis of theory, instead of holding him and expressing – however awkwardly – my feelings to him as a reflection of his own, then he would have had no reason to thank me. The pseudo-theoretically thought-out phrase was of no help because it applied to subjects in the experiment and not to a specific child and, particularly, because those conducting the experiment are not very honest. Insofar as they regard the situation as an experiment they cannot honestly be convinced of what they are saying and their standardised behavioural therapy does not say 'you are a good child' but rather 'you are a child with behavioural difficulties which we want to wean you from'. It is understandable that the children, finding themselves in such a bewildering and contradictory situation, experience even more fear, anger and panic. This is cynicism: 'friendly attention' used for an experimental scheme, prescribed emotional lies.

The report of the psychologist Robert Lane[5] on his work with the autistic boy Robby has quite a different feel about it:

> One day, just after he had crawled through the fence, Robby was pummelling himself with both hands and crying out, 'bad Robbiie! . . . baDD Rob-biie!'
>
> Because of his unarticulated way of speaking, I did not understand him immediately, but after a while the meaning of the words dawned on me. I almost had to agree with him. His nerve-shattering screaming nearly made me get aggressive and I was unable to fathom what had caused the outburst. So I countered his self-reproaches with 'Robby is nice. Robby is my friend.'
>
> [. . .] If anything was needed to bring home to me the futility of my activity [of the therapy with Robby which hitherto had consisted exclusively of walks together, one behind the other, eight metres apart, D.N.], then it was this meaningless, childish nonsense. Nothing seemed to be able to stop him; and so he continued with his self-berating until we had arrived on top . . . and then Robby's self-reproaches stopped just as suddenly as they had begun.[6]

This is not a 'scientific experiment' with a test person, that is, as 'objective' as possible, excluding emotional perceptions, but a consciously experienced scene involving conflicting feelings in a therapeutic relationship. And unlike the children in the human experiment, Robby did not react with increased aggression against himself – of course not, because his therapist's reply was not meant as a 'therapeutic' experimental trick but sincerely. But apparently this reply did not help him either, even though it was not offered as a piece of theory that can be applied in any situation.

It seems that the psychologist only expressed one aspect of his feelings, his positive, ongoing affection, and concealed the other aspect, his anger towards Robby: 'His nerve-shattering screaming nearly made me get aggressive. [. . .] So I countered his self-reproaches . . .'. This is clearly illogical. If the psychologist sensed aggression welling up in him, then this 'so' is not logical. He described his ambivalent feelings, it is true, but he concealed them from Robby and he does not seem aware that Robby must have been able to sense this ambivalence, to hear it in the tone of his voice, and that consequently it must have been difficult for him to believe the affection in the therapist's words.

For months Robby's therapy sessions had consisted of these hikes on the Hundsberg. 'I liked these excursions,' writes Lane, 'even if there was no progress in our relationship.' However: 'he kept repeating [. . .] with an irritatingly, monotonous voice the same words [. . .] his nerve-shattering screaming started to make me feel aggressive.'[7] (Robby had meanwhile got into the habit of saying incomprehensible things to himself.) Robby must have sensed that, notwithstanding his affection, his therapist was increasingly experiencing feelings of emptiness, discouragement and aggression; and, in the light of his life experiences, he must have understood the following: My friend is angry because I am bad. By saying 'bad Robby' he was trying to appease his friend's anger and to tell him how much this aggression made him anxious. It does not help Robby if the therapist believes he should not show him his negative feelings, since these appear to contradict his basic positive attitude prescribed by humanistic psychology.

Now the author provides us with a clue enabling us to understand this scene. From Robby's life history we learn that when he was an infant his mother used to keep herself at the greatest possible distance from him because she really believed that 'bad Robby' was contagiously 'possessed by the devil'. The mother touched her infant 'as little as possible for she was convinced that if she spent too much time with him or got too close to him she would become ill.'[8] Now in his relationship with his therapist, Robby always kept himself at a distance of eight to ten metres, probably in order not to infect and poison him with his 'badness'. His 'badness' exists; it is the desperation and impotent rage, which as a small infant he must have felt towards his mother (at four years of age Robby had begun fires in his parents' apartment and thus fulfilled the phantasy), and which he was now re-experiencing in the counter-transference towards his therapist. And the psychologist was experiencing in his counter-transference the child's feelings which the mother avoided whenever possible, i.e. emptiness, deadly loneliness and rage. Had he not suppressed these feelings and understood how they were connected with the child's life story, then he might have been able to help Robby sooner by saying to him: 'Are you afraid of coming closer to me because you feel you might do something bad to me? You don't need to be afraid because I am strong and can withstand you. And I know, too, that you are not bad even though you feel angry towards me when I do not understand you properly.' In this way the therapist's aggression would have been turned into understanding and the phantasmatic 'badness' named for the child as a legitimate affect.

By repeating his 'bad Robby' – he continued to do this on other walks until, it seems, his trust in his therapist's affection was sufficiently stable – he was insisting that he had something important to say. He sensed the psychologist's aggressive feelings and could only understand them in terms of his own history. So he insisted on communicating something to his therapist by saying 'bad Robby', which he could only say by evacuating his feelings into him just as his mother had once done with him. He did not allow himself simply to be appeased with kind words. Similarly the children who were misused as 'subjects of investigation' may have been hitting themselves as a way of insisting on the need for communication.

It is now understandable why 'under extinguishing conditions' the 'maladjusted behaviour' of some children ceases, but not of all children: with Eileen, for instance, extinguishing strategies had no effect at all. As long as self-aggression remains a means of communication for them, then they are dependent on those who are observing them. Such children will naturally intensify their hitting when they do not feel understood but can still draw hope from the attention they are getting that their message may eventually be heard. Moreover, they will give up when they no longer have anyone to whom they can communicate their distress. It is also understandable why the 'undesirable behaviour' can be more successfully checked and limited by the use of electric shock treatment: a child who is hitting himself because he thinks he is bad will experience such treatment as satisfying his need for punishment – it is the environment which is now inflicting the punishment, so he no longer needs to punish himself. Or when self-aggression is a desperate attempt to use one's own structure to ward off the danger of being flooded by environmental stimulation, as was the case with Eileen, then such an attempt naturally loses significance immediately if the child's own attempts to structure himself are destroyed by electric shock treatment.

In the relationship between Robby and his therapist the consequence of the unsuccessful communication was that for a long time there continued to be little progress. The psychologist complained to his superior: 'I simply can't find a way of getting close to him, of getting him to communicate with me'. The ambivalent feelings in this statement are clear: sympathy and the wish for contact, on the one hand, impatience and anger on the other – 'finding a way of getting him to do what I want him to do'. He still, however, did not understand the significance of these feelings and suppressed the aggressive side, no doubt because he thought he should not get angry with this boy who needed him so much. His superior advised him to try once again with behaviour therapy. He hesitated for a long time: 'the behaviour therapy seemed to me, in spite of everything, questionable in more than one respect. A therapy that aims at breaking down the relationship of trust between therapist and patient to the point that it literally no longer exists, replacing it with a relationship which, to my mind, is more redolent of that between an animal and its trainer, went against everything I held to be good and right. [. . .] I would have found it extremely insensitive to say 'no' to Robby or to give him an electric shock when he was hitting himself during one of his 'bad Rob-biie' phases. I had chosen this profession in order to help people, not to add physical pains to their mental pains.'[9] But eventually he could see no other way: 'And now I had to decide whether a compromise was possible between the high demands of humanistic psychology and the sharply defined claims of behaviour theorists. The longer I thought about it, the clearer it was to me that the basic positions of the two theories were incompatible.'[10]

Of course they are incompatible, as were his ambivalent feelings towards Robby. The two psychological schools represent his ambivalence exactly. Humanistic psychology encourages unconditional acceptance, and this was becoming increasingly difficult with Robby. On the other hand, behaviour therapy represents precisely the opposite, that there was something about Robby he could not accept, something that disturbed him and made him angry which he wanted to get rid of. Unconditional acceptance could not work as he himself suffered from the eight-metre distance between them and from the way they walked endlessly one behind the other in silence. Further, he could sense unconsciously Robby's distress, in face of which such 'unconditional acceptance' would be cynical. He felt that it could not go on like this any longer but he did not realise that Robby himself also wanted change and that, by saying 'bad Robby', he had been trying all along to change something. Since he was deaf to the boy's communication but could no longer defer his own need for more contact, he had to resort to the behaviourists' technical box of tricks. Behaviour therapy now seemed to him the only way of giving expression to anger which, in his friendly 'humanistic' attitude, he believed he should not express. So he tried to get Robby to speak by using their walks or drinking Coke as a stimulus.

> 'Robby, if you would like a Coke or an ice-cream, just tell me. Say, "I'd like a Coke" or "I'd like an ice-cream".'
> There was nothing in Robby's behaviour to suggest that he had heard me, but as we were going right past the canteen, he looked at it with longing – as I did. [. . .] Robby slowed down and there was quite clearly a big struggle going on within him. Eventually he just stood standing there with his head lowered, shuffling his feet on the floor.
> His voice scarcely reached me.

'Have Coca.'

Two words. I tried to get him to say a little more. 'Almost, Robby. Now say, I'd like . . . Coca.'

His face had that familiar, absent look again. Then he repeated, 'Now have Coca!' NOW HAVE Coca!' His voice had a penetrating howl about it.

I did not budge. 'No, Robby. Say, I . . . would like . . . Coca.'

Making a grimace he shrieked 'CAN'T SAY'. Then he suddenly turned round and ran off towards the Pavilion.

The psychologist's reaction to this scene is striking: 'It seemed catastrophic to me, a serious setback'.[11] It seems he had not heard how the boy, desperately torn between wanting to do his beloved therapist a favour and that which prevented him from saying what he was being asked to say, had spontaneously communicated something of his inner strife.

'Can't say!' What a gift! What a lot of love and trust are expressed in this desperate 'shriek', in the boy's personal, rather than prescribed, words! He cannot say 'I'. Of course not; he will not be able to as long as he remains bound by the mother's phantasm that he was possessed by an evil spirit; and, as long as he continues to be afraid of harming his mother or his therapist with 'germs' by being too real, by being a separate 'I'.

But the therapist's feelings of aggression, which had not been worked over and understood but were being acted out in the behaviour therapy technique, made him blind – not to the distress he was causing the child, he describes this in detail for us – but to the impossible nature of what he was asking for, as well as to the communication which Robby wrung from himself in order to appease him.

We are indebted to Robert Lane for describing in such detail his feelings and phantasies with regard to this behaviourist intervention. In spite of such sad scenes in which there is a lack of understanding, his book is an encouraging report on the period of his therapeutic work with Robby.

Equally worthwhile for understanding how behaviour therapy functions for those who are undergoing it and the significance it acquires in their feelings is the book *Kein Kind zum Vorzeigen* by Ingrid Häusler. For Ingrid Häusler her first consultation with a female behaviour therapist was like heaven on earth. After four years of anxiety, despair, and disorientation with regard to the increasing difficulties she was having with her son, it was the first consultation where she felt accepted and also felt confident in the psychologist's competence. Up till then she had only experienced reactions of head-shaking, shock, rejection or concealed blame:

At last I had come across someone who did not raise her eyebrows in disbelief at my description; someone who was familiar with behavioural disturbance of this kind and who had seen many similar children. I got to know a woman who treated Frank, not with mistrust and scorn, but understanding and respect. [. . .] Up till that moment no one had given me support; I had been left completely alone with these problems and now the psychologist was able to help me understand that I had indeed reacted inappropriately. [. . .] Now I had found an 'island in a sea of a lack of understanding'. I learnt the basic principle of behaviour therapy: behaviour that is approved of is reinforced by giving attention and praise; and behaviour that is disapproved of is rendered 'meaningless' by simply being ignored. The consultation gave me a huge boost. Feeling happy that I had at last found the right solution and with a clear idea in my head of how to bring up my child, I left the consultation room.[12]

Certainty, clear instructions, professional competence, together with 'understanding and respect' brought much-needed relief for this mother who was worn to shreds with loneliness and guilt feelings.

Frank had begun hitting himself when he was one and a half years old.

Whenever Frank experienced unpleasurable feelings and wanted to behave 'impossibly', he would immediately begin banging his head against the furniture or the floor. Photos from this period show this clearly: he permanently had a swollen, bluish-coloured forehead. Initially, we were totally at a loss and desperate; I had never thought that a child was capable of such a thing! Frank learnt very quickly that I was afraid of his self-aggression and that I did not know how to cope with it. Unconsciously it was clear to me that the only way of stopping these manipulative attempts was not to take any notice of them any more. I tried that too but then Frank put all his energy into 'drawing me out of my reserve'; he now used his knuckles to hit himself on the forehead and on his nose until he had nosebleeds! Anyone will be able to understand how it was that I then turned round, screamed in his face that he should kill himself and smacked his bottom – in fact I was so desperate that I had to get a grip on myself in order not to lay into him blindly.[13]

Guilt feelings caused the mother so much despair that she could only understand the child's distress as a reproach for being a 'bad mother'. She herself was in distress and experienced Frank as a powerful manipulator (almost as if their respective ages were reversed so that he became her father and she was his abused child). By interpreting the child's behaviour as 'her own incapacity', as she herself writes, 'the resulting self-hate only too easily led to me becoming aggressive with the child. How often have I screamed at Frank out of pure desperation that I might be responsible for his condition!'[14] From early on Frank must have felt that he was the cause of his mother's self-hate, guilt feelings and mental distress; he must have repeatedly experienced how she withdrew into depression, how she inwardly had to abandon him and could no longer hold him. His self-hitting was a way of punishing himself and showing how unheld, how abandoned he felt, and was an appeal for the holding he was so much in need of. (When behaviour therapists say that such 'maladjusted behaviour' by children is used to provoke 'social reinforcement', they are not totally wrong – but they make no mention of the children's distress.)

When the mother punished her son in such situations, he accepted it as if he had been expecting it: 'When I slapped him out of pure desperation, he did not cry. He did not move, he scarcely batted an eyelash.' This made her feel even more desperate, reinforcing the vicious circle of a mutual lack of understanding. This punishment could not work like the electric shocks administered in behaviour therapy, without feeling: the need for punishment could not be satisfied if his mother became even more desperate due to his reaction and her guilt feelings for slapping him.

The mother had at last discovered, in the behaviour therapist, a person who knew other children with similar difficulties. She no longer felt so alone and that she was the worst mother in the world. She obtained a diagnosis, 'autism – a behavioural disorder'. What was threatening for her had now been given a name and there were clear guidelines about how to deal with it. This helped to give structure to her relationship with her son which was foundering into a chaos of anxiety, anger and withdrawal, and so some progress could be observed. Her guilty anxiety in particular became more organised. She learnt that of course she was not actually responsible for Frank's maladjusted behaviour which suggested 'hypersensitivity of the hands and the head' – but she was told that she had reacted inappropriately. Reacting inappropriately in this way was of course normal and understandable; in order to be able to react appropriately in such extreme conditions, she would first have to be initiated into the techniques of behaviour therapy.

The relief that such exoneration from guilt – which, as we know, tends to create dependency, because of the link between the diagnosis and exoneration from guilt – brought to the relationship between Frank and his mother admittedly did not amount to much. The mother also had doubts. 'If he hits himself, we take no notice. If he tries to draw attention to himself by crying or breaking objects, he is given a warning twice, calmly, and in an unequivocal tone of voice; thereafter, he is isolated in a room with few distractions and is only let out once he has calmed down. But I was quite shocked by this method!'[15] When she expressed her doubts, she was reassured: 'I argued that he would have a terrible tantrum in the room and hurt himself. The consultant, on the other hand, believed that in this way Frank would understand the senselessness of his behaviour faster than we might think.' Senselessness? Once again it is neither the child nor the mother who are in control but others, those who 'know'. In spite of all the hate that was bottled up inside her and which does not meet with 'understanding' in such techniques of child-rearing but is simply given an outlet, the mother was none the less able to sense how hard and ignorant the logic of such behaviour therapy is in relation to the child's intentions. She herself found no room in it for her own impulse to comfort Frank when he was hitting himself, no room for the fact that, in spite of all her own despair, she still seemed to be able to sense vaguely how much distress her child was expressing. However, she tried to be 'logical' and so had to put up with new guilt feelings: 'In the street, Frank senses that I cannot react to his self-aggressions so calmly'; in the street she is afraid that passers-by will make remarks about 'the cruelty of the educational approach of behaviour therapy. The result was that this behavioural disorder was expressed primarily in the street.' – 'Behaviour therapy is not a magic solution and should not be allowed to degenerate into an excessive manipulation of the child. We soon understood that no one can act completely logically!',[16] she writes with resignation.

Perhaps there are some people who can be, if not better mothers, at least better behaviour therapists than she was. As the success of her own efforts was limited, she sent Frank to an in-patient clinic for short-term therapy.

> With the help of the system of 'rewards' used in the behaviour therapy, Frank learnt to use a spoon to eat by himself, to put wooden blocks with a hole in them onto a stick that fitted in the hole, to stay sitting on the pottie, to help with getting himself dressed, and not to resist so stubbornly being held by the hand. His self-aggression was diminished by systematically ignoring it, so that it was not necessary to isolate him any more! The unexpected success of the therapy certainly gave me something to think about. Why had I not been successful?[17]

Once again she was faced with the old rivalry – this time not with the hated mother-in-law but with the idealised behaviour therapy institute: 'I valiantly struggled with something like "a mother's hurt pride"'. So it was the same scenario again but with new people, and it was given a therapeutic aura and clear structure so that she could manage it better. The interaction organised by the behaviour therapy now offered the mother's conflicting feelings reliable and institutionally approved outlets which at the same time appeased her conscience and made her feel secure: she was no longer at the complete mercy of her anger, rejection and hate which were tied up in the therapeutic technique of dismantling undesirable behaviour – love and desire for contact were channelled into experimental tests, into developing desirable behaviour patterns. When Frank strictly refused to do the prescribed exercises with his mother but put up with them with the therapist, this insult was more bearable than the mother-in-law's provocative accounts of how Frank behaved so well with her. This professional rival could of course manage better that she could since, as a mother, she inevitably had understandable but, unfortunately, from the point of view of behaviour therapy technique, distorted and disturbing feelings. This is what the system looks like in which the mother and child's chaos and anxiety are so inextricably tied up that there is little hope of any positive development.

With the benefit of the examples of Robby and Frank, the structure of the interaction organised by behaviourist techniques can now be described more generally. A child develops a behaviour pattern by means of which he tries to communicate something to his environment, not symbolically with words and gestures, but in the form of symptomatic behaviour. The communication contains the child's wish, his need to be accepted and understood; and, at the same time, it expresses the child's experience that he is not able to obtain what he wants in the world and to affirm his needs in an acceptable way. A child who is hitting himself because 'something does not suit him' is already assuming in his self-destructive behaviour that what he wants is bad and that he deserves to be punished; and so he is punishing himself for it. Often when children want something 'impossible', what in fact matters for them is not the content of what they want but rather the fundamental experience of being understood and accepted. The environment, rightly enough, feels addressed and experiences the symptomatic behaviour as a provocation. The child thus creates anxiety, anger and helplessness in those around him and takes his revenge. In conjunction with the environmental reaction, the child's symptomatic behaviour becomes a complex enactment. Robby enacted with his therapist the loneliness his mother's madness induced in him; Frank enacted his unfortunate entanglement with his mother's guilty anxiety.

Now behaviour therapy makes no effort to understand such scenarios in terms of the life histories involved. On the contrary, what is intolerable about the symptom is merely viewed as provocation; the counter-transference is not reflected upon in order to gain a better understanding of the interaction and to dissolve the compulsive nature of the scenario but is used against the child defensively and for self-protection. In the behaviour therapy techniques of 'extinguishing', 'time-out', and 'punishment', fear and anger are acted out in the counter-transference. But in this way not only the therapist's feelings but also the child's desires are warded off; the expectation that the environment will be 'hostile' is confirmed, and the scenario is completed by the corresponding environmental response.

It has long been recognised in behaviour therapy that 'breaking down undesirable behaviour patterns' alone is not enough. It would be too cruel to wean a child from his symptoms without offering him a substitute for them. And it would not only be cruel for the child: the therapist's positive feelings and desires for contact would also be frustrated and parents, in particular, would find no therapeutically authorised space for expressing their affection for their child, which might well diminish their readiness to act as their child's behaviour therapist. Consequently, a balance is achieved by 'establishing desirable behaviour patterns'. ('Eye contact', for example, a highly prized therapeutic goal with autistic children, 'gives the therapist [. . .] an intensive experience of contact with the child.'[18]) This should always be coupled with extinguishing strategies. The word desirable contains the notion of desire but it is the desire of the adult world. What the child who is raging or hitting himself wants and needs so urgently cannot be achieved through his own efforts but is given to him in the form of 'social reinforcement' on the condition that he fits in with the picture outlined by behaviour therapy. Then, finally, he will be recognised and accepted. This is why behaviour therapy, in spite of all its drawbacks, can be helpful. In it the child's wish, which is at first warded off by 'breaking down undesirable behaviour patterns', does in the end have its place – it is enacted anew and not symbolised. By coupling the disorganising and organising process the child's enactment is reorganised in an acceptable form so that the child is offered a place which allows him a more pleasant, less chaotically alarming, 'socially reinforced' life.

When Robby eventually began to speak, thanks to behaviour therapy, it was definitely not against his own will; he had already been trying for some time to communicate something with the words 'bad Robby'. It was not just any old thing that he wanted to say but precisely that which had hitherto impeded him from speaking, impeding him moreover from being able to say 'I'; i.e. the phantasy of 'bad Robby'. By putting it into words he was trying to free himself from it. Now, because his therapist did not understand him and could not help him formulate it, he had to learn with the help of behaviour therapy how to speak. His most personal experience, however, that is, of the self-alienation forced on him by his mother's madness, still remained unexpressed. This he could not free himself from, because his therapist was not able to help him formulate his indictment of this madness, and only trained him to use language as 'desirable behaviour'. So he continued to be unable to say 'I' until the therapeutic relation was broken off.

I have frequently heard the argument that the psychoanalytic process is basically nothing other than the unsystematic use of the principles of behaviour therapy. 'A system of rewards is undoubtedly employed by other forms of therapy too; one has the impression, however, that they are given quite arbitrarily so that the optimal timing of learning is not well organised.'[19] There is some truth in this. Here is an example from Winnicott – it concerns welfare work with a nine-year-old boy who often flew into wild fits of rage:

> Did I ever hit him? The answer is no, I never hit. But I should have had to have done so if I had not known all about my hate and if I had not let him know about it too. At crises I would take him by bodily

strength, without anger or blame, and put him outside the front door, whatever the weather or the time of day or night. There was a special bell he could ring, and he knew that if he rang it he would be readmitted and no word said about the past. He used this bell as soon as he had recovered from his maniacal attack.

At first sight this measure does not look very different from the one called 'time-out' in behaviour therapy, the method of upbringing which Ingrid Häusler was supposed to use to manage her sons fits of temper. But Winnicott continues:

> The important thing is that each time, just as I put him outside the door, I told him something; I said that what had happened had made me hate him. This was easy because it was so true. I think these words were important from the point of view of his progress but they were mainly important in enabling me to tolerate the situation without letting out, without losing my temper and without every now and again murdering him.[20]

The difference may seem slight at first but it is critical. Faced with Frank's maniacal attacks, his mother was required to coolly and deliberately use a child-rearing technique whose emotional basis, although she was unaware of it, lay in her own feelings of fear and hate towards her raging son – a task in which she was only partially successful for obvious reasons. Winnicott did something very similar but clearly not as a technique of child rearing; he did it for his own needs in order to cope with his hate and to avoid 'every now and again murdering' the boy. His affection for the boy which persisted in spite of great ambivalence – 'he was the most loveable and the most maddening of children'[21] – was expressed by his ability to keep his impulses of hate under control, but he did find an outlet for them and so did not deny them. He did not estrange himself from them by seeing the act of putting Frank outside the door as a 'scientifically tested, objective technique' to be carried out unemotionally, as in behaviour therapy.

The language used in Ingrid Häusler's report, riddled as it is with the alienating jargon of behaviour therapy, shows how being alienated from one's own impulses, and acting them out, vicariously, in institutional ways that are sanctioned by therapeutic technique, creates dependence on the authority prescribing the technique, as well as how it can influence the mother–child relationship in the most subtle of ways. 'There was now noticeable eye-contact', she writes – there is no longer any mention here of a mother's joy when her child is constantly looking at her. Affects are tied up in reviewing therapeutic achievements; pleasure is found in therapeutic success and no longer in the successful contact between mother and child or therapist and child. Behaviour therapy functions on the basis of self-alienation of this sort, so it obviates the symbolisation of personal wishes and feelings, not only in the child but also in the mother and the therapist. In its place it offers socially acceptable, institutionally supported, 'wished-for' symptoms. The wishes remain nameless and the institution 'Learning Disability' is not called into question.

The newly organised enactment of the old misery with the aid of behaviour therapy guarantees the smooth, conflict-free functioning of those in therapy; it also ensures that parental feelings or the feelings of carers and therapists trained in behaviour therapy are actively brought into play to optimise social conformity. If such feelings were reflected back as counter-transference to the child in therapy, as in the example from Winnicott, they might help him to orient himself better in his environment and would be an expression of solidarity with those who are excluded as well as a critique of the institution perpetuating such exclusion. Used in this way, however, behaviour therapy impedes solidarity.

In the examples I have cited, it should of course not be overlooked that the interventions of behaviour therapy do offer help, afford relief, and provide structure in situations of anxiety, chaos and anger. This is possible whenever they are based on an intuitive understanding of the scenic connections of the 'maladjusted behaviour'. Behaviour therapy can be useful here if it is well thought out and used supportively. If the principal psychologist of the anxious and overburdened mother of an autistic child understands what he (or she) is doing, what he is proposing, and knows that by stimulating the mother he is giving her structured support to deal with the confusion of her ambivalence and especially her hate for her child, then the resulting sense of relief will provide a basis for further development in which the psychologist can accompany the mother and child as they gradually master the symbolic dimension of their interaction, the meaning of the symptoms, and the measures taken to counter them. It seems that some mothers of autistic children succeed in making use of behaviour therapy in this way.

Fear of the void and people making

While behaviour therapy is particularly used with resistant children, i.e. mostly children with autistic or psychotic symptoms, education for those with special needs is preferred with 'Down's children' and 'children at risk'. It is assumed that without such re-education such children will have less chance of developing normally. 'Based on the (average; D. N.) behaviour patterns of a healthy child, exercises [. . .] have been developed which are supposed to stimulate the child who has learning disabilities to acquire this behaviour.'[22]

'As a part of the social system education for those with special needs has the purpose of integrating people with learning disabilities in those areas which are of general interest (to the state).' This means, 'laying down, consolidating or guaranteeing the basic foundations of the child's later usefulness and autonomy. It means, in particular, guidance with respect to the requirements laid down in the educational sector and general knowledge of the normal development which serves as its standard.'[23] 'The aims of education for people with special needs are therefore not (and cannot be) determined by the immediate needs of those concerned and by preventative concerns, but rather by the needs of the state which are the basis for the existence of education for special needs.'[24]

This is clearly formulated and derives from early intervention theory itself, not from polemical writing against it. Remedial education, as the expression of the state's interest in the child, inevitably reduces parents and child carers to being the state's agents. But what is the outlook for the psychical development of a child whose parents have to invest all their energy in the menial tasks of remedial education because they are made to believe that this is the best thing for their child?

I once knew a young man whom I shall call Hans, after the fairy tale 'Hans in Luck', since he was just like the character in the tale.[25] He was born with hydrocephalus but this was only recognised much later so that when the parents were told what the diagnosis was, they also learnt that brain damage had already occurred. The doctor, who, for the times, was very progressive, added that if he was given remedial education, there was still some room for hope. After getting over the initial shock, the parents decided, following the doctor's advice, to give their child as much remedial education as possible. At that time well-organised education programmes for special needs did not exist as they do today but Hans' parents followed exactly the same principles which are used today, i.e. they took the 'normal' developmental profile as a model and took measures designed to bring the boy up to this standard. It was not a case of special exercises; rather the parents, as Bach requires today, 'did precisely what was usual and normal for them, [. . .] only more actively, more intensely, more imaginatively, more unflaggingly'.[26] They succeeded in helping the boy so much that he not only made it to the normal primary school but also, even though he had to repeat one year twice, reached the GCE level at secondary school. The parents had even thought of a profession for Hans for which his particular skills seemed perfectly adapted. When it turned out that Hans had no chance of getting a job in this profession (not only due to a lack of available places) and that finally the only option left was a sheltered workshop for people with learning disabilities, their world collapsed. He was such a well-developed boy and his achievements had amounted to well above what was required by the norm; they had done everything for him, so why were they now being punished like this?

It was clear to everyone who knew Hans that he had learning disabilities. Why? Hans was capable of achievements which some people without learning disabilities are not capable of – so why was he suddenly thought not to be up to the tasks required of him professionally? However, as everyone on the outside could see, but could not bring themselves to tell the parents, it was not just a matter of being able to carry out pre-structured tasks. Growing up and getting on in life involves more than simply being able to solve a complicated puzzle. Hans was not able to make a decision for himself independently and to act without being told what to do. All he had learnt was how to be good, and to do whatever others required him to do. During school breaks he was teased a lot and he would then just stand there smiling naively and his head, which was somewhat too big, would wobble back and forth. Hans never shook his head, never defended himself, and never said 'no'; just as he had never resisted the demands that had been made on him since an early age, and had never learnt to decide for himself whether he wanted to carry out the tasks that he was given to do. His head just wobbled back and forth in such a strange, lost way, all the time, and he would smile so simple-mindedly and blankly as if the capacity to say 'no' had got lost in his not-understanding and in his head wobbling. It was precisely this capacity to say 'no' which he needed in order to become an adult, to be able to act autonomously and make his own decisions.

Admittedly this is an extreme case and it would not be true to say that such a desolate development is the inevitable consequence when parents take charge of the specialised education of their developmentally endangered child. But it would also be illogical to dismiss this awful story with the suggestion that Hans must have been even more brain-damaged than the parents wanted to admit. It remains true that he had sufficient intellectual capacity to reach the GCE level at secondary school. Mental autonomy, however, the capacity to say 'no' is not innate but rather a psychical accomplishment, the lack of which points to a disturbance in early childhood development.

What was it then that impeded Hans from separating, from inwardly setting boundaries to his parents' demands, from learning to say 'no'?

In *Frühforderung mit den Eltern*[27] there is a 'Letter from a Mother' which I want to quote in full here:

> First, two bits of wording which come up over and over again and which offend me: firstly, 'working with the parents' and secondly the proud claim: 'we can save x children from ESN schooling'. Naturally, that is a success for the particular child who is 'saved' and for his parents; I would be happy if my child was one of these children but both these statements always put me in a position which I have great difficulty in accepting.
>
> There is another issue, moreover, I would like to raise regarding the problem of parents. Soon after the birth, the possibility of forgetting

the disability, even for a short while, was taken away from me. The down side of the constant fostering and coercion to succeed and achieve was that I was rarely able simply to accept my son as a child; very quickly I was continually reminded of the fact that he had learning disabilities – that is, above all, that he was someone who was lacking something.

As a mother I have other goals than merely educational ones: I would like my child to be as happy as possible, to feel accepted and enjoy life. Can I achieve this by means of specialised education programmes? Indeed, can they achieve this at all? Is it even a conscious goal of such programmes?

I had role difficulties. Sometimes as a mother I would simply have given way or reacted in a friendly way but as a therapist I felt obliged to act logically and let my attitude be guided by considerations of success. This can make it difficult to be spontaneous and to express feelings. I did not always find it easy to manage both roles and sometimes, for example, I even asked my husband to follow the therapeutic guidelines with the result that he became thoroughly dependent on my information and behavioural standards. When does one recognise the limits of requirements? In the last analysis, of course, we wanted the therapy to go well.

Here is an example: my son had been able to eat by himself for a long time, but for a while he was reluctant to sit on his chair to eat, although I could not see any obvious reason why. I insisted on it and made him go without food because I felt unsure of myself in my role as a mother. Normally, in such a case, a mother would simply take her healthy child for a while in her arms without constantly worrying about whether the child was learning or not. Fortunately, my husband sometimes helped me to free myself from this 'therapeutic constraint'. [. . .]

Most parents find specialised education programmes to be unsystematic. They teach a bit here and a bit there, skills that are sometimes essential, but which might well have been acquired in any case. They exclude the rest of the family, the social environment, individual family styles of learning and, above all, the immense problems that arise with the siblings who do not have learning disabilities. [. . .]

Now, sooner or later, most parents experience feelings of rejection or, at least, doubt. After the question, 'Why have I got a child like this?' comes the question, 'Why do I constantly have to learn, to work on myself and to work with the child?' and so on. I only know two answers:

It is the duty of parents.

Without special remedial education, what is already a terrible misfortune will become an even greater one.

Both motivations are just as valid as, for instance, the comment of a teacher who says, 'You are a bad pupil anyway so if you don't make an effort you'll have to repeat this year.' This may be sufficient motivation for a school report but is it enough to keep parents 'up to scratch' over years in spite of all kinds of frustrations?

Can therapists help us to find a positive motivation? Are they themselves motivated in their own work?[28]

Therapeutic control over parents' feelings – this seems to be the most striking aspect of what Bach is saying. 'The educational efforts made on behalf of people with learning disabilities are characterised by erratic care practices and techniques, which are themselves adapted to erratic learning behaviour. Where special educational situations are involved, special efforts have to be made pedagogically, i.e. something which goes beyond what is usually on offer. [. . .] However, this is not to be understood as something completely different or even as something strange. With people who have learning disabilities what matters is doing precisely what is usual, and normal – only more actively, more intensely . . . .'[29] In reality the exercises recommended by different specialists in special re-education require nothing more than what loving parents do spontaneously with their children.

The first kinaesthetic stimulation involves carrying and holding the baby in different ways. [. . .] By carrying the baby in the ways that are described here, the adult will be stimulating active and varied movements as well as sensory perceptions. With a baby the whole body and several senses are always involved. Even the toes are 'working' too. [. . .]

Picking up and putting down should take place gently and calmly. The baby should be picked up from the diapering table with both hands and laid on the right shoulder so that he is lying with his face against the adult's body. If the adult walks around with the baby in this position and is rocking him a little as he does so, then the baby will also be moving along with the adult's body.'[30] 'Put a shining red ball or a woollen tassel in his little hand and note whether he looks at the object when it comes into his field of vision. You should help him to hold on to the object and to bring it before his eyes, but avoid making any noise so as not to distract him. Does your baby look at the object in his hand for about 2–3 seconds?'

Another exercise: Put your baby in his cot and hold something up for him to try and catch hold of.[31]

These are two suggested exercises from two different educational programmes – both describing interaction situations between parents and child without there being any educational goal. With a child whose development is at risk, however, such exercises should be carried out 'more actively, more intensely, more imaginatively and more untiringly', for it is to be assumed that 'given the same environmental conditions and stimuli the child with learning disabilities has a much greater need for attention and stimulation, since in most cases he is lying inactive and quietly in his bed'.[32] We should understand the 'disability' like the negative of a photo, says Thurmair. 'In pursuing the goal of enabling them to integrate socially in the sense of being able to work, to enjoy autonomy and to avoid or shorten their career in an ESN school, it is necessary to maximise their developmental potential by means of special measures.'[33] The child who is given specialised educational support is regarded, as Holthaus describes in her 'Letter from a Mother', 'first and foremost as someone who is lacking something',[34] and 'what is lacking' should be compensated for by unflagging, imaginative care and specialised education.

Let us imagine for a moment a mother who has just learnt that her child is a child at risk or has 'Down's syndrome', who has to come to terms with the shock of having given birth to an imperfect child, with all the confusion, fear, and guilt feelings involved. She is now told that the best thing she can do for her baby is to give him specialised remedial education. Few mothers will have the self-assurance of Susanna's mother who said to herself, 'Susu gets enough stimulation by playing and romping with me and her brother'. Or, as Karline's mother said, 'I also have an effect on Karline's prognosis, and not only me but also the people I live with, including Karline herself'.[35] So she did not have the child's cerebral paralysis treated in physiotherapy because she did not want to have to put up with the mental strain for herself and her child. Or again, like the mother whose child had to spend the first year of its life in hospital for hydrocephalus operations and who was told that the child's prognosis was very poor and that it urgently needed additional care because it had not yet smiled once. She replied, 'It hasn't had any reason to learn to smile yet. I am going to give it a reason!' – something she soon did.

These mothers had enough self-assurance to trust in their own capacity for empathy with their child's special needs more than in external professional advice. In many cases, however, the parents' self-assurance is undermined by the announcement of the diagnosis. In particular, guilt feelings are aroused by the death phantasies which are mobilised and there is thus a need to make reparation. When professionals then say to parents who have been destabilised in this way, 'The best thing you can do for your child is . . .', the parents are only too ready to fall in with this and will do anything to obtain reassurance and confirmation that they are not in fact responsible, that they are not failing, that they are doing the right thing, and have nothing to reproach themselves for. The words 'you are doing the best thing for your child' function like an offer of absolution: 'We as specialists will absolve you of your sins, if . . .'. This brings into play the unconscious dependency that I have already referred to in Chapter 2 on diagnosis (and Thurmair makes it quite clear what the authority is: the state's interest in their later 'usefulness'), something we have also seen in the interaction organised by behaviour therapy. 'I had role difficulties. Sometimes as a mother I would simply have given way or reacted in a friendly way – as a therapist I felt obliged to act logically and let my attitude be guided by considerations of success. This can make it difficult to be spontaneous and to express feelings.'

And once again Thurmair says: 'What parents want is of little importance as far as early intervention theory is concerned: concrete educational programmes and aims are intended to compensate for the parent's perplexity and helplessness.' 'The parents' interest in their disabled child and his education does not enter into the goals of such programmes. Parental interest is a circumstantial factor that has to be circumvented.'[36]

Thurmair's language is remarkably clear. The parent–child relationship not only fails to be addressed seriously in such programmes; it is even considered as a circumstantial, i.e. as a disturbance factor that has to be taken into account.

> In view of the means that are considered appropriate for the purposes of specialised education, and given the fact that parents have a duty to bring up their children, it has to be accepted that parents have a certain degree of competence. The aim of working with the parents is to give them a role in which their competence is put to good use and developed.[37]

When parents are given the message subliminally that their feelings are a factor of disturbance while, on the surface, the attitude towards them is friendly enough, it is understandable that they then find it hard to accept that 'someone is being friendly and understanding to me because it is his or her profession. As soon as the therapy is over, so also, in most cases, is the interest and understanding.'[38] However, the fact that they are dependent on the authority dispensing absolution means that all this has to be tolerated:

> If the choice is programmes of remedial education with all the attendant problems, or no assistance at all, then, I would not hesitate to choose the former as the lesser evil with the greatest likelihood of success. My inferiority feelings and the conflicts I have with authority which have surfaced again or been reinforced by the birth of a child with learning disabilities are my problem and not the therapist's. I would never accept doing nothing simply because I am unsure of what to do. I would sooner run the risk of doing the wrong thing than take no action at all.[39]

So is this the alternative then? Is Susanna's mother not being active when she plays and romps with her, when she enjoys watching Daniel and Susanna playing together? This alternative seems to be distorted, determined by the judgement of professionals who make the mother believe there is no other alternative. A mother who feels the only alternative to re-education is doing nothing shows that the educational activities are a means for her to ward off subliminal depression and death phantasies which have become unconscious: doing nothing would imply depressive withdrawal, ignoring the child.

The aim, then, of such specialised education is really to establish a defence against guilt and depression. Death phantasies become fixed in the unconscious so that they can serve as a motor turning the parents into a compliant instrument of remedial education programmes at the expense of their own critical capacities.

Environmental death wishes which have been made unconscious – I have already discussed these – can result in the child 'feigning death', being excessively quiet, refusing food, or at least not asking for it, and presenting precisely those symptoms that indicate a need for intervention. 'The children's apparent lack of desire for contact attracts little attention and concern from the environment; it looks as if they do not need it and whenever possible want "to be left alone", in fact need to be left alone.'[40] No one seems to wonder whether the newborn's wish to be left alone is not in fact a sign that it senses the death phantasies of its environment and is trying to protect itself – like Susanna, until her mother had taken her out of the clinic where the assumption was that it was better for a child like her to be put in a home.

Early intervention and its basic assumptions thus prepare the child and parents for what is expected of them: the child becomes a 'typical baby with learning disabilities' who will not develop unless it is given special remedial education. Infants with 'Down's syndrome' undoubtedly also have special weaknesses, but it is of no service to them if, in addition, their vitality is crippled by death wishes that have been made unconscious. This unconsciousness makes parents feel lonely; they are left alone with distressing phantasies and are dependent on the offer of a substitute contact, the promise of absolution. They are ready to do violence to their own feelings and go to great lengths to 'do penance' by giving their child all the educational support they can.

They give their child the educational support that they would have, even if he had not been estranged from their desires by the diagnosis, but now they do it in the name of early intervention theory 'more consciously, more intensively, more imaginatively, more unflaggingly'. What does this mean? They do it more consciously, of course, because they are estranged from their spontaneous impulses; according to Thurmair this is inevitable since parental desires and feelings are seen as factors of disturbance.

Simply holding an infant is enough with a 'normal' child but with infants who have learning disabilities this becomes therapeutic holding. With an infant who has learning disabilities it is not enough just to point at something; at the same time, the seconds have to be counted and practised until the baby is able to look for an adequate length of time. The pleasure in playing with the baby is then replaced by the sense of relief and joy when 'it works', when the baby manages to achieve something approaching normal.

Thus the price of early intervention is self-estrangement and the normative control of the parent–child relationship. The parents' love, and the pleasure they take in playing with their child, is converted into a means of serving the purposes of remedial education, while at the same time the fixed unconscious negative feelings – inaccessible to any reflection – are used to bring the parent–child relationship safely into line with the institution 'Learning Disability'. This way of controlling the parent–child interaction follows a very similar pattern to that which is organised by behaviour therapy. It is no longer an expression of their relationship to each other but a tribute paid to the institution. The joint product is then presented as a normative achievement of the child in the re-education centre rather than being appropriated as a symbol.

'Although my son had been able to eat by himself for a long time, there was a period when, for no apparent reason, he was reluctant to sit on his chair to eat. I insisted he did so and made him go without his food because I was divided between my role as a mother.' An incomplete and therefore illogical sentence – she made her son go without food because she was confused 'between my role as a mother', i.e. she was caught between not being able to trust her own perceptions, the fear of failing, and being left alone with the guilt. There is no symbol for this distress, nothing that those to whom she turns for help might hear. It is macabre to have to read in the same book relating this mother's cry for help that 'early intervention programmes do not take into account what parents want'.

In early intervention, as in behaviour therapy, a dyadic fixation arises without a symbolic dimension. The child is used to reflect the innocence and competence of those who are in charge of him and only receives fragmented mirroring himself; it is not the child as a whole person that is reflected in the mirror of parental affection but rather particular achievements or non-achievements. Since he does not experience himself as a whole person, he cannot free, separate and demarcate himself from the other, from the expectations authority has of him to achieve. Because he only experiences himself in terms of his achievements, a reluctance to achieve results in a loss of self, just as his mother found herself caught in the threatening area of 'between'. Children who have been involved in such programmes give the alarming impression of being marionettes without a will of their own, carrying out the tasks required of them like robots.

A six-year-old girl, whose daily schedule was already like a manager's, came to me for a first consultation. There was no music therapy at the time in the educational programme but at some stage she had had some lessons teaching her to play the flute and xylophone. Although she usually tried to accomplish everything that was asked of her in a whirl of intense effort, now she quietened down, sat there absent-mindedly and was completely inactive. I did not ask her to do anything but just sat opposite her quietly, addressed her by her name from time to time, and placed a box of toys between us. Initially I felt a great antipathy for the studious marionette-like part of her; but as we were just sitting opposite each other this feeling gradually gave way to an unspeakable feeling of emptiness and despair so that I could have cried at length. I saw how her eyes were blurred with tears as she eventually, after sitting together in silence for a long time, put her trembling hands into the box, took out a pair of single building blocks, laid them down in front of her haphazardly and, then, like a 'good girl', put them back in the box again.

She would have been perfectly able to set up an animal scene or a puppet scene if I had asked her to. So after drawing attention to her own wishes by my presence and by pronouncing her name, there remained nothing else for her to do but to show me how she experienced herself, i.e. not with puppet scenes, not in the form of structured, connected experience but rather with single unconnected building blocks, just as her own achievements remained unconnected because she could not give them unity and meaning with her own affective and sensuous reality.

Hans and this girl (I have forgotten her name) are extreme examples, I admit. The pupils at their school found them inept and utterly ridiculous. And behind this 'ridiculousness' lay hidden cruelty, horror and despair in the guise of a clown, Hans 'out-of-luck'.[41]

Most children I know who have had special education have had more luck than the unfortunate Hans or this girl. Their parents managed more or less successfully, as the author of 'Letter from a Mother' also seems to have done, to create islands of spontaneous mutual affection, even if the inter-action was otherwise controlled and standardised. There is general agreement among professionals today that 'overdoing therapy' is to be avoided. Thus 'spontaneous affection' is thoroughly recommended by most theorists of early intervention:

All measures designed to develop and improve the perceptive faculty and motor capacities should be carried out in such a way that they promote the child's emotional and social growth. A colourful environment and friendly atmosphere are important conditions for development. The mother's loving affection for her child promotes his social behaviour and has a positive effect on the child's entire early development. Nothing should be done in a mechanical and silently busy way. The mother should talk to her child a lot, smile at him, sing to him.[42]

The time that is used by the mother or father for kinesthetic stimulation becomes an enjoyable time of being together with the child.[43]

It is paradoxical that even such genuine islands of spontaneous affection, and not simply task-oriented contacts, have become part of early intervention techniques. However, once the phantasm has turned into the private problem of death wishes, parents tend to believe that the only alternative to such interventionist measures is to let their child die and that they themselves can only live by complying with the authority granting absolution. And it is also important that even if parental love finds roundabout ways of expressing itself it must in any case remain under tight control, since too much of it could undermine their readiness, if necessary, to let the child go without food.

What I would like to emphasise here is that early intervention and timely support for parents and children must not have a destructive effect. Kautter et al.[44] have put forward a model of early intervention which gives prority to self-affirmation rather than emphasising achievement. If specialists were aware of the parents' dependence and the relationship of power that exists between them, if, in conjunction with the parents and child, they could work towards breaking down dependency and power, if they could simply help the parents and their child to develop their own solutions to problems instead of prescribing recipes and if they could share the parents' fear of the unknown and sense of emptiness instead of giving them ready-made solutions, then such early forms of intervention might give rise to a critique of the phantasm and genuine solidarity, instead of reinforcing the institution 'Learning Disability'. Even though the essay by Kautter et al. is the only example I know of in the literature which understands early intervention in terms of solidarity in this way, I do know that such models are put into practice here and there. It is important that these are also given a hearing alongside the mainstream of 'people making'.

Chapter 6

Attempts at breaking out

Sound – accompaniment and mediation in the long search for the name

'What's your name?' N. N. asks the new caregiver. 'Claudia', is the reply. It is the wrong answer. N. N. starts talking about her mother. Day-in day-out, she asks Claudia or anybody else she runs into the same question: 'What's your name?' and she always receives the wrong, meaningless answer. Names are meaningless for her as she cannot distinguish between I and you. When, as usual, she does not get an answer, she talks about her mother, about the mother for whom she was 'you' and to whom the question, 'What's your name?' is still directed today. Tell me the name, *my* name, so that I can distinguish myself from you, so that I do not lose myself any longer in you.

(Claudia told me this story several times and every time she told it N. N.'s name escaped me. That is part of the story, I thought, and decided to write it down without asking again what the name was.)

What's 'your' name? Papi, Papi? Endless questions, meaningless, unanswerable questions; so it seems to us at any rate. And because they cause anxiety, threatening our omnipotent phantasies, we think up the most ingenious and laborious methods so as not to have to hear them any longer. We have answers even if they are not the ones that are being sought.

For the most part, therapeutic and remedial rehabilitation programmes are found wanting in the face of the unanswerable, incomprehensible nature of the vital questions of people who have learning disabilities. Their impaired or destroyed capacity for symbolisation seems to us to be an insurmountable barrier; it sets a limit beyond which the therapeutic elaboration of conflicts has to be renounced and education, care and training has to be made available. And so my first question here is: is there really no way within a psychotherapeutic framework of making the destroyed, usurped or withheld space available or helping to create it again?

A second barrier is age: all attempts to do psychotherapeutic work with people with learning disabilities that I know of have been with children and adolescents. And even if one considers the age limit of ten laid down by Bruno Bettelheim, from which he departed only in exceptional cases, as being too rigid, it seems very likely that a thirty-year-old man with severe learning disabilities, who has been in institutional care for over twenty-five years, who has long since renounced his autonomy, will have considerably less chance of extricating himself from the institution of 'learning disability' than if, as a child, he had been offered psychotherapy or a therapeutic milieu, rather than being put in a home.

The second question follows on from this: what can psychotherapy hope to achieve if it no longer selects patients according to their chances of normalisation and integration? What are the therapeutic goals?

Let's take the first question. What do I do with a patient who shows no capacity for symbolisation, who, apart from certain expressions of discomfort and pleasure, is apparently unable to say what he wants and how he sees his life? Someone for whom the idea of having responsibility for one's own life strikes us as being a complete illusion? How can one refrain from telling him what to do?

Wilfried, my first patient, was twenty-nine years old and had been in the institution for twenty-five years. He was a very withdrawn man, of small and delicate build, who usually spent the whole day standing in a corner and would not speak or play. From time to time, though, he would have fits of rage all day long, during which he was capable of wrenching steel doors off their hinges and throwing cupboards around; and, he would bang his head dangerously hard against walls and steel doors. When he was in this state he had to be bound, hand and foot, to his bed with leather belts. This was all I knew about him initially. I was a bit afraid of him (even though I had not seen him in a rage), but felt moved by his withdrawn state.

I was full of good will but lacking experience and skill, and in our first session, I put before Wilfried all the wonderful instruments that were at our disposal. He was not interested in any of them; on the contrary, they seemed to distress him. He became more and more withdrawn. Finally, not knowing what else to do, I held out my hand to him instead of an instrument: 'Look, I am here for you, now show me what you want!', I was saying. He took hold of my hand and took me out of the therapy room into the open air where we went for a walk together. That is how our work together began.

From then on I always went to fetch Wilfried when he was due for a session and he would take me for a walk. He took me on long walks, whenever possible outside the institutional compound. For weeks on end we went for such walks. Every time I came to pick him up, Wilfried tugged on me and could not leave his ward quickly enough; however, on the way back he tried to delay our return, sometimes struggling and making pitiful, choking, whining sounds, but to no avail. I always had to bring him back to the place he so obviously wanted to escape from. We were going round in circles, and it seemed there was no way out.

On several occasions, Wilfried had given me to understand: 'I can lead you by the hand' and, 'I need you to let me lead you' and, 'I want to get out of here' but also, 'I don't know any way out'. There was all this communication but not in a symbolic form; rather, he enacted his communications with me. As a result there really was no way out: wanting out in terms of really leaving the institution was not possible and since he had known nothing else but the ghetto for twenty-five years, once outside he would not really have been able to show me his own way. Above all, however, the experience of hopelessness became deeply engrained because Wilfried experienced it physically over and over again, being unable to talk to me about anything else. His enactment of hopelessness remained unsymbolised, unnamed, and so he was unable to stand back from it and question it.

In the meantime a relationship had developed between us. I was always impressed to see how, when I came to fetch him, discreetly calling out his name across the room which was full of the noise and commotion of all the people packed into it, he would immediately look up and run over to me with his hand outstretched. So I finally felt secure enough to intervene in our distressing enactment. I now understood that our walks *symbolised* his desires.

This was already an intervention. Wilfried's main experience was of standing around on the ward or going out and having to come back. He even had to be accompanied when he went out of the ward, otherwise he would stay hanging around in a corner outside. So, without my intervention, these walks could be nothing more for him than desirable interruptions, though always too short, in his dreadful daily routine.

In order to interrupt the hopelessness and endlessness of our enactment, I now had to *interpret* for Wilfried the desire that was implicit within it. But how does one make an interpretation to someone who clearly cannot use language at all (whether he understood or not, I could not tell; in any case he did not react to language)? I therefore made some modifications to the situation. A few additional observations helped me here. On our walks Wilfried had sometimes bent down to pick up small buttons or stones from the ground, which he would then hold in his hand, rolling them between his fingers until he eventually dropped them.

For me our walks together in silence had been ghost-like and frightening; and, in order to cope with this anxiety, as well as to show Wilfried that I was with him, I began humming songs softly as we went along. Wilfried did not react but I thought I could sense that he did not find my humming unpleasant. Later, an older male nurse told me that Wilfried had known many songs as a child, always enjoyed hearing them, and had even sung them himself. Wilfried did not run away but needed to hold my hand; in other words, he needed a relationship. He clearly suffered on his ward from being exposed to countless and, in most cases, unpleasant stimuli. (Once, after spending some time on the quiet ward, he did not want to go back to his own.)

Based on these observations, I now suggested a game. I decided to work with him again in the music therapy room and arranged the room for his sessions so that it was as unstimulating, calm, and pleasant as possible. In the middle, I placed a round table and two chairs for us to sit opposite each other. On the table I put a collection of small plastic balls. A large cymbal hung from the ceiling near his chair and close to the door. Wilfried accepted this arrangement immediately, sat down on his chair and looked aimlessly at the balls. We sat like this for a while and then I summoned up the courage to give one of the balls a gentle push so that it rolled across the table towards him. Wilfried followed it with his eyes in fascination. When the ball had been still for a while, I rolled the next one towards him, and then another. Wilfried continued to watch very closely; when one of the balls rolled off the table onto the floor, he followed it with his eyes as it rolled under the table or under his chair. But he avoided touching it at all. When, on one occasion, he had to move his leg aside quickly so that the ball did not fall onto it, a peculiar little smile crossed his face which otherwise always looked so deeply sad and taciturn.

In the second or third session, with the same arrangement, Wilfried answered me for the first time: he tried – still carefully avoiding physical contact of any kind – to blow away the ball rolling towards him. He also now began to show interest in the cymbal. He looked at it and drew in his breath a little. Very gently, I gave it a push and the strange, awkward smile on Wilfried's face – it looked as if a mechanism which had been rusting away for years had been set in motion again – showed me that I had got in touch with what he wanted. Together we watched and listened to the cymbal as it slowly came to a standstill.

In this play situation, Wilfried's wishes were contained as an interactive potential and he no longer had to enact them compulsively. The relationship was established with the aid of the round table which Wilfried could make use of if he wanted – he no longer depended on me directly by having his hand in mine. He had escaped for an hour from the noise and overstimulation on his ward and was no longer in a world where he could only exist as long as he held on to my hand; he was in a room which did not make too many demands on him with its strange facilities and did not leave him alone in a void. On the other hand, it offered possibilities for play that corresponded to his interest in small hard balls and soft sounds, without obliging him to take part. And because the arrangement had a symbolic character, Wilfried now had freedom of choice; a way out could be envisaged: if he had decided to reject the relationship when we went for walks together then our going out together would have come to nothing;

but here he could let the balls fall on the floor, did not need to hold my hand, and yet could feel confident that I would stay with him – the room held us together, gave us a common container without chaining us to each other directly.

A first change: as a result of playing together Wilfried experienced that the small ball, the relationship I was offering him, was not lost when he let it fall off the table, that the relationship was still possible even when he rejected it by letting the ball fall on the floor, that he could blow or kick another ball, and that he could also tolerate my 'dropping him' at the end of a session now more easily. Just as the ball was not lost, neither was he; so he no longer had to resist when I brought him back to his ward and could wait until I came to fetch him again for his next session.

Increasingly, Wilfried would kick the balls in my direction as if by accident. Occasionally, if he was unable to blow the ones that were still lying on the table towards me he would push them with the back of his hand. Sometimes I let a ball roll off the table into the cymbal. Wilfried liked this: eventually he allowed himself to pick a ball up with his hand and to throw it at the cymbal. This now made a ringing sound that was not as soft as before. The cymbal gradually came to a standstill. Wilfried loved to set the cymbal swinging either by throwing a ball at it, or with his foot, or sometimes with a wooden hammer I gave him, and then he would listen to it entranced. Now I felt encouraged to make another interpretation, to intervene again by structuring the game. From Wilfried's withdrawn responses to my offers of contact, I had noticed his reluctance to touch our materials with his hands, with the palms of his hands, and how important it was for him to be able independently to determine the degree of closeness and distance in our relationship. It seemed to me now that the structure the table offered was too rigid. By now our relationship was so secure that the quiet room that remained unchanged and the play materials which were always at our disposal, provided enough security in themselves. So I got rid of the table, put myself in a corner, and left it to Wilfried to decide where he wanted to be, whether he wanted to remain sitting or standing. I placed the balls on the floor, along with other smaller and bigger ones made of different materials, near the suspended cymbal. Wilfried's rusty smile when he first saw this arrangement told me that my interpretation was right; now he could join in our work quite independently. We kept this arrangement for a considerable length of time; with growing courage and increasing pleasure and liveliness, Wilfried was able to discover his own forms of play and discover his own desires. Let us leave him to play now and ask ourselves why this man who had severe learning disabilities and for years, even decades, had only loitered in corners, occasionally rolling small stones between his fingers, was now able to take a lively interest in playing.

He had gained space for playing and continued to do so increasingly, that much was clear: by throwing things, by knocking the cymbal so that it swung more, by making the balls rebound harder off the cymbal the ringing sound became even louder. It was the material that gave him space. It replaced the need to have his hand held. Certainly, Wilfried could have continued going for walks with me like this but the limits set by reality destroyed this real space over and over again. But now the walks had taken on a symbolic character and the space that Wilfried had now acquired was the free area of his phantasy which no one could destroy, for it remained with him as a memory during his dreadful daily existence. His small stones and balls represented this space for him.

The material was not chosen fortuitously, even if at the time I could not have given satisfying reasons for the choice I made. Judging from the only recognisable signs of interest in materials which Wilfried manifested, I chose the small balls, and later added the bigger ones. They were not heavy and shapeless like the little stones which Wilfried held between his fingers, but light and round – a structure making them suitable for the most varied uses. Balls can serve as missiles or (as was the case with Wilfried and me) can express cautious attempts at *rapprochement*, and they can also (as a symbol of the breast) be licked and put in the mouth. Because of their appearance, the way they roll, or by being used with other objects, especially instruments, they can be invested with many different symbolic meanings by anyone playing with them, either singly or multiply.

For Wilfried and me, the balls thus became mediating agents creating space for the beginnings of a potential relationship, rather than the immediacy of holding my hand. The balls rolling quietly between us told a story which we both understood. It is less easy to explain why I included the cymbal, suspended from the ceiling, as the second play item in the music therapy with Wilfried. We could also have thrown the balls at a drum, a standing cymbal or a xylophone. But the soft rocking movements and the sound of the cymbal slowly swinging to a standstill seemed to me best suited for representing the atmosphere of the symbiotic relationship which I offered Wilfried and which he so thankfully accepted. The cymbal swings like an infant being rocked, it continues to reverberate for a long time, just as the almost defenceless infant's psyche 'reverberates' when something has disturbed the symbiotic security. The cymbal had become Wilfried's subjective-object in which he found his experience – experience from early infancy – reflected; and the cymbal allowed Wilfried to remain grown-up while reliving these earliest experiences through it. The cymbal allowed for possibilities of symbolisation which went beyond the ball game, enabling Wilfried to gain a bit more independence and space. In addition to the story of our relationship, of our cautious *rapprochement* and the reluctance to relate, I can now also speak of what happened in Wilfried when he felt moved by my willingness to relate to him: the cymbal began moving within him as it did between us; and, like the cymbal, it took him a long time to refind his balance again. The cymbal also said something about me as a 'symbiotic part object'. It hung on a stable leather band allowing it to swing quietly and holding it securely – this secure holding pleased Wilfried who did not stop smiling: he wanted to be held like this too. But for Wilfried, this desire to be held was in reality inseparable from the anxiety that his space, the distance he needed, would not be respected and that he would be overwhelmed just as he was constantly on the ward. So the cymbal had to continue swinging for a long time so that his inner distress and experience of being overwhelmed could 'swing itself out' with it, i.e. be soothed, giving him confidence that things could be different, that in this protected room he could enter into a relationship without immediately being overwhelmed by stimuli and demands. Because the cymbal established a limit between us and, at the same time, had a transitional function linking us by its movement, by the sound it made, now, when he wanted to start the cymbal swinging he could pick up the balls and throw them at it. He could allow for intimacy and tactile contact because the cymbal reassured him that, in spite of the strength of his desire for tactile contact, the palm of his hand would not stay glued to mine.

The large cymbal hanging by the long leather band symbolised a symbiotic relationship for Wilfried, giving him a sense of being held and contained as it 'swung out' the external stimuli. This was repeated in the experience with the sound that we made with the balls and the baton. By tapping the instrument a warm, sonorous sound, endlessly dying away, envelops, moved and contained us. Wilfried knew that his fear of closeness and his desire for distance was being respected.

Here is another example: Eileen and I were kneeling on the floor, side by side, with the large cymbal suspended from the ceiling and hanging between us. She was making complicated figures with her hand in front of her eyes and was totally absorbed in this activity. Eventually, I gently tapped the cymbal. Eileen stopped what she was doing, looked at the cymbal rocking gently and started rocking slowly with it. I felt caught up in this movement, as if I was at one with it, and thus at one with Eileen too. The symbiotic relationship which, in her own peculiar way of throwing herself at everyone, Eileen both wanted and yet could not enter into because her complete incapacity to trust an object relationship was expressed only too clearly in the arbitrariness of object-choice, was created here by the reliable instrument. Moreover, Eileen had decided to hug me less often which I understood as her first tentative experiments with non-arbitrariness. It seemed as if she was withdrawing her affection from me but this was in fact a first sign of object constancy. In this way the instrument took over an important mediating function; it was absolutely reliable, indestructible, always in the same place, and, above all, Eileen could see a reflection of her rocking in it.

The light tapping of the cymbal was like a gentle shock interrupting Eileen in what she was doing. The cymbal was rocking; it was also disturbed by the shock and was trying to find its equilibrium again. This reflected Eileen's inner life; for once, she was not alone in her efforts to regain her equilibrium following the interruption. The interruptions which she experienced with people were more abrupt; most of her caregivers were not even able to allow her time to rock herself back into a state of equilibrium, let alone show sympathy towards her in her state of shock. The daily routine on the ward was too hectic for such slow experiences. When Eileen rocked in synchrony with the cymbal she was calm and seemed very concentrated. These were very intense moments. Eileen was no longer completely alone, she had the cymbal with her. By silently, gently, swaying along with the instrument, without Eileen noticing it, I was able to establish the beginnings of a very delicate, scarcely noticeable relationship with her in which her experience of losing the ground beneath her no longer had to be faced alone.

Another game: Eileen had a plastic ball which she liked throwing away from herself. I would keep fetching it and giving it back to her. She seldom threw the ball in my direction, throwing it more often at the cymbal and then needed time to rock with the ringing sound until she was ready again. Eileen was becoming happier and happier, laughing and jumping with joy, happy to see that the ball always came back and that the cymbal always found its equilibrium again. They were indestructible; unlike her environment they made no demands on her and they were completely reliable and transparent. Under these conditions she began to speak more. The ball said nothing, did not interrupt her and the cymbal answered when she wanted it to. Through this activity with the ball and the cymbal, which she found meaningful, she now tried to bring the shock-like, piercing orders which all too often wrenched her out of her monotonous, lonely experience, into the context of a relationship. Perhaps they could be worked through after all; perhaps they would not always be incomprehensible and did have a meaning that she could understand. This was my hope as Eileen now repeated all those commands whose meaning she had never had time to understand, trying to bring them, like the cymbal, into tune with her experience.

The main reason why Eileen was referred to me was because of her dreadful, incessant head banging which seemed to involve no affects. After a few weeks of music therapy – in the meantime the caregivers had watched me working with her and then continued our 'indestructible' ball game – she had stopped this almost completely and was in general much happier. She had learnt that an answer was possible, that her throwing away did not necessarily destroy the relationship.

When working with people who suffer from such severe learning disabilities, it is important that the forms of play and materials used are felt to be indestructible and reliable. By 'indestructible' I do not of course mean an objective quality: the cymbal can be 'destructible', for example, because it will break if it is used as a swing; on the other hand, a really fragile material, such as balloons, can nonetheless signify 'indestructibility'. Materials must therefore always be chosen for the significance they may have in any particular therapy situation. What is also important in most cases for the meaning 'indestructible', is that the materials are easy to handle and that the sounds are produced by the patients themselves, otherwise a failure could destroy this quality of meaning.

So it is a question of the quality of experience, in particular the experience of the infant in the first weeks and months of life. M. Balint has called this period:

> . . . the phase of the undifferentiated environment, of the primary substances or the phase of the harmonious interpenetrating mix-up. [. . .] The best illustration for this state is the relationship we have towards the air surrounding us. It is difficult to say whether the air in our lungs or in our guts is us, or not us; and it does not even matter. [. . .] The air has to be there for us in adequate quantity and quality; and as long as it is there the relationship between us and it cannot be observed, or only with very great difficulty; if, however, anything interferes with our supply of air, impressive and noisy symptoms develop in the same way as with the dissatisfied infant . . .
>
> The air is not an object but a substance, like water or milk. [. . .] There are a few – not many – more such substances [. . .]: water, earth, and fire; with some others [. . .] such as sand and water or plasticine. Their chief characteristic is their indestructibility. You can build a castle out of wet sand, then destroy it, and the sand will still be there; you can stop the jet of water coming from a tap but, as soon as you take your finger away, the jet is there again, and so on.[1]

In working with patients who regress to these phases of development, Balint continues, the analyst himself has to take on the quality of a 'primary substance' to a certain extent. 'He must be there; he must be pliable to a very high degree; he must not offer much resistance; he certainly must be indestructible, and he must allow his patient to live with him in a sort of harmonious interpenetrating mix-up.'[2] Something similar is also true for the music therapist's work with people who have severe learning disabilities. An essential difference, however, is that the regression of a patient in psychoanalysis is generally temporary and reversible, occurring on experiential levels while an awareness of one's own adulthood and independence is simultaneously preserved. The regression can therefore be symbolised and worked over therapeutically. This is seldom the case with patients with severe learning disabilities who are often just as dependent as infants. However, they are not infants, and in most cases their level of sensory-motor development contrasts strikingly with their mental development. Treating them as infants would mean blotting out the potential of this developmental discrepancy. While in psychoanalysis the possibility of symbolising regression is guaranteed by the conditions of the setting (session times, speaking, etc.) in which the analyst treats the analysand in every respect as an adult, in therapeutic work with people who have severe learning disabilities the therapist has first to lay the ground for a symbolic dimension, i.e. by introducing suitable materials into the therapeutic relationship. The immediacy of the two-person relationship, beyond which these patients have never been able to develop, or to which they have regressed as a result of a trauma, can thus be resolved in a triangular situation involving patient–materials–therapist, patient–symbol–therapist; and, once it can be symbolised, it can be contained and worked over.

An infant is unable initially to offer any intentional resistance to the long period of dependency on the two-person relationship; however, from its initial resistance expressed purely vegetatively, it eventually develops a capacity to say 'no' by means of which it defends, demarcates and asserts itself. Wilfried and Carmen have not been able to learn this 'no' and yet they have not remained infants: their defensive manoeuvres are attempts at self-affirmation by means of which they seek to extricate themselves from the two-person relationship on which they are dependent, yet without really being able to become independent. These forms of defence, which operate in their lives as long as there is no change, are rigid and thus impede any change. If Eileen, for example, had indicated just once that she wanted to continue playing ball, even though she threw the ball away, her caregivers would have recognised the misunderstanding and responded to it (just as they did after they had watched me doing it). But Wilfried and Eileen had to cling to their defence because it was their only means of expressing something that they were unable to say in any other way as yet. Wilfried used his autistic withdrawal and his bouts of anger to achieve the attachment, the symbiotic relationship he needed, but could not tolerate, because his only experience of it was one of being overpowered and attached with leather straps. Eileen's seemingly symbiotic form of defence of thrusting herself on others was designed to provoke the response 'Eileen – no!' which she herself was unable to say, i.e. 'I, Eileen, am saying no!' The therapist can now begin to work with these rigid, self-destructive and badly damaged forms of self-affirmation, sensing in them the presence of dammed up vital energies which give him (or her) the hope he needs to be able to work with such hopeless people. Their rigidity points to the merging-into-one-another experience of the two-person relationship; they become symbols which the therapist can interpret, the basis of his therapeutic activity, by means of which he will try to create the foundations and the space for his patients' own capacity to symbolise.

Now the choice of materials is important. They must be capable of symbolising the infant-like quality of experience of those with severe learning disabilities and, at the same time, correspond to their actual age;

they must be simple and transparent and yet be capable of representing complex interactions. Of course, priority is always given to the materials, if there are any, which are chosen by the patient himself. Any restriction of the choice of materials or therapeutic technique can only result in further restriction of the damaged, constricted or broken possibilities of communication which people with learning disabilities have at their disposal. The therapist must therefore be prepared to make use of any play material, however unlikely, as well as the most abstruse forms of play which the patient may bring and be capable of using creatively. Consequently, my aim here is not to promote music therapy as an exclusive way of working psychotherapeutically which excludes other forms of play and other materials. But in working with patients with severe learning disabilities, experience shows that sounds and rhythms take precedence over other materials. There are several reasons for this: sounds and rhythms accompany the beginnings of life. 'Already the disturbances of intra-uterine equilibrium as a result of being shaken about, knocked, etc. structure the continuity of embryonic life through rhythmic interruptions. They can be contained in the resulting vibrations', just as the cymbal hanging on the leather band allows the ringing sound to slowly fade away.

> After birth, sounds and rhythms of movement accompany both the ongoing continuity outside the womb in the 'primary substances' as well as their time-rhythm structured interruptions, i.e. in the form of a steady background noise interrupting the silence and the child's crying as a response to intolerable external stimuli or bodily tensions impinging on him and disturbing his equilibrium. In the reciprocal play between the partners of the mother–child dyad, such acoustic sensations, if in harmony with the immediate situation, can be experienced either as soothing and sleep-inducing or as passively received or actively produced signals. What is important is that the noises are in tune with the experience but they can exist separately, even though the child is at first unaware that they are separate. Crying is not hunger or physical discomfort but is part of this experience and is an appeal for it to be removed in a satisfying interaction; a creaking door signals the arrival of the careperson . . . sounds and noises have a 'function of social orientation', they also begin to represent in the child's experience the situation of which they are a part.[3]

The symbolic potential of sounds and rhythms makes it possible then to symbolise the earliest forms of life in psychotherapy with people who have severe learning disabilities.

If patients are to be able to make use of this it is important that the sound creates and really produces the experience it potentially symbolises; and, that this symbolic material is in tune with the patient's still barely

differentiated capacity for experience, without itself detracting from potential differentiation. Sound is a very tactile, enveloping, overpowering
experience; our bodies resonate with it. The ringing sound of the cymbal
really interrupted Eileen's activity, echoing her experience on the ward
when she was asked to do things; its reverberating echo enveloped her with
friendly vibrations, establishing the beginnings of a symbiotic relationship
and symbolised all this at one and the same time. This was more helpful to
Eileen than if I had held her. Like Wilfried, she was then free to determine
the duration of this process of finding her equilibrium. She could turn
away, ignore the sound, free or separate herself when she wanted to; and
return if she needed the cymbal and its ringing sound again. The ringing
sound helped her to practise symbolically the interaction form of 'separation and relating', as an infant would do, without having to give up her
physical independence as an adolescent. But, however much sound may
symbolise early infantile experience, it is also adult material. It can be
highly differentiated and, at the same time, quite unstructured; or its
structure can be so simple and transparent that it does not demand too
much from people with learning disabilities while being, more than any
other material, in tune with their psychic experience, without pinning them
to it. Right at the beginning of my relationship with Inge – whom I shall
talk about in more detail in the next chapter – I created a symbiotic
atmosphere by listening to taped recordings of harpsichord sonatas by
D. Scarlatti. She was able to respond to the music as a protective envelope
of friendly vibrations and it was clear that she did not feel the need to
withdraw as much as usual. For me, however, the dismal marking of time
and rigidity of this music symbolised the endless, hopeless repetitions, the
relational situation between Inge and me, which was moulded by her earlier
experience with a mother who, all too often, was unreachable and unavailable. How far Inge was aware of this sophisticated symbolism I do not
know, nor does it matter: it was contained as a potential development in the
non-differentiation of the primary substance providing her with potential
space.

Sounds and rhythms thus allow for both undifferentiated fusion of the self
and the object and their differentiation. This is not only important for the
patients but also for the therapist, as the example of Inge shows. The
counter-transference feelings which I experienced in my work with Inge were
expressed in Scarlatti's music; and, if it enabled me to create Inge's first
experience of space, of being held, it was also because I understood my own
feelings better and felt contained through the music, through its meaning in
the process of re-enacting Inge's early experience. The music, the sound,
helped me to tolerate, on Inge's behalf, the dreadful loneliness and fear of
death which had left her numb and which I was now experiencing in the
counter-transference. In my work with Wilfried, sound helped me to tolerate
the boredom and the taboo on touching and, with it, his hidden feelings of

anxiety and murderous anger, so that he was no longer left alone with these feelings. Even though I did not initially receive an answer to my offer of a relationship, the sound nonetheless confirmed that I was there and that I was making such a provision. The sounds, the music, must also express for the therapist what she is as yet unable to communicate to herself and the patient in any other way: her holding, her being there, her ability to tolerate not understanding, as well as her understanding. Without this possibility she would have to react to the lack of response with anxiety – or with defences against it – anxiety of not existing because she is not recognised, fears of losing herself in the sense of unending emptiness and hopelessness. Indeed working with people with learning disabilities, whose capacities for relating are still at the 'phase of primary substances', produces strong feeling responses in the therapist: deadly boredom, leaden fatigue, feelings of emptiness, 'unreality' states, an inability to concentrate and indifference, all forms of defence against fears of death, murderous anger and deep despair.

Anxiety and defences against it in the therapist's counter-transference arise from the undifferentiated nature of the relationship. Nothing is familiar, nothing can be taken for granted; even the most minimal levels of understanding have to be achieved out of this diffuse, indeterminate, formlessness. The counter-transference feelings themselves are thoroughly diffuse and, at first, scarcely identifiable: feelings of anger are not directed at something or someone in particular, feelings of despair have no definable cause; rather the anger is object-less, limitless and potentially over-whelming. What causes the therapist such anxiety is the threatening sense of loss of self faced with a person whose incapacity or reluctance to share the load of a relationship along socially pre-determined lines threatens to undermine his or her own organising capacity.

Wilfried and Eileen, however, needed their therapist to participate in the diffuseness and formlessness in which they have to spend their lives so that they can elaborate their own structure, their own desire for living.

> It is only here in this unintegrated state of the personality, that that which we describe as creative can appear. This if reflected back, *but only if reflected back*, becomes part of the organised individual person-ality, and eventually this in summation makes the individual to be, to be found; and eventually enables himself or herself to postulate the existence of the self.[4]

What Winnicott says with respect to psychotherapeutic work with neurotic and psychotic patients is valid in an even more elementary way in psycho-therapy with patients who have learning disabilities. Here too, a central factor in therapeutic progress, as the examples have shown, is 'reflecting back', interpretation and its preliminary stages: giving back what has been thrown away; picking up of what has fallen down: elucidating tonally the small, at first barely noticeable, spontaneous, gestures, and the first signs of personal organisation with the help of suitable materials. Only when the therapist, 'indestructible' like a primary substance, is able to take over for a sufficient length of time these very early mirror functions, can patients inwardly establish, appropriate, and integrate such early structures, and then perhaps experiment with further steps on the basis of these foundations which have finally been acquired.

Let me return now to Wilfried. He had now become boisterous, drawing attention to himself. In particular, he had taken to throwing the heavy wooden balls vehemently at the cymbal, as well as the drum, the xylophone, the piano keys – instruments he came across in the room without my presenting them to him. A year had passed and in between a few things had happened. Shortly after we began playing together, I was absent because of illness; when I returned, I found Wilfried attached to his bed, squealing, sucking in air and banging his fettered fists. He was enraged. I sat down beside him hoping that, in spite of all his distress, he could still sense that I was with him. It was painful to see him strapped down like that, struggling with the straps. I said his name softly and he listened. I held out my hand to him and he tentatively gave me his bound hand – as if it might stick otherwise – and opened his fist a little. With my other hand I tapped the palm of his hand gently and tickled it. He smiled, withdrew his hand and then reached out to me with it again. He could allow this intimacy of contact now because he was tied up and in a state of anguish; otherwise, he would have rejected it, however much he desired it. There were one or two other occasions, after I had returned from my holidays, when I found Wilfried having a fit of rage. The last time it happened, an observant nurse recommended that I take him to music therapy in spite of his angry outburst, and it really was all right. Afterwards he did not need to be tied up any more. It was the last fit of rage I saw him have. I then realised that since starting his music therapy Wilfried had always 'thrown a tantrum' when he missed the therapy – his oasis – which allowed him four times a week to experience his boundaries and to express himself in a relationship. Whereas his rages had previously overwhelmed him for no apparent reason, they now acquired a meaning in the context of our relationship and became a means of communication. They enabled him to express helplessly, and still in an unsymbolised form, his need for intimacy; intimacy where his boundaries were respected and protected against impingements. Once I had understood this better I began to incorporate in the therapy the game with the palm of his hand – another interpretation. When he had stopped playing and noisily sucking in air, I went over to him slowly, always ready to move away again if he signalled that that was what he wanted. I tickled the palm of his hand, patted it with my hand and clapped my hands; he held out his hands and, with my help, began clapping his hands, smiling roguishly. When he had had enough, he pointed his hand towards my chair and so I left him alone with the cymbal and the balls. Soon after I took an organ-pipe in with me – I had had this idea because of the sound of him sucking in air. He clearly liked its soft, deep tone, felt confident enough to take hold of it himself and to blow in it, and was pleased with the deep tone he could make with it.

Wilfried's ball throwing and kicking became increasingly purposeful: when he wanted me to come to him, he became more boisterous, or made sure that the balls rolled in my direction. He did not do this directly but he developed his own technique of sending the balls to me by making them rebound off instruments and walls. So there was still an object between us which the ball rebounded off, as well as the sound of the rebound, representing a third party, a boundary symbol and a symbol of the desire for contact bridging the boundary.

At first, it was difficult and tiring for me to get involved in Wilfried's play with sufficient attention to pick up the small signs of his readiness for contact. But things were different now because of the interaction forms that had emerged during his bouts of anger; that is, anger had now become a real affect in our relationship. Wilfried was able to set boundaries, to challenge them, and ask for what he needed; and, if I was not careful, Wilfried made such a noise with the balls and instruments that I could no longer ignore what he wanted. His bouts of anger on the ward ceased – in fact, he did not have any more angry outbursts during the whole last year of our work together because he could now vent his anger on me before it overwhelmed him. Because I interpreted and symbolically satisfied his need for a containing, reliable relationship, he was able to integrate the affect of anger as an interaction form into his personality. It was no coincidence that Wilfried now also used the other instruments in the room, i.e. the piano, xylophone and drums, in order to attract my attention: the sounds they produced were better suited than the rising and falling sounds of the cymbal for expressing what Wilfried wanted to tell me. 'I am here. You there, listen to me!' Drum and piano sounds are unequivocal, clearly defined, individual sounds. Now that Wilfried had acquired a sufficient sense of his own boundaries to be able to assert them in our relationship – for example, by using gestures to distance me if I got too close to him instead of withdrawing himself – he could actively challenge the boundary between us and make his desire to relate to me clearly understood. He had now found his own contours in our relationship, just like the sounds of the drum, the xylophone and the piano he used to assert himself. Our relationship had developed from a 'harmonious interpenetrating mix-up' to an ever more clearly defined interplay of symbiosis and separation between two individuals separating from each other.

Both the process of sounds, 'unending', 'indestructible' noises – including rattling, clapping sounds etc. – swinging themselves out, as well as clearly defined sounds, form a basis for self-discovery, for name finding. Out of the unsophisticated nature of the substance-like sounds and noises, tones begin to emerge as the first objects. They accompany the emergence of human objects from the undifferentiated state of symbiotic fusion. To the extent that Wilfried was able to sense his own contours, to experience himself as a separate individual in relationship to his environment, he could also more clearly recognise me as being a separate person from him, albeit to a limited extent. He had begun to see himself as a subject who wanted things from the environment because he had had a reliable experience with me showing that his desires could serve to build a bridge spanning separateness. Now these contours which had been sensed and played with in therapy needed to be integrated as inner ideational images, self and object representations. Here, too, sound and rhythmic materials prove to be particularly suitable for accompanying this further step along the path towards finding one's own name: sensing one's own boundaries, trying out one's own capacities of being active in the world always requires courage and confidence. People like Wilfried, Inge and Eileen whose only experience of such attempts is one of failure, being dropped, banging their heads against brick walls, however such expectations may have come about, have little idea how to make use of new space to which they are unaccustomed. On the contrary, they continue to cling to the old numbness, for it is the only thing which has enabled them so far to survive in a hostile world. That is why it is important that, with the materials available, play emerges out of gestures of rejection, i.e. that the ball makes a sound when it rebounds and rolls a bit, whether it is allowed to fall or is thrown in a particular direction; that the cymbal makes a ringing sound if it is touched; that the rattle makes a noise when Inge waves it or drops it, like with paper or a spoon. Unlike sand or plasticine, for example, which can only be used to create specific objects, and which simply remain substance-like if they are not used for this purpose, such materials make it possible in an extremely unsophisticated and diffuse way for an autonomous, structural and symbolic organisation to emerge. They provide reliable and indestructible responses – aided by the fact that the music therapist untiringly gives them back – to the gestures by which people with learning disabilities reveal their inner destruction and total hopelessness; i.e. dropping things, losing things, throwing things away, tipping things over, making a sound which symbolises being dropped, losing oneself – in other words the most fundamental experiences of people with severe learning disabilities, infantile psychotics and autists. The sound of the instruments is saying: 'my falling is audible and so I (and you, the one who has let me fall) am really here', whereas the gestures of people with learning disabilities are saying, 'I am lost anyway'. Eileen could hear this when she dropped a ball onto the cymbal; she could remember this experience of being lost and, at the same time, she experienced for the first time the opposite experience of getting a response, being accepted and reflected. Or, in the sound of an instrument that she had thrown away or tipped over

Philippa could hear what she was unable to experience with her mother: 'Listen, I have survived your murderous anger'. The loneliness, the loss of self, the overpowering, destructive, murderous panicky anger of the person in a rage are shared and given their first symbolic structure, even if such patients have still not reached the point of wanting to share something because they are lacking the confidence and experience that their over-whelming experiences can be contained and their suffering relieved.

It is only when the experience has been sufficiently integrated so that there is an answer to the quasi-involuntary, accidental, purely vegetative gesture, just as the infant's crying acquires meaning by being responded to, can the next step be undertaken in the independent creation and sharing of symbols: intentional production. Instruments are then used intentionally to make sounds, a rattle is first shaken before it is thrown away again, a drum is not just touched but given a little tap. Wilfried now plucked up the courage to produce sounds on the organ-pipe which hitherto he had done in an involuntary, noisy way when he was angry and longing for closeness, security and being held – he was clearly trying to 'keep himself together'. At first they were timid, deep, warm, intermittent sounds and, later, long-drawn-out sounds full of yearning. They were products arising from the contours of the 'primary substance' air which, now that he had acquired space, breathing space, he could give up consciously because he was confident that there would always be enough of it for him, just as his therapy, which he needed like air to breathe, would always be there for him.

At this point I am going to make a pause in my presentation. In the therapeutic case of Chapter 7, 'A child without behavioural difficulties', will be able to go into certain issues in more detail; others must, however, remain open to discussion: what I am reporting here is based on first attempts and certainly not on a time-tested and proven therapeutic pro-cedure. My concern is to stimulate not to indoctrinate – and, perhaps, to be a little provocative.

It may seem provocative to some that I have so unhesitatingly drawn on psychoanalytic vocabulary to elaborate my work but psychoanalysis may be considered as *the* therapy form, *par excellence*, of 'the mind'. Nonethe-less, I want to point out that my way of working is psychoanalytic not only with regard to the foundations of my understanding but also in that I claim, with the help of this understanding – through 'interpretations' and by structuring their play – to allow patients to find their own way.

The basis of the work is respect for the patient's autonomy, however damaged it is, however shaken his desire is. I could scarcely have thought of such a meaningful and original solution to Wilfried's problem as he himself found after a long period of work: establishing contact by means of the wall as a third party over which he sent me his ball-messages. He could only find this solution, however, because I had had confidence from the beginning in his wish for contact and in his capacity to find a way. With this confidence, which initially there was little reason to have (although more than with some other patients with severe learning disabilities), I kept the relationship going until he was able to establish it himself.

In psychoanalysis, the working alliance between therapist and patient is the starting-point for their work together. It is understood that, within his possibilities, the patient also assumes responsibility for the therapy. There is also a working alliance in psychotherapeutic work with patients who have learning disabilities; here, too, patients must take on responsibility for the work that is done together in that they come to the therapy wanting something, i.e. with their own desires. Often, a verbal agreement is not possible; with patients who have severe learning disabilities it has to develop gradually in the course of recurring encounters. This can demand a great deal of patience – the case study of Inge ('A child without behavioural difficulties') may give a sense of how much patience is needed sometimes. It appears then that this desire evolves very slowly from initially shadowy outlines to increasingly distinct contours, like a photograph in a developing bath, until the patient can acquire a stable experience of the reliable, recurring play area as a space in which he can move autonomously.

Sometimes, however, the working alliance is achieved very quickly. Once in the U-Bahn I met a social worker I knew who was with one of her clients, a girl with learning disabilities. While the social worker was talking to me, the girl was fidgeting restlessly and saying to herself: 'Empty out the water, empty out the water'. The social worker explained to me that, whenever she had the chance, the girl loved splashing water around and letting it overflow onto floors. The girl gave me a very meaningful look and repeated, 'Empty out the water!' I replied: 'We should try to understand why you always want to flood everything!' I shall never forget the look she had on her face: with wide-open eyes she gave me a long startled stare and then sat down for a while very quietly, almost rigid. It was as if my words had struck a chord in her which even she was not aware of, let alone those around her; a chord which she now listened to with astonishment, disbelief, full of fear and anxiety, as well as desire.

This could have been the beginning of a therapeutic working alliance: the desire to be understood – in spite of the anxiety and doubt – could be clearly detected in her eyes. I have seen such deeply astounded and often startled looks in quite a few therapy situations.

It is often people with learning disabilities who have psychotic (autistic) structures that arrive so quickly at an understanding (even if it can take a long time before they can trust their understanding). It is as if the proposition: 'Let's try and understand together the importance of this for you?' were able to create in one instant an image of the destroyed space which, although it is immediately lost again, leaves behind it a vague hope and longing on the basis of which the work can continue.

On the whole, work with patients with infantile psychotic structures is different, more lively and absorbing. It is easier to relate to the ruins of destroyed space than to wait with often endless patience and just be there until a lively area of play can grow in place of one which is lacking or uninhabitable. In my second case history 'Possessed by the devil' (Chapter 8) I will speak about a child with a psychotic structure who had less severe learning disabilities than Wilfried or Eileen. With this child it was possible to communicate verbally as well as by playing with puppets; consequently, the way of working was similar to psychoanalytic play therapy even if instruments and sounds played an important role. Such work along the lines of analytic child psychotherapy is frequently suitable for such patients (and is used increasingly as the therapy progresses), and usually they know very well which materials and forms of play are good for them. As the working methods of psychoanalytic therapy for children are well known, I do not intend to go into them here except in relation to the account of Filippa.

Respect for the patient's autonomy, however destroyed or curtailed it may be, is central to the way of working. Wilfried's and Eileen's ways of surviving are to be respected as 'resistance' (as it is called in psychoanalytic therapy), that is, as rudimentary forms of the capacity to say 'I'. This respectful attitude manifests itself in the way the therapist, instead of seeking to get rid of such symptoms, tries to understand them as an enactment and to communicate this understanding through interpretations. The therapeutic situation is an enactment that is increasingly dominated by the patient's experience providing the therapist knows how to wait in readiness rather than intruding with his or her own wishes, fears, convictions, thereby usurping the space. This means that, as a therapist, I regard all my feelings and impulses as counter-transference and try to understand which role I am playing in the patient's enactment. However, the feelings and desires which the patient brings to the therapy, I understand as transference: I am not really responsible for looking after him, the therapeutic situation is clearly separate from the patient's everyday life in which his problems have developed and in which they continue to exist. Although, unlike the neurotic patient in psychoanalysis, patients with learning disabilities are initially, and often for a long time afterwards, unaware of the difference, it is nonetheless there and is highlighted by my therapeutic activity in which I seek to understand all acting out in the therapy, including, when necessary, actual provision of care, in terms of both its scenic and symbolic meaning.

When I knew Mirko he was a nine-year-old boy who only uttered a few sentences, mostly echolalic, and who kept his mother in a permanent state of terror by throwing missiles at her. He was able to hit her on the head with incredible precision with the result that she had to keep an eye on him almost the whole time. At first he could only tolerate the music therapy situation if I held on to him and listened to music with him on a tape – or rather, this was all I could do, as I was so afraid of his dangerous missiles too. I could sense in the counter-transference that alongside this fear I had feelings of murderous hate (if he were dead, then I would not need to be so afraid), a sense of guilt, and an awareness of being thoroughly inadequate as a therapist because I did not have my hate and fear under control and could only act them out by holding him.

Fear, hate, feelings of guilt and inadequacy also determined the mother's relationship to Mirko. She had not wanted the pregnancy, saw herself as completely incapable as a mother, hated herself, fearing the child and the demands he made on her. The situation was far too much for her and after Mirko's birth she sank into a deep depression from which she could not climb out. She simply functioned 'like a robot', but was inwardly absent. The child began to terrorise her from very early on with his missiles, making her even more depressed than she already was.

He was now repeating this with me in therapy and I was experiencing the mother's distress in my counter-transference: the sense of things being too much, fear of my own hate, fear of the child who was behaving so 'odiously', a sense of being stuck in these feelings, a sense of impotence so that there was no space for playing together. And then I understood that the fear that was making me hold on to Mirko was a response to his own fear of not being held. Fear of not being held . . . a deadly fear of a therapist who was so tied up in her own anxieties that she left him alone, just as his depressed mother left him alone and could not hold him. I realised that he would go on throwing things as long as he had to force me to hold him physically, since he had no experience of a symbiotic holding relationship with a strong mother.

Now there was something I could do: he needed holding, holding physically. For him the situation was still indistinguishable from that of being alone with his mentally absent mother. A symbolic dimension first had to be established but without depriving him of my actual holding; so I went over to the piano with him, held him on my lap, guided his hand, and asked him which song he wanted to play. He asked me for 'There Comes a Birdie' and I guided his hand with mine. I had to do this over and over again, hour after hour. In the end I felt secure enough to leave him for a moment in order to switch the tape recorder on; I explained to him clearly what I was going to do and that I would be back very soon. He did not throw anything at me but I could hear him playing around on the piano which he had never done before. I quickly turned the recorder on, waited, and he started playing, at first hesitantly but quite recognisably 'There Comes a Birdie Flying'.

When he had finished he turned round towards me, gave me an inquiring look (normally his expression was always full of anxiety and unfocused) and also looked at the tape recorder. The distance between us was suddenly no longer bad as his inquiring look enabled him to bridge it; and I told him that I had recorded his playing. I ran the tape back, put it on replay, and when Mirko heard himself, he rushed over to me with joy. At last his voice, which was normally so deep, precocious and compassionate, sounded like a child's, a happy child's voice: he had found himself. This sad song, evoking his loneliness, enabled Mirko to appropriate his own story. It was his own story: his experience was constituted by sadness and loneliness, by the great distance between his mother and himself and for the first time he felt this was being reflected. With the song he was finally able to say 'I': 'I am so dreadfully lonely; I can never go to my mother because she is unreachable except by means of my "missile letters"; that is who I am, and by playing this song, I, Mirko, am introducing myself to you. I exist; and the world is no longer unreachable because my loneliness and my unhappiness in it can be shared because I can listen to my song, because you listened to it.' He also showed me the longing and love he felt for his mother – feelings which had hitherto been bound in his dangerous throwing of missiles and could not be experienced directly, but which he could now take home with him – even if a lot more time would be necessary before there was space for them between him and his mother.

This scene bears witness to the transition from pure acting out to symbolic holding in therapy. A working alliance was created in which the boy began to cease to see me as a pure copy of his mother and to make use of me as a third party who made a recording of him and played his song back to him on the tape. This helped him to find out that the circumstances which had hitherto determined his life did not have to go on for ever, providing he could learn to formulate his longing in an audible and understandable way.

The fact that this is already a form of transference is important for me since, as a therapist, I cannot claim to offer the patient a 'better home'. Unlike Bettelheim, who believed that his autistic patients were best cared for as far away from their parents as possible so that they could have better experiences than they had had previously, I do not think that this is always necessary. After all, parents find themselves in a mutually destructive relationship with their child not because of malevolence but because of distress. Through joint effort – regular consultations with the parents, or by working together with the care-persons in institutions – the vicious circle of the 'derailed' interactions can gradually be broken if, parents, caregivers and therapists can be made aware of the roles they play in the enactment of soul murder.

Bettelheim's 'Orthogenic School', which claims to offer autistic children a 'better environment', may be understood as a deluded attempt to avoid dealing with the institution 'Learning Disability' so as to deny the shame and guilt about its own participation in it. Not only a better home, but an island of good people and love in a world full of badness: this is the concept of denial on the basis of which Bettelheim's School, under his charismatic leadership, has achieved impressive results. It is not a coincidence, however, that the first of the three therapeutic case histories in *The Empty Fortress* was broken off by the parents after their child had made noticeable improvement, and the case report amounts to little more than a complaint against these parents, for there is no place in it for their distress. They are held to be responsible, omnipotently hindering the School from carrying out its saving work. While I am criticising this here, I do not wish in any way to detract from Bettelheim's contribution as a whole. The failure of Laura's therapy simply reiterates clearly the institutional power of 'Learning Disability', and the lesson to be learnt from this is that only reflection, and not denial, can lead to any real progress. Admittedly, this is easier said than done.

Reflection has to begin in the therapeutic work with the patient, in which the therapist understands him/herself not just in terms of his helping role, but also as an agent of the institution 'Learning Disability'. It also means recognising, feeling and interpreting the hate and anger of people with learning disabilities as well as his own role in the therapist–patient relationship. I have shown how difficult this can be with the example of the ending of Wilfried's therapy. Reflection is even more crucial in working with parents or those in charge of a child. Great pains must be taken to work over guilt feelings. In most cases this means initially that I as the therapist have to assume the role of the authority granting absolution, with all the complications that assuming such power implies. Only gradually, as the relationship grows, can this initial dependence be resolved through mutual insight into the mechanisms of guilt feelings, responsibility, and being overstrained. This is only possible when the parents are sure that I do not presume that I can do things better than they can.

In the work with Susanna and her parents the situation became difficult when the parents began to suspect that, alongside their conscious good will and their critical eye for social grievances, they were not strangers to the phantasms of 'Learning Disability'. During several sessions they found me hard and rejecting; they were beginning to fear that I might damage Susanna and the possibility of the therapy being broken off hung heavily in the air. Then they had a major dispute about relatives. The issue was whether these relatives secretly rejected Susanna because she was 'Mongoloid' or whether they could trust in their good will. Finally, the mother told me that at an early stage in our relationship (at the time Susanna was only a few weeks old), I had told them how my first encounter with a 'Mongol' infant had provoked powerful feelings of rejection in me, which had shocked me considerably. When I spoke again about this experience and added that I had been horrified at the time to realise to what extent, in spite of all my conscious efforts, I was still conditioned by social assumptions, the situation became less tense. When I next met the parents, in their flat, the mother asked me to put Susanna to bed. Susanna did not like this at all and cried, but then fell asleep soon after. When she cried, I felt extremely guilty and I realised immediately that the mother now needed to see how I could be hard with Susanna too: like that, she did not have to feel so guilty herself and could feel more confident that causing Susanna day-to-day frustrations of this kind did not mean she was unwittingly participating in society's mechanism of delegating soul murder.

Working with parents can be very onerous, depending on the burden they are saddled with. Under some circumstances, my position as a singular music therapist without the authority of institutional backing is too weak for me to be able to endure the parents' guilty anxiety and needs for absolution. This is especially true when parents have been intensively caught up for some time in the usual guilt-exonerating proposals.

After preliminary discussions, and Ingo's first play session, and a short time before the impending amniotic test during her new pregnancy, Ingo's mother (see Chapter 4, 'The enactment of soul murder') decided to let Ingo start music therapy as soon as possible. What I was offering him was rather different from the various forms of remedial help he had been proposed up till then. It was therefore important for Ingo that, for once, there was no attempt to manipulate the fact that he had learning disabilities; what mattered was for him to be taken seriously in his own right and to have the opportunity to work through the conflicts he had previously put up with on account of his disabilities. In particular, she hoped that he could work on the feelings of anger and fear which she suspected he harboured due to the strong death wishes she had felt towards him during the first year and which he had probably sensed. Both during and after the amniotic test, which had involved complications, I had several telephone conversations with her during which I noticed how, in her distressed state, she was clinging increasingly to the phantasm, and so was losing contact with the thoughts and wishes she had so clearly and openly formulated for Ingo up till then. When she rang again one year later it was on the suggestion of the doctor who had endorsed her application for music therapy. I could tell immediately that our contact was less positive than the year before. In the meantime, Ingo had been given so many different forms of remedial education that I also had doubts whether the addition of this session of music therapy was likely to be of any help to him. While discussing again the aims of my work with the mother, I found it was almost impossible to talk about things that she herself had said the previous year. She then decided against the music therapy: there had been a misunderstanding from the start, she had always imagined that I would use rhythmic exercises to promote the child's motor functioning. She did not feel that what I was offering was right for Ingo. It was clear to me that now that her death wishes had been re-mobilised as a result of the amniotic test, she could no longer tolerate the idea that Ingo's conflicts with her could become a theme of the therapy.

If we still hope to be able to help in such muddled situations, much depends on the conditions of the therapeutic setting. Ingo's mother might have been able to accept my offer if the doctor, as my superior, had been able to support my work rather than just inquiring about it: a doctor, an institution, can offer more reassurance in a situation where societal guilt is being acted out than a young, unknown music therapist working in private practice. Unless one only wants to work with children whose parents, for whatever reasons, can cope better with the insecurities of a private arrangement than others, then it is necessary to have an external institutional support which can lend the provision of therapy more authority and security. However, this would have to be an organisation in which all the rules and modes of relating were continually being reflected upon and were well thought through; otherwise, it would be very easy for things to happen as they did in the Institute for Outpatient Music Therapy where I worked with Filippa (Chapter 8, 'Possessed by the devil'). The distress and anxiety of such severely disturbed patients and their parents provokes both in me and in those with whom I work, major counter-transference responses which, if they are not understood and worked through by the group as a whole, very quickly arouse society's tendencies to exclude such *lebensunwertes Leben*.

Notwithstanding all these conditions, it is of course the therapist's personal motivation that is the most important factor: what drives me to do this difficult work of all things? It is quite clear that it scarcely provides the gratifications which psychotherapy otherwise can offer. Quick, clearly visible, demonstrable successes are rare; one always has to reckon with setbacks, with the possibility of therapy being broken off, and long stretches when there is no apparent progress, no movement. The work is often boring and frustrating; for the most part it is exhausting and can even affect my private life. Sometimes I am faced with real dangers that have to be weighed up carefully beforehand and, under certain circumstances, measures of self-protection have to be taken. Furthermore, it is uncertain whether the therapy is in the end at all helpful, especially with older patients with learning disabilities whose hopes have foundered over the years; or whether one's own strength and the possibilities at one's disposal will be adequate to survive the therapy, as long as is necessary, through all the crises and dangers which are not always foreseeable; and, finally, whether something unforeseeable will not make me myself break off the therapy prematurely.

Why then, when there is so much that speaks against it, would anyone do this work at all, and even do it with pleasure? Phantasies of different kinds may be involved, such as phantasies of grandeur or phantasies of saving people; there may be longings for fusion and regression, longings to escape from the terror of having to perform and the compulsive activity of everyday life into the symbiotic holding of the therapeutic space; fears of failure are easier to tolerate if one knows that success can hardly be expected and that the patients in their state of hopelessness do not expect or require the therapy to 'bring something'. Such phantasies are not forbidden and in fact always form the basis of therapeutic work; but, it is important that as a therapist I am aware of them as counter-transference responses to the institution 'Learning Disability', otherwise they can have a detrimental effect on the therapy. While omnipotent phantasies of grandeur determine my work, my personal leaning is to specialise in working with autistic children whose aura of being special I then hope to share. Such a choice is justifiable but when the reverse side of this, i.e. despising those who are well-adapted, is not properly worked through, then the therapist's projective identification can lead to blocks in understanding. Or, if I bring my own yearnings for fusion, which is part of the work with children who have severe learning disabilities, then there is a danger of my overlooking or misinterpreting the patients' often weak signs of readiness to free themselves from the symbiotic situation.

There are sufficient grounds for declining psychotherapeutic work with patients who have learning disabilities – reasons which lie not with the patients but with ourselves and our capacities, fears, limits and desires which are determined by socially organised defences. The reasons are justified on a personal level but projective labelling 'unsuitable for psychotherapy' is too readily used to cover them, and this is the point I wanted to make here. In any case, in order to be able to do such work profitably for both my patients and myself, I have to be able to enjoy small things like being fascinated by a rolling ball or listening to the clang of a cymbal. However difficult and exhausting this work may be, it is a source of quite unusual and positive experiences. One can accept that doing psychotherapy with patients with learning disabilities will only lead in exceptional cases to them being able to live independently of institutional regimentation. But is it not already a satisfaction to see that, after two years of music therapy, Wilfried has now gained so much space that he can sometimes get the often overworked caregivers to participate in a game of football? He knows, moreover, how to make himself popular by using his roguish smile to make contact with others. He was thus one of a small group of men with severe learning disabilities to be selected to leave the institution in order to live in a community in the country which offered more human ways of living. Wilfried's newly awakened longings will have a much better chance of being satisfied here than in the institution.

Chapter 7

A child without behavioural difficulties

Inge, like Wilfried, was one of my first patients. I worked with her for two years, five times a week. Seldom have I had to tolerate so much discouragement and boredom in a therapy; seldom has a child tried my patience and desire to understand so severely. And yet, or probably because of this, long after the therapy had been broken off, I looked for an opportunity to take her on again under different conditions. Inge and Wilfried have taught me a lot more than any institutional therapy training and I shall always be thankful to them. My grief at having to leave Inge and my wish to hold on to the beautiful experiences which I shared with her moved me, shortly after the therapy ended, to write the following report. I am giving it again here in only a slightly modified form, even though it clearly records how much difficulty I had in coming to any understanding at that time and just how little I understood.

Emerging from a state of numbness

When I began the music therapy with Inge she was seven years old and had just been taken into the institution. After the long illness and eventual death of her husband, her physically disabled mother had suffered a nervous breakdown and, even after recovering, did not feel she was in a position to take care of her daughter any longer at home.

The new patient proved to be an 'unproblematic case'. She was easy to manage; she was dry and clean provided she was put regularly on the toilet; she was relatively undemanding and expressed no needs; she showed no disturbing 'behavioural traits' and always seemed satisfied with what was offered her. Although she was one of a number of well-behaved patients, she nonetheless received a surprising amount of attention.

Admittedly, Inge did have one striking feature: she was an unusually beautiful child. Everyone wanted to have contact with her, but she would not have contact with anyone. This was an insult that could not be accepted so easily. Consequently, she was given therapy; someone on the ward was given the special responsibility of looking after her, and home visits to her mother were arranged. Finally, when nothing seemed to help (after four months of music therapy), a case seminar was convened.

Inge was put into care with the diagnosis 'severe mental retardation with mild locomotor retardation, probably as a result of brain damage in infancy of unknown causes'. Now I will give a few details on her history: when she was born, her mother was thirty-seven and her father thirty-nine years old. She had a brother, three years older than her, who had developed normally. Inge was born one month prematurely, after a complicated pregnancy, was frequently ill during her infancy, was late in learning to walk and could not stand up from the sitting position. Her father was said to have given her a great deal of care when he was alive but he apparently became very difficult, behaving, especially after the onset of his illness, as if he was the third child of his wife who herself was ill. According to the medical file, her brother played with Inge 'on a level involving intense bodily contact' and sometimes she really seemed to enjoy it. Apart from this, hardly anyone had succeeded in establishing contact with the child. Inge had not learnt to speak at all.

Inge's main activity consisted in waving back and forth or in crumpling paper, plastic bags, plush, spoons, or else round or plastic revolving objects. Furthermore, she enjoyed handling water, sand, hair, and small solid balls, although this never developed into a recognisable play activity. Now and then she reacted pleasurably to noises such as splashing water, hand-clapping and the rustling of paper. If someone made these noises for her, she would sometimes spread out her arms and clumsily wave them around, sometimes laughing and squealing a little too, while moving stiffly from one leg to the other. Sometimes she would do this for no obvious reason so that one could never be certain whether she was really responding to the noises or not. Generally speaking, Inge spent the whole day quietly and unobtrusively, thoroughly indifferent to what was happening around her. Now and then she would make vocal sounds, the rudimentary nature of which was particularly reminiscent of the sounds made by infants in the first weeks of life. She often masturbated by pressing her drawn up legs together while lying on the floor or bed. She would often sit in a corner (but never, of her own choice, on the floor) – in the music therapy room there was a large armchair for her – draw up her legs and stop her ears for no apparent reason. Inge could not stand on one leg, found it difficult to negotiate steps, particularly when descending, and could never pull herself up from the floor without help. At one stage a mild cerebral palsy was even suspected. Inge reacted to loud music or a hectic atmosphere and, sometimes, to going to the toilet, by bursting into tears; occasionally, she would cry for no obvious reason so that one could not be sure whether the supposed reasons for her crying really had anything to do with it.

After visiting Inge's mother in her flat, a few months after Inge had been taken into the institution, the person in charge of her ward reported that the mother had cooked a big pudding which she spoon-fed to the child. As the pudding was being eaten, the spoon remained the only means of contact between mother and daughter while the brother gave Inge a lot of attention 'on the level of bodily contact' during the visit.

In the music therapy I endeavoured from the start to create an atmosphere which I thought would be pleasant and secure for Inge. First, I experimented with pre-structuring measures. I played tapes on which I had recorded the sounds of running and gurgling water, waves and other sounds of nature; or I brought along music with me which seemed to correspond on an affective level to what I was experiencing with Inge. Particularly important for me were Domenico Scarlatti's harpsichord sonatas (from which I learned that Scarlatti had dedicated them all to his unhappy beloved whom he had followed to Spain when she was to be married to the King of Spain. It was precisely such a situation of inaccessibility which was being enacted in the relationship between Inge and me). After a period of getting to know each other, I tried to create a safe situation just by doing things together. The beginning and ending rituals, as well as the room with the armchair, which we never changed, provided a framework which held together what we were doing even when it seemed to be utterly meaningless and arbitrary.

Going on the preliminary information I had at my disposal, I gathered together materials which I thought were likely to interest Inge: solid balls made of different materials and of different sizes, either singly or several together in different containers (tins, tambourines, etc), water in a large bucket, rattles, clappers, paper and spoons. We played standing up or sitting on the floor. I drew Inge's attention to these things by waving or rattling them in front of her and then held them out to her or rolled them to her if she put out her hand. She would take hold of them but, in most cases, only to drop them again immediately, as if unintentionally, and I would then begin the game all over again. I made rustling sounds with paper for her and sometimes she would come over to me with joy and snatch at the paper. She tore a few strips up, waved them around and threw the rest away with indifference. She would scratch the rattles and clappers 'casually', and then drop them as well. If I held my hand out, then she would sometimes hand the instrument back to me. For the first time, after more than three months, as she was giving the instrument back she looked expectantly at my hand. This was the first sign of development, which I was very happy and excited about. Now Inge was able to anticipate my rattling, clapping and rustling.

Inge and I played with solid balls, sitting mostly on the floor. I would let the balls fall into a bucket of water, onto a cymbal or a tambourine, with several of them rolling around in the tambourine; or, I would tap and scratch one of the larger balls and then roll it towards her. Inge would pick it up, scratch it or put it into her mouth, finally letting go of it heedlessly; with increasing frequency the ball would fall, as if fortuitously, in my direction. For a while, at least, all these games made her happy provided she did not decide to withdraw completely, which, to my discouragement, happened all too often. At some point, mostly fairly rapidly, she would lose all interest in such games, start masturbating, or coil up on the floor or in her armchair with her hands over her ears. It was then up to me to find the next game that was likely to arouse her interest. There were repeated sessions when the only thing that held her interest was splashing water and where she spent most of the time in her chair. I found such sessions particularly wearing. Inge only looked at me, or rather through me, rarely, and even this was fortuitous and fleeting. When something made her happy, she looked first at the instrument, then at my hand, yet seemed not to notice me myself. When she met people outside the therapy situation she persisted in her indifference and showed no signs of recognition.

Things went on like this for about four months. Hardly anything seemed to change. I could not understand Inge's changing willingness to play, nor her occasional crying. Increasingly, I felt listless, unable to concentrate; the sessions dragged on endlessly and bored me. Had I perhaps overestimated what Inge and I could do when I began this work with her? Were we not dealing here in fact with an insurmountable organic handicap? Or was the stagnation due to my doing something completely wrong? My self-confidence dwindled noticeably. It was in this situation that the above-mentioned case seminar was set up. There was general sense of perplexity, a sense of impasse and not being able to go on. By speaking about this state of perplexity and discouragement, I regained a bit of my courage, and, feeling that I was not prepared to give in to the onset of resignation, insisted that there had to be a way of understanding Inge's withdrawals, her inaccessibility and her stagnation. I suggested that Inge's movements away from me should not only be accepted but even encouraged, for only then would she be able to develop the confidence which she was so clearly lacking, which also made itself felt in the case seminar in the form of perplexity and a lack of self-confidence. An observation was then made which for me became the key to understanding: sometimes in the past, Inge had fallen down while running around in the garden and had sat there for hours completely 'indifferent', for she could not get up by herself and her lame mother could not get to her because she did not have the necessary assistance. My advice made good sense and from that moment on I was acknowledged as being Inge's specialist. This brought with it both a sense of obligation and encouragement and was crucial in helping me get through the next six months; it took that long until the tiniest alterations of detail in our play signalled the beginnings of a process of development. (Seldom had I been so lucky to have the support of my mainly 'learning theory' oriented colleagues, but rarely had I needed it so much either as with Inge!)

We had found a few new games without, however, giving up the old ones (indeed, we kept these up throughout the entire length of the therapy). I now threw the ball to her frequently in such a way that it bounced on the tambourine on the way. Once she had it in her hand, she began to throw it back to me with increasing regularity, at first, as if unintentionally, but then clearly aiming to do so, and sometimes over the tambourine that was between us. Another game was to make a ball run through a pipe and fall into some water or onto a drum. The invisible ball could be heard rolling inside the pipe. Sometimes Inge directed her gaze at the end of the pipe where she expected the ball to come out. When she handed me instruments, she tended to look up more often from my hand to my face. I had the feeling that she was beginning to see me as a whole person. In her encounters outside the music therapy, she also now sometimes showed vague signs of recognising people. When she was sitting on the floor in therapy and was unable to reach an instrument or ball directly, she did not ignore it any more as she had done previously, but even made attempts to get hold of these things. (She could not crawl but she began to pull herself forward a bit with her legs.) I observed all such changes with great delight as they seemed at last to confirm that my efforts for Inge were not in vain.

It was just when these developments were taking place that I was due to take my summer holiday. When I returned, Inge was ill and for nearly half a year it was not possible to continue the music therapy because she caught one bout of flu after another and was visibly deteriorating. The doctor was very concerned and perplexed because there was actually 'nothing wrong with her'. I assumed that I had failed her at a critical time and so visited her regularly. When we were able to work, if at all, less happened, for the most part, than in the initial phase of her treatment. Often, she would just sit on my lap and we would pass a ball or a scrap of paper back and forth to each other. During this period I often sang songs and tunes to her which I made up, especially when I had to visit her on the hospital ward. There she occasionally greeted me from afar – these were great moments – laughing, with her arms wide open; but mostly she was completely apathetic. During my visits our games were confined to exchanging vocal sounds and it was never clear whether Inge could even hear me. She just liked stroking my fur coat, which I wore regularly to please her.

At times she would pull my long hair. It was a very sad time during which I was often on the brink of giving up; only the support of colleagues and the rare wonderful moments when she greeted me kept me going.

When Inge was well again, and could come regularly, we were able within a few weeks to get the whole process of development going again. I now introduced a few songs, one of which, the Hoppe-Reiter song, acquired particular significance as a farewell game. The reason I chose this was the vague impression I had that Inge's vocal expression was, on the whole, a little more structured now, as well as the fact that I had noticed that she now often looked at me in the face. She soon got to know the song, clung on to my hair, and gave me a happy laugh as soon as the final lines of the song ('then the rider goes plop') came, whereupon I gently let her fall over backwards. If she was in a particularly good mood, there were times when, in a state of jubilation, she let herself fall without holding on, quite confident that I would hold her. Often she did not like to wait for the end of the song and, laughing, let herself fall backwards repeatedly.

Together we discovered another game: I ran out through the door of the music therapy room and disappeared out of sight, making myself heard clearly around the corner with a rattle. She followed me hesitantly and for an instant a joyful expression of recognition came over her face and she laughed with delight when I reappeared shaking the rattle. Eventually, I could hide without needing to draw attention to my presence with the rattle.

We continued to play all the usual, well-known games, but now Inge was much more purposive and happier in her play. Sessions during which she completely withdrew became less frequent, but still occurred nonetheless. I still did not understand what these withdrawals were connected with and felt disappointed in such sessions.

At this stage in the process I had a probationer with me, called Bernd, who already knew Inge from a practical placement he had done on a ward. After a period of passively sitting in on the session, I let him take over the therapy and took part in the sessions myself as co-therapist. This was not easy and I felt jealous – in fact I wanted to be able to share Inge's joyful participation in the games during sessions for which I had had to do so much groundwork, for so long, and with so many setbacks. Initially, there was a look of disappointment on Inge's face when she saw Bernd, and not me. In addition, I had some misgivings about letting a probationer take over the therapy at such an important stage. A determining factor in my decision was that I was planning to leave the institution and hoped that Bernd would be able to continue the therapy after that. After the initial disappointment, Inge soon accepted the new situation.

During the final six months the long-awaited success began to manifest itself. Inge began to develop so quickly that I was quite beside myself with joy. The shadows cast by the prospect of the impending end of our work were correspondingly darker. I tried to deny my sadness, investing hope in the continuation of the therapy with Bernd and in the fact that I would be able to come back in a year's time (I had decided to go to London to be trained as a music therapist, as I had no qualification, in the hope then of being able to take up a post in the institution which would be more advantageous for my work than my current status as an untrained beginner). I was not aware that Inge must have noticed my inner struggles, my sadness, and my parting. I thus tried to protect myself against guilt feelings and in so doing saddled myself, first and foremost, with guilt.

Although up till then Inge had generally not responded to sophisticated sounds – a few exceptions had been the games in which she had at least been able to tolerate the tambourine notes which served to illustrate the rhythmic structure of our ball games – now, within a short time, she developed an interest in playing on the drums, and then the xylophone and piano as well. She drew my attention to her new interests in a peculiar way: she walked past the instrument, waving a drumstick, and produced a note 'quite unintentionally'. I picked up the drumstick as soon as she had dropped it as usual and began to play on the drums or the xylophone for her. An expression of joyful surprise appeared on her face. Inge steered my attention towards the piano because whenever she sat on her chair which was near the piano she always 'needed' to support herself by leaning on the keyboard. Soon she clearly preferred the harmonically sophisticated instruments, the xylophone and piano, to the drums. Inge guided my hand or let her hand be guided while playing; sometimes, if I stood behind her and gave her support, she would even play a few notes of her own accord. One day I had the impression that Inge's vocal sounds were suggestive of the Hoppe-Reiter song. I was not sure of this, however – as usual I could hardly believe my ears – until a few days later, with the same sounds that had always seemed to me like those of a tiny baby, Inge quite perceptibly intoned the refrain from 'Obladi-Oblada'.[1] I could scarcely believe it: I had not known until a few months before whether she was even aware of her surroundings at all, and here she was singing a hit song which was in vogue years ago! We could now hear her intoning this and another hit from her childhood regularly in fragments, and occasionally some words were even recognisable. I was over the moon!

When Bernd and I had tracked down copies of the hits and were able to play her the recordings, the response was overwhelming: she lifted up her little skirt and, with her legs apart, swayed from one foot to the other, clearly trying to keep in step with the rhythm of the music, beaming at me with joy. (If anyone makes the reproach, as in fact happened once at a music therapy conference, that working for so long and so intensively with a child until she 'can at last play the xylophone' is an incredible waste of time and money, then I can only say that I would give up the whole world to see such a happy face.)

Soon after Inge had mastered the xylophone and piano, she began to explore the surroundings of the music therapy room. My game of hide-and-seek had showed her that there was a world outside, too. Now she began to open the door, whereas before she had never showed any signs of wanting or being able to do this. She did it hesitantly at first, finally daring to take a few steps outside. When she then heard me coming after her, clip-clopping in my wooden shoes, she began running, laughing and shouting with joy, and she loved it when I went ahead of her and whisked her up in my open arms.

Once Bernd had taken over the role of therapist, she eventually took hold of his hand during a game (this was also a new active step on her part); or she would go ahead alone, clearly confident that he would follow her. She explored with curiosity all the floors and open doors in the area. I accompanied these explorations by improvising with her hit songs. She came back later when she heard me playing 'Obladi', stood for a while next to the piano, watching me proudly and radiant with joy, only to run off again laughing, almost immediately.

It was at this time that Inge showed signs at long last of 'maladjusted behaviour': now that she could open doors by herself, she often went into the kitchen and nibbled at cakes and biscuits if she could find them.

The parting was sad. It turned out that Bernd would not be able to take over the therapy. I did not know how we should prepare Inge for this news; helplessly, I simply brought cakes with me to the last session which she broke into crumbs, eating a few of them indifferently and 'losing' the rest. How right she was, too! I felt miserable, as if I was doing something unforgivable.

I met her a few more times after her last session, during my last days in the institution, and in these encounters she responded quite differently: she saw me coming from afar, looked incredibly surprised and then ran towards me to take me by the hand and drag me towards the music therapy room. I would never have thought that she would be able to find her bearings so well in the large grounds of the institution! The last meeting took place when she was in a big play enclosure with other children from her ward. She recognised me through the fence and ran over towards me; she stood by the fence, laughing, but then the expression of indifference reappeared on her face and she turned and went: she could no longer come to me.

Inge reacted to this separation as she had done the year before, by falling ill again.

Psychotherapy without words

I was able to infer very little from the little I had gleaned about Inge's early childhood. One thing seemed certain: her mother was hopelessly overworked. She was temporarily bound to her wheelchair (whether she suffered from cerebral palsy or from multiple sclerosis was not known); she was working, and had had to take care of her severely ill husband shortly after Inge's birth, as well as a toddler and a particularly demanding infant, which Inge had certainly been as a result of her premature birth and fragile health. Although I hardly understood the importance of it initially, the first central thought which came to me during the therapy was in fact related to this: 'Inge always remains where she is, immobile'. She would always stay in a pre-adopted or assigned position until someone got her out of it and had not developed any capacities which would have allowed her to move by herself. She could walk, but she could not sit down or get up from the floor (as we were nearing the end of the therapy she began to show signs of being able to do this), she found steps awkward to manage and could only do so when someone was with her. A key to understanding this was provided with a story from her past: once when Inge had fallen over in the garden, she remained sitting for hours because her mother was unable to come to her aid. Clearly, only by remaining in a state of indifference and inner numbness could Inge avoid the experience of symbiotic dependence which must have seemed life-threatening for her because, as a 'symbiotic part object', her mother had frequently simply not been there. But it was precisely because it was impossible for her to experience her real dependency on her present, yet unavailable mother (neither the father who worked all day nor the brother who went to a kindergarten could take her place), that she was hindered from trying to separate. As such attempts are regularly linked with failure, i.e. a relapse into even greater dependency, this was a risk Inge could not take without the reliable presence of a supportive mother. Because she had to avoid experiencing dependence at any price, all steps towards perceiving the environment and autonomy were barred.

The things Inge showed a preference for, like sand, water, plush, hair, rotating and swinging movements, as well as noises made with materials suggestive of sand and water, made it easier for her to remain immobile by helping her to avoid or disavow separation experiences. Inge tried to remain in the experiential form of the 'primary substances' and the experience she lacked most was that of indestructibility. Her mother was not indestructible: all too often she had not been able to help, and Inge must have had the impression that her behaviour, her falling over, had destroyed her mother. And she was also not indestructible because she tortured herself with guilt feelings when she had to leave Inge alone like that – so she was probably unable in such situations, even by talking to her, to keep the relationship alive. In order to remain in this state of indifference, which had long been contradicted by the state of her sensory-motor development, Inge warded off, whenever possible, any experience which disturbed the 'harmonious interpenetrating mix-up', or which threatened to break through her denial of the object world. This explains why she cried when she heard noises which were too loud for her, as well as the partial improvement she had made in practical skills in daily life in comparison with her psychical development. She was now able to get dressed and undressed by herself with little help, but could still not open any doors.

Now Inge's 'indifference' and stagnation in the music therapy are understandable. If, for instance, in the ball game, she had not let the ball fall in my direction 'accidentally' but had done so on purpose, she would have made herself dependent on me by expecting me to pick the ball up and throw it back. Only after I had rolled or handed the ball back reliably on countless occasions – in spite of considerable feelings of boredom and discouragement – and she had not been destroyed (at times the game was purely confined to giving and taking while I held her on my lap – at these moments she could not even tolerate the space between us) was she able to make a game out of her apparently haphazard losing of the ball. In this context the apparently insignificant change that occurred when she handed back a ball or an instrument, of looking at my hand expectantly, may be understood as a first step towards acknowledging symbiotic dependence.

The only active forms of behaviour which Inge showed – stopping her ears and masturbating with her thighs pressed together – involved closing bodily orifices, shutting herself off against possible impingements from outside. At times, I had the impression she was retreating from the stimuli I was producing; for example, if these were no longer confined to limits that were acceptable for her because, due to my impatience and worry about being a bad music therapist, I was allowing myself to be drawn into an active-seductive role. This is a role that the brother may have filled in her infancy – his games with Inge 'on the level of bodily contact' were probably determined by sexual excitation, which is not surprising for a 'normally developed' child of his age. For Inge, who had no possibility of elaborating genital excitement, this may well have been sexually traumatic. As she was not even able to tolerate the external demands made on her, how could she reconcile the demands of such intense stimulation on her own body with her laboriously sustained denial of any kind of object world, including her own? So she attempted to cope with the stimulation and ward off further excitement by completely shutting herself off, evacuating the tension through masturbation.

My therapeutic method of working was frequently one of groping in the dark – only gradually, and only after the therapy had ended, was I able to develop a partial understanding of Inge's problems and of what had transpired between us. However, it was precisely this groping and my readiness to let myself be guided by Inge that had apparently allowed things to develop in the right direction.

My preliminary diagnostic ideas allowed me to infer that I first had to offer myself to Inge as a reliable symbiotic object to relate to so that, in the security of the symbiotic situation, she could take her own first steps of development. The games that were so central to almost the whole of the first year of treatment need to be understood against the background of this objective. Her basic structure was largely the same. I took a non-directed and seemingly fortuitous movement of Inge's as being a form of giving; I picked up what she dropped, thereby giving a structure to these goings-on. This continued with me reproducing her haphazard noises for her, holding out the instrument to her, rolling the ball back to her. By having her incidental movements accepted and returned to her, they began to acquire significance and meaning for her. This was her first experience of play. Here I was taking on what Winnicott calls the mirroring role of the mother and psychotherapist. When Inge began looking, first, at my hand holding the instrument, and then directly at my face, this was a clear indication that we were now relating at a symbiotic level. By gazing into my face, she could find herself mirrored there and experience herself for the first time in the union with me as an entity separate from the environment. At the same time her gaze, full of expectancy, showed that she was beginning to 'use' me in Winnicott's sense of the word. On the basis of this dual unit, differentiation into self and object representations, i.e. the process of separation and individuation could begin. The games we were beginning to play ushered this process in. The game with the pipe or tube gave Inge her first experience of something she could not feel or see, but could still hear. The logical follow-up to this was the game of hide-and-seek where I myself now vanished outside her field of vision and tried to keep myself alive in her memory by producing clapping sounds. The way she followed me hesitantly showed how she was trying to build up an inner image of me. Her game of running away was a reversal of this situation, her first active step of separation. Here too, it was very important that I signalled my 'survival' of this step with the clip-clopping sound of my shoes as I ran after her. Another step in this direction was structuring the process of throwing the ball back and forth by means of the tambourine. The ensuing sound was different from our usual sand and plush sounds due to its considerably greater sophistication; and, it was the first and, for a long time to come, the only one of its kind that Inge could accept without needing to withdraw. Its most significant difference from the sand and plush sounds was its poignant brevity: it no longer had the potentially endless and indestructible quality of the ball game but was unmistakably limited. It thus represented a first separation process. Its limitation gave the tone the characteristics of an object and allowed it to take the position of a third party in our relationship which – so I thought – would represent our playful interaction in Inge's memory and so be able to replace it for a while. This expectation was confirmed as Inge discovered the drum 'by chance', which was her own way of being cautious. There was a clear expression of recognition on her face. An important step towards separation had now been taken: Inge was able to bring one of our play situations to memory when it was not a present reality and, what is more, did so in my presence. Our relationship had now acquired a past, a history, which we could mutually tell each other by means of the drum tone. It had become a symbol of our particular interaction. In this symbol, self and object representations were as yet undifferentiated.

From here things could develop quickly to the next stage: as Inge's interest was awakened by more and more clearly defined tones which could be experimented with in the music therapy, she discovered singing by herself. So she was able to suggest the first hit song 'Obladi' and could recognise it on the tape. The happy expression on her face was one of recalling something that had been missed for a long time (I saw the same expression on her face when I visited her there a year after leaving the

institution). The context in which this occurred showed all the characteristics of early triangulation; that is, the period of pre-oedipal development in which the father or another person, other than the mother, is
clearly perceived in his or her own right. The father acquires importance as
the one who can protect the child from the mother who, because she is still
a symbiotic caregiver, seems threatening to the child in his attempts to
separate from her. At the same time, the father is the one who the child can
turn towards as a first 'other-than-mother' object. He helps to keep the
yearning for, and simultaneous fear of, the symbiotic mother within
tolerable limits – fear of falling back into symbiosis and of being punished
for abandoning her. A number of factors suggested the onset of triangulation: Inge's capacity to differentiate between Bernd and I, expressed in the
look of disappointment on her face as he went to meet her in my place; the
jealousy that I experienced in the counter-transference, but also the decision
to let Bernd take over the therapy in the first place; the increasing importance of triangular situations in play between therapist and patient, with the
tone, drumstick and cassette recorder as the third party. The emergence of
songs in this situation allowed me to infer that these were connected with
Inge's memories of her father. The touching gesture of lifting up her skirt –
the opposite of shutting herself off in masturbation – was also suggestive of
this. Be that as it may, it is certain that the introduction of songs enabled
Inge to begin to bring into the therapy memories from her early childhood
on a symbolic level and not simply through acting out. This event could be
understood as the beginning of a therapeutic working alliance. The triangular structure occurred again in the Hoppe-Reiter game. This time the
song represented the third party by ushering in and accompanying the
mutually shared situation with self and object representations still united. It
enabled us to work over the earlier traumatic experience of the long holiday
separation. I dropped her, and yet I picked her up again. At the same time
the song was also an invitation to Inge to leave behind the symbiotic
situation with me in which she would fall over backwards. Inge's joy in
letting herself fall over was a clear expression of thrills, a reaction to
awareness of the separation of self and object. That is to say, her self was
now able to expose itself with confidence to the anxiety-producing and
pleasurable situation of abandonment, of letting itself fall over. It could
give up the safety of the ground beneath it, confident in the continuity of
relationship, in the object's capacity to wait and hold, which could now be
perceived as separate from the self.

Thrills were also recognisable in Inge's laughing when she ran away from
me and heard me running after her making a rattling sound. Here, more
clearly than in the game of hide-and-seek, this rattling acquired the
significance of a first symbol with differentiated object representation. A
further step in the differentiation of self and object representations were
Inge's extensive walks which she took in Bernd's company while I showed

her that I was still there – now I always stayed where I was – at the piano. These walks also allowed her to explore areas where my piano playing was scarcely audible or could not be heard at all. She seemed to do this intentionally because she showed a preference for such places. Now she could leave, escape from the sphere of 'plush', of infinity, of indestructibility (my uninterrupted piano playing), by herself: a clear act of 'destroying the object' and of aggression which I survived, something she could at last have confidence in. When she then came back and greeted me at the piano, she was clearly proud that she had asserted herself like that. A precursor of this 'destruction of the object', setting the latter outside the omnipotent control of the self and also outside the symbiosis, was the 'indifferent' dropping of play materials which, for such a long time, had been her only activity.

The aggressive aspect of her throwing away movement was dominated by her fear of being abandoned and concealed in her 'fortuitousness'. A clearly aggressive intention was, on the other hand, already recognisable in her dropping of things during the Hoppe-Reiter game; her habit of holding on to my hair was certainly also determined by her continuing lack of trust, but the aggression was clearly noticeable and quite painful for me. In the further step she took of breaking through the limits of my audibility on her explorative walks, it was possible for her for the first time to experience real trust and real separation. I have already looked at the role which sounds and rhythms can play in therapeutic development in Chapter 6, 'Attempts at breaking out'. Nevertheless, at the risk of repeating myself, I would like to outline once again their significance in Inge's development. The shift of meaning which these materials underwent in her psychic development, and which makes them so suitable for psychotherapeutic work with people with learning disabilities who do not speak, was clearly visible in this therapy. First, the 'plush' sounds, including the taped music, formed a tremendous space in which Inge and I could encounter each other. She filled the emptiness between us with friendly vibrations and enveloped us in a mutual touching. Thus they provided protection against loneliness and external impingements, creating a symbiotic atmosphere. These potentially unlimited noises were now subject to interruptions because Inge let me give her the instrument or because she dropped it. By picking up the dropped instrument, her subjective-object, I was picking her up, the one who was always dropping out of our relationship.

Through the interruption of sounds Inge had her first experience of self-determined temporal organisation which did not have to founder in the indifference of humdrum daily existence. She created a past and ultimately, with her expectant gaze, a future too. So the potentially infinite, indestructible, symbiosis-creating sounds uniting us became precursors of the emergence of memory which became possible with separation and triangulation.

Being held by sound allowed Inge the space, when she felt like it, to distance herself from me. It was both real holding – through the vibrating air

– as well as symbolic holding. It could reproduce and represent her situation. Sound thus offered itself as a transitional phenomenon. In the therapy with Inge it was of the greatest importance that both the audible as well as self-produced sounds, even when they were 'unintentional', could acquire such meaning. With such transitional objects self and object representations are still united, but as they become differentiated, they can be of decisive help. In the evolution that occurred in the different games – including the pipe game, the game of hide-and-seek, the game in which I ran after her with my shoes clacking and the explorative walks accompanied by my playing the piano – the 'plushy', persisting, reliable sounds became the first symbol for Inge which had the unmistakable character of an object representation. At this time Inge began to discover individual tones by herself. These helped the organisation of a self-representation. This found clear expression in the songs: Inge used them to present herself with her own identity, her own history separate from mine, in the situation that we created together. By including the songs in my piano improvisations, Inge could feel she had a place in my memory, just as she could bring me to mind through the plushy sounds. It is worth noting how the passive experience of the quality of the sounds coming from outside contributed to the formation of the object representation, while the active bodily experience of producing sounds supported the formation of the self-representation.

Final farewell

Barely a year after I had left the institute, I returned to visit Inge again. It was still unclear whether I would ever come again, although I would very much have liked to on account of Inge. She recognised me immediately and she had that overjoyed look on her face that I recognised from the time when she had rediscovered her songs. She ran towards me, and wanted to leave the ward with me; but, when I did not follow, she turned away 'with indifference', only to try again immediately. I felt torn inwardly: I was also happy to see her again and pleased that she recognised me after so long; naively enough I had never imagined this situation. What was intolerable was the idea that I might have to disappoint Inge.

One and a half years later, there was renewed hope that I would be able to take up the work with her again. I visited her again, without really knowing. She recognised me this time, too, but reacted quite differently: after a quick look of recognition, she turned away resolutely and remained lying with her back to me. I waited, sitting next to her on her bed. Eventually, she turned towards me again, with a look which seemed to say: 'Am I really to believe that you are there, are you not an illusion which will suddenly vanish again?' (the meaning of Inge's behaviour was so much clearer to me now – I wondered how much emptiness and withdrawal I might have been able to spare us, if I had been able to understand more at the time of the therapy). She showed a flicker of joy at meeting again, then turned her back once more, making a game out of this coming and going. Then she stood up and her gaze fell briefly on the mirror next to her bed; when I stood behind her, she recognised us in the mirror and laughed. I introduced us to each other: 'That is you, Inge, and that is me, Dietmut'. 'Nnge-Nnge-Nnge', she replied, and I remembered that towards the end of our work she had begun to pronounce her name in this way. I had so often tried to bring her out of her infinite loneliness in this way. We both laughed and we had a few moments of real happiness together: she, a rather vain girl, going through puberty, and I, unable for a few moments to deny that I might have to give her up for lost. Eventually she went over to the door and stood there on the threshold. There was a great tension in her – even a passing caregiver was able to sense this tension – revolving around the question: 'Will I be able to get out of here?' Unlike me, she saw that we would not be able to overcome the fence that the institution 'Learning Disability' had put between us. She turned round resolutely, lay down on her bed again, and stayed there with her back turned towards me. I respected her decision and left. This was the last time we saw each other.

Chapter 8

Possessed by the devil

I worked with Filippa at the Institute for Outpatient Music Therapy. When I took up my position there, I was full of enthusiasm about the facilities which seemed to correspond entirely to the framework I had imagined as being suitable for my work. The children were treated free of charge and the therapists were paid for the most part with public funding. I had been employed with the idea that I would take on children with learning disabilities as well as autistic or infantile psychotic children. This very much corresponded to what I wanted and so I overlooked the fact that, since the opening of the Institute a few years earlier a whole string of colleagues had already worked there before me and after a short time had all been dismissed or had resigned. My recent unemployment was an additional reason for me to overlook this. Soon, of course, I was faced with the same difficulties which had been the stumbling-block of my predecessors.

A short while after taking up the post, I began the therapy with Filippa. Whereas previously my therapies had gone calmly and smoothly (just one case of an adolescent with a learning disability had been difficult and caused offence – after giving in my notice, I was able to find an arrangement for continuing his therapy), the work with Filippa and her mother was likely to affect the whole Institute. I would have needed the support of those in charge of the Institute – instead of which, however, I reaped reproaches. I was forbidden from continuing my work with the mother in the Institute for several reasons: first, it was felt that this woman was not worth my trouble; secondly, the sessions with Filippa were 'too noisy' and, also at times I could not prevent something getting broken. So we were banished to a small room with no windows. I was willing to continue the therapy but being sidelined like this exceeded my limits of tolerance. I managed to make a temporary arrangement for the therapies to continue to be financed through the Institute, while looking simultaneously for a way to continue privately. But Filippa's therapy ran aground due to the strength of this institutional counter-transference reaction, the latter being closely reflected by the fate ascribed to those with learning disabilities by the institution 'Learning Disability'. This was confirmed once again in the case of Filippa and her mother; i.e. that unruliness and aggression, which Filippa acted out, result in exclusion.

The therapy failed, though, not simply because of the reaction of the Institute, but also because I could not extricate myself from the panic involved in the counter-acting out of the Institute's management, as well as in the relationship between mother and child, allowing myself to be caught up and dominated by it in my therapeutic work. I should have been more cautious, slowing down Filippa's furious work tempo so as not to overtax the mother, who herself was so severely disturbed that Filippa played an indispensable role in her defence against psychotic anxieties. It is not that I would have overlooked this, but the anxiety of the impending dismissal which hung over me, just as the illness hung over Filippa, took away the sense of calm I needed to cope with the chaos of the destructive organisation of this mother–daughter relationship and to consider carefully the right moment to interpret Filippa's distress, without overtaxing the mother, as well as how much waiting and holding back the child could have tolerated without experiencing it as another trauma.

The reproach might be made that under these conditions I should never have taken on such a difficult therapy, and that, given the severe nature of the mother's disturbance, it was questionable whether, even under better conditions, therapy should have been undertaken at all. If I had been more cautious or, at least, had attempted from the outset to avoid the possibility of therapies being broken off, it would have spared me such bad experiences (whether it would have been better for Filippa is not altogether clear), but it would also have prevented me from gaining the experiences I have written about in this book. I did not have to break off all the therapies; however, I found that the relationships which were ended meaningfully owed their success to circumstances which, because of the conditions created by the institution 'Learning Disability', cannot be taken for granted, whereas the circumstances surrounding the failure of Filippa's therapy, as well as Inge's, even if they may seem extreme, are a good illustration of institutional reality in all its awfulness (characteristically, Maud Mannoni also presented the case of a recent therapeutic failure in her book *The Backward Child and His Mother* – probably for similar reasons). My hope in publishing such experiences is that my readers may have a better hope of avoiding the mistakes that I made.

Gaining space

The beginning was already a breathtaking experience. Filippa, as I shall call her here, rushed into the introductory consultation in the therapy room and immediately started throwing instruments around. She was raving and screaming and could not be calmed down, and the observer (my superior, who told me later that I was going to be working with this child) was barely able to make contact with her.

After reading my superior's report I was very tense, a week later, when I met Filippa alone for the first time. Filippa, who was almost six years old, was brought to the consultation by her mother. She was a stocky little girl and marched energetically past me with big, dark, wide-open anxious eyes, in the direction of the tubular bells and began hitting them hard. I greeted the mother and offered her a seat, then turned to Filippa and asked her: 'Is that you making all that noise, Filippa?' She cringed awkwardly in distress. 'Making music', she said, despairingly. I was shocked: why had I said something so aggressive and why was naming the aggressivity in her play so threatening for her? As if by way of an answer, she stopped playing, lay down on the floor, and her eyes fell closed. She made desperate efforts to keep them open. I built a screen around her out of tubular bells on which we each played a little in turn. She struggled fiercely against falling asleep but finally – while I covered her with a blanket and tried to soothe her fear of falling asleep by singing her a lullaby – succumbed.

At the most, five minutes had passed, and in this short time Filippa had already completely captivated me with her energy, her anger, and her despair.

I now turned to the mother and said that I would also want to see her alone so that we could get to know each other, and so that she could tell me why she wanted Filippa to have music therapy. She thought she could tell me there and then. Since I hesitated, she added, 'Little Filippa is sleeping soundly now. And anyway she would scarcely understand what I am saying. She understands very little in general.' In spite of my uneasiness – something gave me the definite feeling that Filippa understood very well, but that her mother needed to believe otherwise – as soon as Filippa's regular deep breathing indicated that she was fast asleep, I sat down with Frau L. and listened to what she had to say.

The pregnancy and birth had gone normally. In the fifth or sixth month after the birth, and several times after that as well, the parents had noticed Filippa having 'a first mild convulsion' which came as a shock for them at the time. In the second, and particularly the third year, during which Filippa was alone with her father, the fits became more frequent until she finally had a convulsion almost hourly and then started turning round and round herself, 'as if she had someone clinging onto her neck'. Her father had held her for hours on his lap 'in expectation of the next fit'. Frau L. said that she sometimes had the impression that Filippa 'was possessed by the devil'. As I asked more questions, Frau L. said that Filippa sometimes behaved in ways which were 'not her' and which she herself was clearly unhappy about.

When Filippa was two years old, the conflicts between the parents had become intolerable (from Frau L.'s account I inferred that her husband's excessive sexual demands, coloured by infantile needs, were driving her away) so that, in the end, Frau L. fled with her then seven-year-old son from a previous relationship, leaving Filippa with her father. It was only one and a half years later – meanwhile she was pregnant again – that she took steps, with legal help, to have custody of her child. With tears in her eyes and full of self-reproaches, Frau L. reported how, on her arrival, after one and a half years, Filippa had been in a state of complete neglect, just running round in circles for hours and, apart from 'Mummy', had uttered no other words. When she caught sight of her mother, she stopped her circular movement, called out 'Mummy', ran over to her and clung onto her tightly.

Because of her epileptic fits, which in the meantime had become very frequent, Filippa had to go into hospital for several weeks (the father had not sought medical help). As the effect of the medication prescribed for her there soon began to wear off, the mother took her away on the advice of a non-medical practitioner, trying unsuccessfully to treat the increasingly serious fits with homeopathic means. A vicious circle set in: for four-to-five days Filippa became increasingly 'restless' and then on the sixth or seventh day had about seven or eight grand mal fits after which she was always totally apathetic for one or two days until the cycle began again. The mother did not say any more about the character of the 'restlessness' and something stopped me from asking any more about it.

When, in spite of the healer's efforts, Filippa's fits got worse and her mental development was showing clear signs of being retarded (she still spoke very little and was primarily preoccupied with running water), Frau L. finally returned to a doctor but did not see the prescribed drug treatment through since once again its effect soon wore off, and so she again resorted to natural healing. Again, Filippa's condition deteriorated so alarmingly that Frau L. was obliged to return to the child neurologist who had already treated Filippa. (This was the doctor whose report I was given to read.) The doctor announced the diagnosis: he had found 'individual sclerotic brain cells', said Frau L., and prescribed a treatment of heavy medication against convulsions which put an end to the fits immediately. This had occurred shortly before my first meeting with Filippa. Since then, she had been a transformed child, calm and docile, said Frau L. She had great confidence in the doctor who had helped her so much.

After being asked explicitly once again about her daughter's difficulties and problems, Frau L. said that Filippa spoke badly, did not have a good memory, and, in particular, had no sense for time intervals. Otherwise, the difficulties were slight. (Later, I read in the doctor's report that a short time before being put back on medication Filippa had been having a lot of tantrums which involved throwing objects, and especially chairs, around.) Further, she had attacked her little brother violently, indeed dangerously; was constantly running away; just repeated a few stereotyped phrases, forming two- or three-word sentences; often spent a long time at the water tap, and frequently spent hours bending over a chair masturbating. After taking medication, the 'maladjusted behaviour' disappeared completely at first, but then gradually reappeared as the shock effect of the drugs wore off. She hoped that by the time Filippa started school in two years time (Frau L. hoped to be able to delay this by one year) she would be able to go to a normal school. I asked her if this was something she hoped would result from the music therapy and she said yes, it was. When I stressed that I could not promise this at all, but that I was willing to try and that I would tell her frankly what I thought the hopes and chances for Filippa were, she quickly added that she was not concerned about whether Filippa succeeded or not 'as long as she got better!'

Following this first encounter with the mother and child, I had the opportunity of reading through the medical report. The diagnosis was dismal: tuberous brain sclerosis – a rare but usually progressive illness involving symptoms of epilepsy, skin deformity and brain cell sclerosis. Concerning the announcement of the diagnosis there was a terse note in the report: 'the mother was informed about the progressive nature of this illness and its likely consequences and took it in without much emotional reaction'. These, then, were the 'individual calcified brain cells' which Frau L. had spoken about! The doctor's scarcely veiled antipathy for Frau L. was evident in the report. I could barely recognise in it the sensitive, good-natured woman whom I had spoken with shortly before, who seemed to care so lovingly for her sick child and who had spoken to me so frankly and full of sadness about her sense of guilt. The report presented a picture of a slut who was indifferent, incapable of parenting, neglectful of her children and responsible for Filippa's 'behavioural disorders'. Understandably, the doctor was furious with Frau L. for the irresponsible way in which she had acted with Filippa's medication and felt his own competence had been slighted. I decided to trust my own sense of the situation, especially as I was not overly confident in the capacity for understanding of this doctor who had not asked himself why Frau L. had acted the way she did and who had clearly confused the mother's lack of reaction to such an awful diagnosis with indifference. (What should she have done then? Broken down in front of him?) Furthermore, I found Frau L's doubts about orthodox medicine quite understandable as its effects had been very harmful for Filippa: the doctor had made the prognosis with an air of absolute certainty which was unjustified given the current state of medical knowledge; moreover, Frau L. noticed that the drugs, and particularly the shock caused by their being introduced too abruptly, was also harmful for Filippa.

However, my suspicions were aroused by the fact that in spite of (or even because of) her mild manner, at times Frau L. clearly evoked strong feelings of aggression in other people – even my superior had spoken about her in a rather unfriendly way. What also set me thinking was the childlike trust Frau L. had shown in the doctor from whom she had already fled once to the non-medical practitioner, and who had discriminated against her so much behind her back. In addition there was Frau L.'s tendency to deny realities which were too much for her: not only had she minimised the dreadful diagnosis in her phantasy to 'individual sclerotic brain cells' but she had also referred to the serious problems with Filippa as 'slight difficulties', remaining silent about many issues in spite of my questions. In the light of all this I expected – rightly as it turned out – that working with the mother would, at any rate, be no less difficult than the therapy with Filippa.

First, however, I had to cope with the reality of this diagnosis myself. After reading all the literature I could get access to, and after a number of discussions with doctors, I simply knew that a progressive deterioration was not certain and that Filippa's mental retardation was clearly more serious than the diagnosis had led one to expect, even allowing for an eventual progression of the illness. As the illness deteriorates progressively in some cases but not in others, and, in some cases, stabilises itself at some point, whereas in others it can be fatal, and, as there seem to be no known organic causes for these differences, I assumed that the child's mental situation, in particular her capacity to come to terms with the illness and to struggle against its progression, was not without relevance for the course of the illness. The task of the therapy would therefore be to support Filippa in her struggle against the terrible illness; but, for such a struggle, Filippa's mental and emotional situation offered the most inauspicious circumstances imaginable.

The farewell situation following the initial meeting with Filippa and her mother gave me the first key to understanding. Frau L. lifted the sleeping child up gently from the floor, woke her and said, 'Don't hit now, Filippa'. I said goodbye to Filippa, promising her that I would be waiting for her there at the same time the following week. A ghostly smile crossed her face.

'Don't hit, Filippa' – Filippa 'make music' and not 'noise' – and yet when I call it 'noise', then she was overcome by sleep as if it were a punishment. A death sentence; for a fear of death underlay Filippa's desperate efforts not to fall asleep. It was better to assume that Filippa was consumed with anger: anger with her mother who had abandoned her, who had left her behind as a pledge to the father, probably for the excessive sexual demands which Frau L., not without a sense of guilt, was thereby escaping from. Indeed, Filippa's compulsive masturbation may have been a sign of severe sexual trauma. Anger, too, because her mother had had another son, depriving Filippa of a large part of the mother's love (by throwing and hitting things, Filippa forced her mother to give her, if not love, then at least attention, because she had to protect the little baby from dangerous attacks).

When, once again, she was not given her medication, Filippa's wild tantrums increased daily, culminating in a series of severe, self-destructive fits. I assumed, however, that Filippa experienced these as a punishment and death threat for being bad, so that her apathy the following day may have been not just the result of bodily exhaustion but also a kind of death-feigning reflex. The medication intervened in this deadly cycle of rage and self-punishment so powerfully that Filippa must have experienced it as a duplication of the death threat. She was suddenly deprived of her liveliness, namely, her bodily excitation through which her anger found expression (and which was therefore her most important means of expression), and this could only be understood as a punishment for her 'badness', the bad-ness of the raging, screaming and masturbating little girl. It is understand-able that after this shock she was initially 'like a new person', compliant, calm and easy to handle; it is also understandable that when I named her anger ('are you making all that noise?'), she was scared to death. Her experience was that whenever she was promised help, she was killed for her badness (whether by the withdrawal of medication or the sudden use of it).

In the next session, Filippa immediately confirmed the correctness of my assumption that guilt and phantasies of punishment were involved. This time she was wilder again, screaming and hitting herself as she was brought to the session and as soon as she saw me she demanded: 'Play with water'. Then at the sink she said, 'Wash finger away – wash Filippa's finger away'. I sat down with her, watching her for a while as she let the water run over her finger, watched it draining off, and kept repeating, 'Wash Filippa's finger away'. Finally, I asked her if anyone had told her that her finger was bad and dirty. 'Yeah', she answered. So I said, 'But that's not true, your finger is nice, your finger is very clean, Filippa is nice, I am quite sure of that'. She glanced at me sideways for a few seconds strangely as if she wanted to make sure that the person who was saying this to her was really there. Then, when I asked her to, she was ready to come to the music room where for a while we banged around really aggressively with batons on instruments and other objects. (Unfortunately, there was no running water in the therapy room; in the lavatory there was just cold water and no heating, which was why I always tried to make the therapy room the place of play.) At the next session I brought Filippa some white soap in a white container. Again, to begin with, we played the game with water and once again I told her that her fingers were nice and that she did not have to get rid of them. She enjoyed playing with water and soap but the fingers were still there and were very clean. Once, she suddenly held out her hand to me saying: 'Kiss'. Then she took the soap with her into the music therapy room where for a whole hour she held on to it like a mascot and wanted me to play some 'music' for her on the piano. While I was doing this, she ran around, calling out from time to time, 'Hello *Frau*' and I replied, 'Hello Filippa'. Sometimes she came up very close to me, leaning on me lightly, to hear me whisper in her ear, 'Lovely Filippa, Filippa is very nice and clean'. Then she smiled in a way which, on her face with its terribly distressed expression, made a strange, distant and unreal impression, as if what I said to her had sounded unreal.

> At one point she pointed to one of the pictures on the wall in the room (children making music; she pointed to a child in red, playing the trumpet) and said, 'That is a man . . . mustn't wash finger away'.
> 'No, because Filippa's fingers are fine.'
> 'Filippa, mustn't break things.'
> 'No, you haven't destroyed anything.'
> 'Filippa mustn't hit.'
> 'Sometimes when Filippa is very angry, she lashes out.' Filippa then lay down backwards on the floor, with her frock up so that her panties were showing, opened her legs wide – an almost obscene looking position – and kicked vigorously with one leg several times in the air.
> 'Yes, kick him away.'
> She glanced at me sideways, rather shocked, and then continued kicking.
> She now pointed at me and asked, 'Who is that?' and as I said my first name, she repeated 'Hut'. (Since Filippa usually only used words when she could pronounce them properly, it seemed to me that this idea she had of my name was not meaningless.)

Mostly, however, she called me '*Frau*' or occasionally 'Mami' too; only in the last months of our work did she gradually learn to pronounce my name properly.

The reasons for her anger now became clearly recognisable: when I had a few words with her mother before the session began, or greeted her sibling, and especially when I ended the session, she would get angry and throw instruments around or hit me; during the sessions, however, she made a concentrated effort to make me aware of how distressed she was.

In the following session Filippa's anger acquired a structure which could be named for the first time. She hit the drums and said:

> 'Filippa, mustn't hit.'
> 'Filippa is hitting the drum. Filippa is hitting the drum because she is angry.'
> In her play with water which followed she no longer talked about 'washing finger away'. Instead, she adjusted the flow of water from the tap so that it was as weak as possible.
> 'Filippa is making finger wet . . . *Frau* make finger wet too!' 'Ooh, it tickles nicely!'
> 'Tickle.'
> With her hand on her genitals she then went over to the window and said, 'I want to go out'.

At this point I want to make a pause in my description to cast an eye back over the process once more. In the breathlessness of writing, the atmosphere of this therapy with Filippa has come back to me: from the outset it was as if Filippa had to win a race. It seems to me that she knew only too well that the illness (and, as will become apparent, the threatening conflictual situation with her mother) was following hot on her heels, and she was running for her life. I have never known a child to struggle with so much energy as Filippa did to discover something new in each session, without a pause. Unfortunately, how right she was became only too clear as time went on.

So what have we been working on in these first five sessions? 'I want to go out.' This was the first time that Filippa, who otherwise spoke of herself only in the third person, used the 'I' form. (The caregivers in the kindergarten could scarcely believe that she had really said this.) Filippa is not bad and dirty; the *Frau's* white soap helps her to make herself spotless and the *Frau* also helps her to recognise that her anger is not bad but justified. She is justified in being angry when the *Frau* ends the session; when she hits the drum; when she stamps away 'the man'. And she is also not bad when she enjoys the 'tickling feeling' of the running water and making her finger wet (masturbating) – because the *Frau* clearly also enjoys that, and because Filippa's finger is nice and clean enough for 'Hut' to kiss. More and more, I suspected to my horror that when Filippa had been left alone with the father, he had sexually abused her, and that Filippa's excessive masturbation was the result of a sexual trauma which had awakened her genital pleasure prematurely and exploited it. Filippa's sense of guilt, which was why she had to wash away her 'bad' (used for caressing herself) finger, probably resulted from a prohibition of her mother, but it could only be so oppressing because Filippa felt implicated – guilty = dirty – through her own experience of pleasure in the 'bad' thing which her father had done to her (and which she continually repeated in her painfully compulsive masturbating). Consequently, she could hardly feel her anger towards her father who was so bad for her.

Now that I had named the anger she was expressing by pummelling the drum, finding it justified rather than bad and dirty, she no longer had to 'wash away' her finger, but could separate her own childish pleasure in tickling from the scene of sexual abuse, recognising it as her own, and thereby gaining a bit of her identity as a little girl. 'I want to get out': out of this hellish cauldron of anger, fear, compulsive over-stimulation and guilt feelings.

Meanwhile, I had another consultation with the mother during which she clearly confirmed my suspicion that the father had sexually traumatised the child; she herself had long suspected this to be the case. I also spoke with her about the diagnosis and together we formulated the hope that, with the help of music therapy, Filippa would be in a better position to defend herself against the progression of the illness. When I realised towards the end of the consultation that there was little time left over for her herself, she said there was nothing to talk about anyway. When I asked what she meant, she burst into tears. 'Everything has been a bit too much for me recently,' she said desperately, 'and sometimes I just do not have enough energy left for Filippa even though she needs it so much!' For Filippa, but perhaps also for herself? Responding to my question, which was too much for her, Frau L. spoke of problems of daily life, which were certainly bad enough, but compared with the awfulness of what she had just been speaking about so calmly, they seemed almost marginal. Quite clearly, I had demanded too much from Frau L. in this discussion because I did not realise how much energy it was costing her to keep up such an appearance of calm. Soon I realised that this experience of things being 'too much' had been one of Frau L's own central childhood experiences. I set up a new appointment with her as soon as possible, which was to be a session expressly for her.

The sixth session with Filippa began chaotically. (After the session, the next consultation with Frau L. was arranged, which, because of the chaos, in fact did not take place.) Filippa was not picked up at the kindergarten and brought to me as usual by her own mother but by another mother, and I found her screaming and raving in panic, probably afraid that she had been abandoned by her mother again. When her mother walked in late, Filippa was so beside herself with despair that she simply thrashed about wildly with her arms and legs and wreaked havoc in the music therapy room. I asked the mother to stay in the room. After this wild tantrum – I tried to avoid any serious damage and just waited – Filippa discovered the dolls in the box which, since the last session, I had laid out for her on the floor; the adult dolls and the child dolls lying next to each other. As in the last session, she now began trampling back and forth on the dolls, but visibly only stamped on the adult dolls. 'Yes, just stamp on them, those bad, nasty, adult dolls', I said to her. (What would the mother make of this interpretation, I wondered rather uncomfortably?) Gradually, Filippa's trampling abated a bit and she eventually began abusing the dolls with the legs of a chair. I took the princess doll, sat it on a little doll's chair and drew Filippa's attention towards it: 'Look, this is Filippa-doll sitting on her chair!' Filippa knelt down and looked at 'Filippa-doll' with a yearning, imploring expression and said, 'That is a girl'. After looking at her at length she picked Filippa-doll up carefully from the chair and laid it on the floor next to the chair and then began squashing the grown-up dolls and the baby doll with the chair. I said to her that Filippa-doll's chair had to squash the grown-up dolls because they were so nasty to her and that she also felt she had to mistreat the baby doll because the baby deprived her of her mother's love. She now wanted to 'play with water' again. Once she was in the bath, however, where her mother was not looking on, she said:

'*Frau* hurts Filippa!'

'Bad *Frau*, she hurts poor Filippa.'

'*Frau*, mustn't hit.'

Saying so, she looked at the wall. I hit the wall and said, 'There, I am hitting her, the nasty thing!'

She hit it too and together we started hitting and kicking and stamping on the floor with mounting rhythm. As we did so, a smile of relief crossed her face, suggesting she was beginning to relax.

After this session, which Frau L. had sat in on partially, I was glad that I was able to arrange another appointment with her fairly soon as I was concerned about how she may have reacted to my interpretations. Frau L. brought several small children with her to this appointment so that the parents' room, which was usually used for consultations, was not free. 'We can go in the therapy room', she suggested. Unfortunately, it was occupied as well, and so I had to make some room for us in the office in spite of the sour faces and disparaging remarks. What a scenario: once again, and this time quite literally, there was no room for Frau L.! And once again, I was unable to prevent Filippa from becoming the centre of the discussion. Frau L. reproached me for completely over-interpreting Filippa's behaviour. What I called Filippa's anger, she could not see at all. 'That is not Filippa, that is not anger.' 'Filippa is a good girl.' I was shocked. I could hear a veiled threat in what she said: 'Anger is not allowed! And if that is what you call it, then Filippa won't be coming to music therapy any more.' When I survived her attack, which was fairly mild but contained a strong under-current of aggression, but did not conceal my dismay, the situation became less tense; at the end of the consultation Frau L. was able to express some of her own anger that the time for our meeting had been cut short by the chaotic way it had started, as well as her jealousy of my next patient who had just arrived.

I was shocked by the aggression which I could hear in Frau L.'s reproach that I was over-interpreting Filippa's behaviour; and even more by her attitude, 'This is not Filippa, Filippa is a nice girl' – I had hardly ever met such a guileful child. So that was it, then: when Filippa was angry, which was the affect she experienced most, her mother did not recognise her at all; 'that is not her' but an evil spirit which has taken hold of her. For Filippa, this was even worse than the lack of reaction stemming from a sense of guilt which I had already sensed: so when the angry Filippa searched for her image in the maternal mirror, she saw nothing but a black hole and must have had the feeling that she did not really exist (hence her 'yeah-yeah' and her quick sideways glance when I made interpretations seemed to say: it can't be, but it *must, must* be true!). Consequently she was driven, ever more desperately and compulsively, to force any reaction whatsoever; and, even if it meant punishment, she needed to get really angry in order to feel that she existed. So in addition to the experience of fits, episodic illnesses and the shock of medication, for Filippa the threat of the death sentence was even more prevalent. As far as her mother was concerned, when she was angry she simply did not exist; she was merely air.

But this anger, which for the good-natured Frau L. did not exist, was projected onto others – the doctor, the director of the Institute, and also me. She made others angry by frequently being late, especially after Filippa's sessions, and also through the hostility she provoked in the Institute, which I then had to put up with. Gradually, in the following consultations, I got to know parts of Frau L.'s life-history – a bizarre and dreadful series of catastrophes – which helped me understand why it was so important for her to deny her own anger, constantly provoking it in her environment; and, why she lived out this anger by projecting it into her daughter's wild tantrums.

For Frau L. therefore, Filippa's anger was unconsciously the incarnation of everything 'bad' that she had to expel from herself, which was why her good-naturedness always seemed somewhat unreal. But, in spite of the catastrophic situation of their relationship, Frau L. loved her daughter just as she was, with her own psychical possibilities. If this had not been the case, Filippa would not have been able to participate in the music therapy with such intensity and energy, and, likewise, would not have been able to take in my interpretations with such gratitude, as if they were good milk. Because of this love, Filippa could not be bad, but Frau L. needed the phantasy that Filippa was 'possessed by the devil' whenever she screamed, had wild tantrums, and masturbated. Of course, this phantasy contained, even if in a coded form, the truth that Filippa's anger was only so uncontrollable and overpowering because it was magnified by the mother's projection of her split-off anger ('That really wasn't Filippa, it was "the devil"') which Frau L. had to banish from herself, subjecting Filippa to it in the form of a bad introject.

The underlying threat, 'If you name Filippa's anger, I will break off the therapy', was thus a warning: be careful how you deal with my denial of anger, think twice before you put my precarious mental equilibrium in question, because I will not be able to tolerate it. This made me anxious, yet I could sense that because of her energy and her tremendous will-power, and because she felt threatened and driven by her dreadful illness, Filippa's pace of activity was far too much for her mother who at last had found a kind of inner equilibrium and peace in herself (I was not yet aware that this was at Filippa's expense) which she had always lacked and which she would only give up with great difficulty.

In Filippa's therapy the dolls, which I had introduced as a symbol, became very significant in the period that followed. In the last session they had given her the opportunity of expressing her anger symbolically rather than simply acting it out. She made the transition from actually trampling them underfoot to mistreating them symbolically with the doll's chair, after I had offered her a self-representation in the form of a Filippa-doll. In the next session I placed a female doll next to the Filippa-doll on the chair. Filippa picked the female doll up and used it to torment the Filippa-doll, while I continued to show my sympathy for the poor Filippa-doll. Eventually, I could not stand it any longer and took the female doll away from her, putting it on the little chair with the Filippa-doll on her lap. Filippa watched this doll scene intently for a long time, and then asked me for 'chair . . . lap'. Sitting on my lap she now took a male doll and threw it away angrily. Later she made the male doll wet. 'Now the man has wet himself', I said to her. She found a flower and said to it, 'There, little flower . . . it pricks . . . it's bleeding . . . that is a man'. Only later did I learn that 'making little flowers' was Frau L.'s expression for Filippa's masturbating. The man wets himself, 'little flower' pricks and blood is coming: I could scarcely have heard Filippa speak more clearly of what I increasingly had to understand as her actual experience.

In the next session, Filippa again spent part of the time throwing the male doll angrily against the wall, crying without tears and was clearly very distressed. Again and again she sought assurance from me that I still thought that Filippa was lovely and that her finger was perfectly clean. Then she wanted to go to the bathroom. There she tried to impale Filippa-doll on a blue hook that was much too big for the delicate little doll. Then she made the doll all wet. 'Poor Filippa-doll, has the bad man made her all wet?' I said to her; whereupon Filippa became very distressed again, crying painfully, without tears. 'But now Filippa has washed the Filippa-doll and it is nice and clean!' 'Yeah, yeah yeah', she said, as if she was trying to wake up from a bad nightmare. Then she sat for a while on my lap and looked very oppressed. I rocked her and asked, 'Poor Filippa, are you feeling very sad?' She got back on her feet, took a few steps away from me, and then suddenly ran towards me in order to cling on to me desperately. Pointing at the blue hook, she said vehemently, 'I don't like that, the blue one there!'

So that was it: running up to mother, after one and a half years of waiting. Only now could Filippa tell me what had dumbfounded her at that time, what had been so dreadful during the period of waiting: 'I don't like that, the blue peg there', the peg that is much too big, on which Filippa-doll was impaled – the penis-hook on which the 'man' impaled Filippa when she sat on his lap; the penis-hook, which was much too big for her, the little girl, so that she noticed 'it's bleeding'.

Was it purely coincidental that after this session Frau L. made us wait for a particularly long time? I waited in the parents' room with Filippa, who was whining with anxiety, impatience and anger, and promised her, 'I will wait here with you until Mummy arrives'. And when she was showing signs of throwing a tantrum, I said, 'You always have to wait so long for Mummy; she is always so late, bad Mummy!'

From then on Filippa tried hard to keep her anger under control. On several occasions, as she was on the point of throwing an instrument around, she hesitated, holding it for a while at an oblique angle.

'Fall down!'
'Filippa is holding on to the drum, so that it does not fall.'

She now walked more frequently along the border of the round carpets in the therapy room as if she wanted to conjure up limits, and the mother reported that the same thing happened at home and on walks; i.e. these were magic attempts to find limits and to set limits herself to the experience of being overwhelmed by anger. She had now reached a point where she could establish her own structures and invent her own games.

All the games we had played up till then had acquired their symbolic meaning and structure either as a result of my interpretations (banging on the drum, rhythmic kicking, playing with water) or had been my suggestions (playing with dolls). It was only by means of such symbolic structuring that Filippa could develop a more sophisticated expression of herself and her feelings. Until the session when she began mistreating the little dolls with the doll's chair, instead of actually trampling on them, Filippa must have experienced her anger as completely annihilating. Annihilating for the mother, because by not reacting in such situations she showed that she was really not available for Filippa; and annihilating, likewise, for the self (barely separated from being a symbiotic part-object of her mother); for the very real experience of self-annihilation in the series of severe fits at the climax of her temper tantrums must have undone all of Filippa's attempts to differentiate between phantasy and reality.

That Filippa would have been quite capable intellectually of forming and using symbols, as well as of making sophisticated use of language, was clear from her wide-awake participation in the music therapy; from her rare, but perfectly correct use of the word 'I'; and, especially, from her astounding understanding of language which contrasted starkly with the mother's belief that Filippa understood very little. On one occasion, as Frau L. was bringing Filippa to a session and telling me a few things about her own history, she began speaking circumspectly about 'that time there in . . .' (the period with Filippa's father) and Filippa screamed at her mother angrily, 'Mummy, go away!' and threw something at her head – since then she had learnt to accept such situations because she had already noticed that my talks with her mother could also bring her some relief. I often observed her precise reactions like this to my interpretations in the therapy, which often involved a really complex level of language. But they were reactions; Filippa could only make active use of her intelligence and her understanding of language to the extent that I created space for her in the therapy with my interpretations and suggestions for games. Ostensibly, during

Filippa's development, her capacity for symbolic expression had been demolished, hindering her, long after the terrible period of being abandoned, from being able to work through her bad experiences verbally and playfully and from differentiating between phantasy and reality. The result was that her violent feelings overwhelmed her and were turned against herself.

By reconstructing the history of the relationship between Filippa and her mother, we can understand how this may have come about. When Filippa was a little over two years old she probably began to see her mother as a rival to her father. She would have wanted to take her mother's place with her father and may often have thought, 'Mummy, go away!' just as she said to her mother when the latter was telling me about this period; and then her mother did in fact give up her place by actually going away. The wishful phantasy turned into an awful reality: not only did her Mummy go away, leaving Filippa alone with her father, but her father really took Filippa for a substitute wife, responding to her childish wish for fatherly tenderness with his adult male sexuality. Filippa thus fell into an unbearable whirl of rage, anxiety, sexual excitement, guilt and abandonment. She must have had the feeling that the bad situation was the product of her childish desires which had involuntarily become bad; worse still, what was phantasy had now become inescapable reality. The transitional space between phantasy and reality had suddenly been destroyed, i.e. the space in which Filippa could potentially have learnt to play, sing and speak. Instead of play and activity mediating between her inner and outer world, Filippa was at the mercy of her own affects, her father's abuse and the dreadful illness which was now rapidly gaining the upper hand and absorbing all the meanings that Filippa could no longer work through. The fits which now became so frequent were a manifestation of her rage towards her father who was abusing her and her absent mother, as well as being a manifestation of her self-punishment for the 'bad' desires of her sexual excitement which had become a reality. A period of illness probably followed, as is often the case in times of severe emotional crises. This was a further shock for Filippa, a real, and not simply phantasised, threat of the death sentence. Illness and psychic catastrophe were meshed like millwheels and set in motion an inevitable process of development which threatened, inexorably, to grind Filippa slowly into the ground.

When the mother eventually took Filippa away from her father, who was abusing her, and took care of her herself, things did not get better. Firstly, Filippa had to go straight into hospital where, abandoned by both her parents now, she was subjected for the first time to the shock of the drug treatment; secondly, when she was eventually home again with Mummy, the space for playing, which she had acquired during the period when she was not having her fits (she had begun playing and speaking again), was once again destroyed. This was not just because her fits, which she was probably using to express her anger towards her mother – anger her mother could recognise in no other way – were gradually returning again, but particularly because her mother now stopped her from taking her drugs in order to seek a 'miracle' cure from a non-medical healer which was supposed to liberate her 'possessed' child of her devilish possession as well as of the temper tantrums which Frau L. was unable to link up with Filippa's dreadful experiences.

In order to make the structure of the mother–child relationship, which was so life-threatening for Filippa, more understandable, I now propose to recount some details from Frau L.'s life history. Frau L. was an only child of a mother who was addicted to medication; and, according to Frau L., was always 'in the clouds' and barely capable of dealing with practical reality. Accordingly, the juvenile court had taken her child away from her periodically, sending her to the grandmother, with the result that strong feelings of jealousy developed between the mother and grandmother. Ostensibly, however, these feelings were hardly ever given expression. Torn in this way between the different people who had her in their charge, the little E.L. was forced prematurely to come to terms with reality, and was even obliged to take care of her constantly intoxicated and euphoric mother. Her father had never known Frau L., as he died before she was born. Once, during the period when the little E.L. was at the oedipal stage, her mother had had a lover for a while, a chemist, who provided her with a lot of drugs, while he was having a seductive effect on the little fatherless girl. Whether Frau L., like Filippa later, was really sexually seduced by this man who represented her painfully missing father, I do not know; however, it does not seem improbable.

Frau L. was involved in a similar but even more fatal constellation of relationships during her adolescence. Once again the mother had had a friend, who was also addicted, but who had left her when he got to know the daughter, with whom he immediately had a passionate relationship resulting in the birth of Frau L.'s eldest son. Frau L.'s mother was wildly jealous. The relationship broke down and the man went back to Frau L.'s mother, but then returned again to Frau L. because he could not stand seeing how Frau L.'s mother had in the meantime seriously deteriorated both mentally and physically. Now the mother was suffering from the illness which left her completely gaga within two years and eventually led to her death. Frau L. took flight in the marriage to Filippa's father and soon got pregnant again. The mother and daughter's joint lover then committed suicide in a grisly fashion. Her mother died from sclerosis of the brain, which was said to have resulted from a misuse of medication, without being reconciled with her daughter, all of which caused Frau L. a great deal of suffering. (Frau L. had never been able to pronounce the name of Filippa's illness – she invented the most complicated names of illnesses in order not to have to pronounce the awful words 'sclerosis of the brain'.) After the terrible deaths of her mother and her friend, Frau L. tortured herself with intolerable guilt feelings, and these then got mixed up with her guilt feelings toward Filippa so that, in her unconscious phantasies, she was her mother's murderer as well as the cause of her daughter's terrible illness.

Filippa was thus implicated in the history and phantasies of her mother in a way that was life-threatening for her. It was not just that Frau L. tried to achieve with Filippa what her own mother had failed to achieve, i.e. freedom from addiction to medication. It was much more that there was a repetition of the history of oedipal rivalry from which Frau L.'s mother had taken refuge: first through addiction, and later in the terminal illness, leaving her daughter to the lover and to cope with the guilt feelings alone. Frau L. likewise now took flight from her husband's sexual demands and the conflictual oedipal situation, exposing Filippa to sexual abuse by her father. In so doing, she obliged Filippa to assume the role which her own mother had evaded through addiction – Filippa became a mother figure for her unconsciously, emerging victorious from the situation of oedipal rivalry to have an 'adult' sexual relationship with the father-husband (who, like Frau L.'s much idealised father, who had died before her birth, was Algerian). Understandably, in the light of her childhood history, this had been too much for Frau L. She often told me that she longed for a 'purely platonic' loving relationship with a man.

At the same time, however, through projective identification, Filippa represented for Frau L. a negative image of herself as a little girl neglected by a crazy mother and exposed to paternal seduction. So Filippa had to carry all the feelings which Frau L. needed to evacuate so as not to break down under the pressure of mental stress. These included feelings of hate and anger towards her own mother who had put her in such an intolerable situation; her murderous phantasies and jealousy; her will to live; her capacity to defend herself which she unconsciously believed had driven her mother into illness and death; and, her lack of reality-sense – she believed it was not so much she herself who 'lived in the clouds', as her own mother had done, but Filippa. (Much later, months after the music therapy had been broken off, Frau L. said to me: 'It is not good for Filippa to be with ghost-seers; she needs people who have their feet on the ground a bit' – apparently, the late fruit of our discussions; too late, perhaps, for Filippa.) There remained nothing for Filippa to introject as a self-image but these projections. This was not only because the mirroring she got from her mother was distorted, but also because this reflection fitted in so fatally with her mental and physical reality that there was no space left for questioning or repudiating it.

Consequently, the most important thing in the music therapy was for Filippa to acquire space, an area for play. During this early stage of the therapy I felt as if I had to fight off with great, flailing movements everything which threatened to overwhelm Filippa so that she could at least begin to acknowledge it. Hence my massive and, at times, risky interpretations and playfully structuring interventions. The latter were also undoubtedly provoked by her astounding ability to use her 'extremely limited vocabulary and three-word sentences' to communicate her distress; and, moreover, she seemed to want them as if they were an elixir of life. They allowed her to have the entirely new experience that the mother's introjected projections, by which she was, as it were, possessed, were nameable. And, by being named, they could also be negated: Filippa is not nasty, bad, and dirty but nice and clean; she is often angry too, and with good reason. It seems improbable to me that Frau L. had really said to Filippa that her finger was bad and dirty, as I had said in my first interpretation. But it was precisely because of the non-symbolic quality of the mother's unconscious projections that Filippa found herself so directly and unavoidably at their mercy. If 'someone' did not say this to her then there was no one and nothing for Filippa to repudiate. The mother's introjects were really 'the devil' for Filippa. Only 'someone' can lie; she could only defend herself against 'someone', but not, against the 'devil' which held her in its grip, which 'brought her down', without her understanding how or why. So, instead of the bad introjects, this first interpretation, like my verbal interpretations in the early stages generally, offered Filippa other, better, and more constructive introjects which she immediately took in as she had the bad ones before, i.e. good milk instead of the usual bad milk. They enabled her to find the strength and courage for the next step towards autonomy of self-experience and symbol formation. 'Filippa-doll', representing the newly discovered 'nice Filippa' who wanted to live and feel and experience, created the necessary distance between us so that together we could see Filippa's destructive phantasies no longer as 'the devil' but as conflicts that could be worked through. But this little doll game was nonetheless my suggestion and Filippa could only use it with the help of my playful encouragement. The play materials demanded a degree of differentiation between self and object for which Filippa was not yet ready, as her language use clearly indicated: '*Filippa nicht hauen*' can be understood (in German) actively as well as passively, and, 'fall down' can mean both that Filippa lets the instrument fall and that Filippa, like the instrument, 'falls over' during a fit. Filippa therefore needed to find other materials, more suitable for her, in order to make herself independent of my presence.

Filippa chose sound as her material. This allowed for the fusion of self and object, as well as their differentiation, and could be experienced both symbolically and concretely. The tubular bells, representing the holding symbiotic relationship – Filippa had observed them with the same insistent look as my doll arrangement – fell over because Filippa was angry and threw them around; they rang because Filippa made them ring by throwing them around as an expression of her anger. Furthermore, Filippa could hold them. She could also hold the symbiotic relationship with me; she did not have to destroy it and herself with her anger and her fits because, like the tubular bells, I had reliably and repeatedly survived her aggression and responded to her.

In one of the next sessions I laid Filippa's sweets out in front of her. What gave me this idea was the way she had looked with yearning at the tubular bell game; and, her absorbed listening, as if I was nourishing her with sounds. She discovered the sweets, went straight over to the box of toys, and took out the cow:

> 'What is that?'
>
> 'It is a cow, which gives nice, good milk.'
>
> 'Filippa mustn't throw cup in.'
>
> 'You don't want to throw the cup in, because you need the milk in it, but sometimes you are very angry with it and you think it is bad, and then you have to throw it away. When the *Frau* hurts you, you feel you have to hit her too.'
>
> 'Yes!'
>
> She took a sweet for herself, sat on my lap, once again wanting me to play something for her on the tubular bells; she then played on them with her feet. Then she walked around the room, putting her hand briefly between her legs. Because she threw me a fleeting look of guilt, I said to her: 'that's nice and warm!' She then put her hand between the bars of the radiator and said 'hot'. She got back on my lap again, pointing to the 'man', painted in red, on the wall, curling up her shoulders as if in a sudden state of fright.
>
> 'Filippa is afraid of the red man and thinks he may do something to her, but I am holding Filippa tight and making sure that the man on the wall does nothing to her.'

Now she lay down on the floor and wanted me to tickle her, laughing happily and tickling me in turn. She had once again rediscovered a bit of her childish pleasure because she knew that I would not abuse her, that I would protect her from the man on the wall, and that it would not get too hot between her legs. Her whole demeanour was now so joyful and relaxed, in a way that I had never had the slightest glimpse of before. She took the male doll in her hand and tickled it, giggling; then she threw it away violently. As if waking from a bad nightmare, and without looking at me, she said 'go and fetch it!' It sounded echolalic, as if it might have no meaning and remain unanswered. I did what she wanted as quickly as possible. Now, alternately, she threw the male-doll and drumstick violently against the tubular bells, the cymbal or the drum. Each time there was a sound, and each time, I reliably fetched the object she had thrown away. Filippa invented a new variation and was becoming increasingly joyful. Laughing loudly and wantonly, she called out 'Ooh-ooh', throwing her voice and hearing it reverberating first as an echo (the instruments give a strong echo), and then again in my answer 'Ooh-ooh' – a completely new and inspiring experience. The strong, noisy Filippa, who had hitherto always felt she was abysmally bad because her mother never recognised and accepted in her, or in others, any feelings other than soft and tender ones – never demanding feelings – experienced something that resonated with her own voice! 'Ooh-ooh', she called out, and sometimes 'Papa' too; Filippa rediscovered her child's love for her father, cruelly destroyed by his sexual abuse of her.

Filippa could now awake from the nightmare of not being recognised by her mother, of the latter's lack of resonance with her. After the session, Filippa ran away from her mother, who had come to collect her, and was picked up by the police two hours later while she was taking a walk along the river. She was still rejoicing and calling out 'Ooh-ooh', which was the first object, the first transitional object that she could take with her, giving her independence from me and her mother, and serving as a symbol of her energy and zest for living which for so long had been bedevilled. Since this session she has clearly been more relaxed outside the sessions as well; she hardly ever attacks her siblings or other children in the kindergarten, plays happily, humming to herself, and has been much more co-operative than ever before.

Waiting (for the next session) now became a theme for the first time. When, as usual, after a session, Filippa did not want to stop and was reluctant to go with me to the parents' room, I asked her whether she could not wait until we saw each other again at the next session. 'Wait', she repeated angrily, following behind me. So in the repeated separation-situations with me a bit of her anger towards her mother, who had made her wait so long, could be experienced and elaborated. This made leaving-situations easier for her and she no longer demanded, as she had done sometimes before, '*Frau*, come too!' The ground was laid for a constructive working-through of the impending holiday separation. To this end I again made use of the dolls playing a scene in which *Frau*-doll left Filippa-doll alone in her chair, with Filippa-doll missing her and *Frau*-doll coming back again after a while. Then I explained to Filippa that I would soon be going away on holiday but that I would be coming back. By way of illustration, I hid behind a curtain, calling out 'Ooh-ooh' loudly. At first she ignored this game, but, then, she said, 'Do that again' and, then, with a painful expression: '*Frau*, don't go away!'

'The *Frau* is not going away now but soon it will be holiday time and then the *Frau* will not be here; after the holidays we will be able to make music again.'

In the next session Filippa asked to play the farewell-game again; she played the curtain game, exchanging roles, and then carefully began making a big pile of instruments in the middle of the room. I said to her: 'Filippa is very angry that the *Frau* wants to take her holidays, but she also knows that the *Frau* understands this and is not angry with her and that, after the holidays, we can play again with all the instruments.'

Frau L. was also able to take a step forward in recognising Filippa. This was plain to see in her reactions to Filippa's expressions of anger when parting. Once, Filippa just stayed staring in front of her rigidly and could not be induced to go home. 'Are you feeling very sad, now?', Frau L. asked her, whereupon Filippa, clearly relieved, jumped up and went with her. On another occasion, as I was leaving, Frau L. laughed understandingly when Filippa followed me angrily and I said to her: 'Yes, it is horrible of me just to take my vacation like that, isn't it!' It was evident that our talks had helped Frau L. to begin to be able to accept her own wishes and feelings that she projected onto Filippa because she felt they were 'bad' and 'unrealisable'.

A storm brewing and catastrophe

After the holidays Frau L. reported that initially things had gone very well with Filippa at home. However, when she returned to her hometown with her children to visit an uncle and his wife, Filippa had gone wild again and behaved 'as if she was possessed'. I inquired about the relatives and learnt that the aunt was afraid of Filippa and that the uncle was in contact with a medicine man and ghost-seer whom he had consulted about Filippa. This 'spirit man' asked if he could have a piece of clothing belonging to the 'possessed child' so that he could exorcise the evil spirit. So she gave her uncle a pair of Filippa's panties.

A shiver ran down my spine when I heard this story: how symbolic – giving Filippa's panties to the spirit man to be exorcised! No wonder Filippa had flown into a wild rage again. Frau L. sensed my shock and herself began to doubt her belief in spirits: 'The spirit man said that Filippa's playing with water could be explained by the fact that spirits do not like water. What do you think, is that true?' I could sense her anxiety in this question: would I simply try and talk her out of her spirit phantasy which contained so much truth in it for her? Or would I also play the ghost-seer, thereby weakening her contact with reality still further? In my answer I tried to be conciliatory: 'In my rather un-poetic language, I would probably say something similar to the medicine man, namely, that with the water, Filippa is trying to wash away what she considers to be bad in herself.' Frau L. heaved a sigh of relief on hearing this answer.

She further recounted that, when they were visiting the uncle, there were occasions when Filippa was so enraged that she had gone for her throat, 'her life centre', trying to suffocate her. On top of that Filippa had got into the habit of clearing out all the cupboards in the flat. Sometimes, she said, she had had to scream at the child, she was so nervous. Apologetically,

Frau L. added: 'I'm not normally like that. I am someone who doesn't get angry easily. But it was all simply too much!' Once she even hit Filippa. Filippa had burst into tears, really sobbing deeply, like any other small child would.

I was glad she had screamed at Filippa and even that she had hit her, for it was much better for Filippa at last to have a direct reaction to her anger, to be able to cry, instead of being oppressed by tearless despair.

Frau L. also told me about worrying developments regarding her other children, and, as I often did, I tried to steer the conversation round to talking about how she herself was feeling, for I knew that she had had a rough time of it lately. 'You're not telling me again that I am using myself as food for my children, are you?' she asked casually, laughing; 'You know, I'm actually quite happy myself, it's just my character!' As I indicated that the consultation was about to end, Frau L. told me quickly that she had heard about a new healing method, a 'flower therapy', which she wanted to try out for Filippa. I felt as if the ground had been cut from under my feet.

Subsequently, I asked myself what it was about this that had made me so anxious, what it was that had given me the feeling that the 'centre of Filippa's life' might now be at stake. I could not really explain it. I then recalled that Frau L. referred to Filippa's masturbating as 'making little flowers', and I also recalled the story of the underwear for the 'spirit man'. Perhaps it was something to do with driving out the devil? This would be logical, since Filippa's anger and sexuality were the 'devil'; perhaps it was a question of driving out Filippa's vital energy? At the same time, the shocking thought occurred to me that Frau L. might once again begin acting in the way suggested by the doctor's report, that is, by stopping Filippa's medication, giving up medical treatment in favour of the 'flower therapy'. Jealousy also seemed to be involved, and I recalled numerous situations of jealousy between Filippa and her mother: Frau L.'s jealousy of Filippa's relationship with me ('we can go in the therapy room'), even if she was unable to admit this desire consciously; the constant danger of a rivalry between Frau L. and myself over Filippa; the jealousy of the Institute's management regarding my commitment to Frau L. and Filippa ('Is it really necessary to do so much for these people?', had been their reproach). Frau L. had told me about her husband's, i.e. Filippa's father's, mad jealousy, and of childhood stories of how she was torn, to and fro, between her mother and grandmother; and, how, at the grandmother's instigation, her mother temporarily lost the right of custody. At that time I did not know anything about the situation of jealousy surrounding the common lovers.

Although Filippa did not seem as happy as she was before the holidays, in the period following them she developed new forms of play so energetically that, at first, my concerns faded into the background. Filippa's main preoccupations now were clearing out the instruments (getting rid of the introjections symbolically); dirtying the therapy room as well as cleaning it up again compulsively; and, stepping on areas of the floor that were uneven and points that represented borders for her – all of which were attempts at structuring, containing, coping with her violent feelings and affects. Now, tapping on the instruments, which had played a role from the beginning, became the central form of play. For hours on end we tapped on the temple blocks, which had recently become her favourite instrument:

> 'That thing there is pricking again!'
> 'I'm going to hit you, you nasty pricking thing!'
> 'Nasty *Frau*.'
> 'The *Frau* is nasty to you and hurts you, does she?'
> 'Filippa must hit!', she cried and started hitting the instruments hard.
> 'Too hard!' she cried out and, while I was hitting the instruments hard, I also cried out, 'Too hard'. And then she did it again, crying out jubilantly:
> 'Too hard!'
> 'Too hard!'
> 'Too hard!'

All her joy and energy was expressed in this 'too hard'. It stemmed from a frequent prohibition of her mother who had wanted, with these words, to get her out of the habit of hitting too hard, speaking too loudly and crying out. (At this time there were increasingly frequent complaints in the Institute that the therapy sessions with Filippa were far too noisy, intolerable to have to listen to . . . .) Frau L. herself never did anything 'too hard'; she always spoke softly and under her breath – Filippa's voice, however, was strong and sonorous (when she was being brought to see me, I could always hear her a long way off saying, 'Where is the *Frau*? Where is the *Frau*? Hello, *Frau!*'), her gait full of purpose. Her eyes sparkled with zest when, together, we played the instrument 'too hard' and it responded with its sound, with a rhythmic structure, and we were being quite boisterous together. Most of the time we played alternately, imitating each other's rhythms; and while I was playing, Filippa would step back a metre or two, skipping and whirling, and then return to make the sound again. 'Too hard': at last it was no longer 'the devil' but Filippa herself who wanted to live, who defended herself, and who was now discovering that it was all right, that it was not 'bad and dirty'.

In retrospect, I wonder whether I should have been more cautious at this stage of the therapy; whether Filippa's vehement re-appropriation of her vital energy at this time had not been too worrying for her mother; and whether I had not driven her into her defensive panic reactions by my lack of caution. I do not know. At the time I was never able to tell how I could restrain Filippa without giving her the feeling once again that there was no place for her liveliness.

Recently, at home, Filippa had been provoking frequent conflicts with her elder brother B., who rejected her violently. She would continually go to his room, open the door, and each time he would scream at her 'Go away!', pushing her back, and slamming the door in her face. She would cry bitterly and then try again. That she went on repeating this experience with her brother is an indication of how much Filippa must have missed having her mother set boundaries (and thus possibilities for identification). However painful this experience of being pushed away was for her, it was, nonetheless, a response, and she was able to learn something new from it. Once, on the day the disastrous cycle began all over again (i.e. when the mother had begun to reduce the medication again), she had had a wild tantrum in the kindergarten – for the first time in a long while – and had hit and knocked over other children. In the end a worker shut her out of the playroom. When, after a few minutes, he let her in again, she ran up to him and kicked him as hard as possible in the shins, shouting at him: 'Go away!' The staff were amazed and delighted – they had never seen Filippa so purposefully and, clearly, justifiably angry and it was the first time they had ever heard her saying anything like this.

The disaster: I happened to learn from Frau L. that, during the last few days, she had been with Filippa to see the healer, a specialist for the Bach flower remedy Frau L. had told me about. The specialist had not only prescribed certain flower remedies, but had also recommended that Filippa's drugs be gradually reduced. Frau L., who had long been denying her mistrust of the doctor, whose disapproving attitude she must have sensed, accepted this recommendation only too readily. For her, the doctor was now 'bad', whereas the healer appealed to her by promising a 'miracle', something I had not done. Her anxieties concerning chemical medicines, which were understandable given her dreadful childhood memories of a medicine-dependent mother, broke loose and found an alibi in the healer's recommendation. (Although I am being critical of the healer here, I would like to point out that I am not trying to play the competence of doctors and healers off against each other; this was happening much more in what Frau L. was doing to Filippa on account of the distress caused by her anxiety and guilt feelings. This was a situation in which the respective specialists got entangled, in most cases unsuspectingly, without realising the damage that was being done. It was also very difficult for me to keep the right distance in the dreadful dynamics of this murderous relationship between a mother who, with all her own weaknesses, really loved her child, and a severely ill child whom even a much less disturbed mother would have found it difficult to cope with.)

I learnt from the kindergarten that during this period when Filippa's hope was dashed by the shock resulting from the withdrawal of drugs, provoking once again regular and severe fits, outside the therapy she regressed to the chaos of the time before she started taking drugs and doing music therapy: she screamed, went wild and mistreated small children; and, once again, would mostly spend her time standing by the water tap which she had not shown much interest in for a long while. Clearly, she must have experienced the withdrawal of medication as a punishment for the new zest for living she had discovered in therapy. In the music therapy she tried at first to counter the disaster by working more intensively. In these sessions she repeatedly requested: '*Frau* sing!' Initially, I did not understand and sang her songs, and she got angrier and angrier with my obtuseness. 'Sing – about the man!' she eventually ordered me: so it was her story that she wanted me to sing, the story of the little girl who was abandoned by her mother, who was made a woman by her father who was 'too hard'. Filippa also asked for interpretations quite consciously and proceeded in the following period to dictate to me, while I sang for her, how the words should continue.

Although in this first period of the disaster, Filippa made considerable progress and showed few signs of her impending breakdown during the music therapy sessions, I became increasingly distressed as a result of the news of disastrous events at the kindergarten. Frau L. now had a completely euphoric and reality-denying attitude towards Filippa's illness, and I could once again see the flickering look of anxiety on Filippa's face. Frau L. talked to me more and more now about the other children, particularly about B.'s suicide threats, which he had recently been making frequently. In order to be able to manage my feelings in relation to this chaotic family and to be able to look for solutions I began to write 'Notes on Family L.'. As it is difficult for me to write about this period, I am simply going to write up a few of these chaotic and very emotional notes which may be the best way of getting across how I felt in my work with Frau L. and her daughter at this time.

> '*I am beginning to understand what 'It's all been a bit too much for me recently' means. Now, it's me who is feeling things are too much, who would like to scream with anger and helplessness and go wild like Filippa. Frau L. seems to want me to heal the whole family . . . B.'s suicide threats, the little boy with eyes full of unhappiness, and signs of the onset of severe disturbance . . .*
>
> *Signs of impending disaster: Filippa is now undergoing the recently announced flower remedy therapy (probably a mild form of exorcism). A great shock when Frau L. told me about it: 'Bach flower remedies' to reinforce the denial of Filippa's illness ('making little flowers' is what Frau L., calls Filippa's painfully driven masturbating in her language devoid of aggression): it could mean the end of music therapy. Jealousy of the healer who does what I cannot do – promise a miracle. In the end, this seems easier than dealing with Frau L.'s mistrust and disappointment just at a time when things are not going wonderfully. Anxiety for Filippa,*

for whom this total denial could mean a rapid and fatal acceleration of her illness – fading away like the scent of a flower . . .

Jealousy . . . be careful not to get entangled with the healer in the goings-on between Frau L.'s mother and grandmother. This will be difficult, for worse is coming:

The flower remedy therapy is supposed to gradually replace the anti-convulsion drugs. This is far too much for Filippa! She is far from being able (in spite of 'fall down') to defend herself against the fits and to keep her anger under control without medication. Filippa flipped out and went wild on the day she received a reduced dose for the first time as well as when she was initially examined by the healer. She is clever, knows exactly what is going on – if only she could make her mother understand!

How am I going to explain to Frau L. that she shouldn't do this? It is all so reminiscent of her own history.

Still, she said recently (the day Filippa went wild again): 'Today I could have smashed everything to bits.' If only she would do it!!! Instead of cutting the ground from under her child's feet. She is now having phantasies of putting Filippa in a home – the important thing here is that she wants to make room for herself and the other children. Is sacrificing Filippa really the only solution?

The scenes with Filippa and her brother B. How Filippa always wants to go to him and is turned away, standing outside, and crying bitterly until the next attempt. Isn't this Frau L.'s own story as a little girl, begging on heaven's door to be let in to see her father whom she had never known, and who had left her at the mercy of her mother who was unable to cope with life?

'Incest' – the word that suggests itself to me regarding Frau L.'s quasi-incestuous relationship to Filippa's father.

Incest – racial shame. Frau L. always stresses the Algerian temperament that was so incompatible with her Northern temperament. So Filippa's life, the product of absolute sin, is lebensunwertes Leben.

Death on her heels.[1]

It was as if she wanted to shake someone off who was plaguing her, clinging to her, said Frau L. about Filippa's fits. An exact observation, at the price of believing in spirits.

The burden this child has to carry is unimaginable: illness, her mother's projections, the phantasy of racial shame . . . and how one leads to the other: the fact that tuberous brain sclerosis is very frequently inherited . . .

. . .

[Later] Filippa was clearly having a bout of illness. Hardly surprising. The white spots were spreading considerably; skin changes slightly visible around her nose.

Frequent gestures recently: Filippa clasps my face in her hands 'tenderly', with a teeth-gnashing smile, twisted with anger. Still, she does have her anger more 'under control' than before – but at what price?! And Frau L. can't see the disaster; her euphoria regarding the Bach flower remedies is limitless. Filippa, get lost . . .!

B., says Frau L. (he has to express her destructive wishes against Filippa), wishes Filippa would die.

. . .

[Still later] Filippa needs her medication again, otherwise she is lost. Just as she does when she feels dead scared, she has already abandoned herself compliantly. (Not surprisingly the withdrawal shock has given rise to the severest round of fits yet – the healer interpreted these as a typical worsening of symptoms, a sign of healing setting in.)

Ghastly to see how Filippa is being destroyed.

Screaming with anger – it wouldn't be enough . . .

[Still later] Filippa isn't gnashing her teeth any more, and Frau L. says that her behaviour has improved so much. Yes, the child's dying a thousand deaths and the mother can only see that she is getting quieter and quieter, for heaven's sake, you miserable bawler, Filippa, get lost!

Getting in touch with the healer was of no avail: she celebrates Filippa's compliant self-abandonment as her 'miracle'.

Just how much I was contaminated by the child's fears of death and the mother's panic-driven euphoria is clear from reading these notes. Writing them up as well as discussing them with colleagues, enabled me to gain a certain distance from the projective identifications which had assailed me. In this re-enactment of Frau L.'s inner strife, I could see that the only hope was if I did not get too entangled, if I did not take the euphoric mother (the healer) away from her as, in the past, the grandmother had tried to deprive Frau L.'s mother of the right of custody. I also needed to be able to offer her the holding she had never had for her chaotic feelings and anxieties, in which euphoria and magic hope could have a place alongside her perception of reality – for she needed both. It was clear to me that without support from the Institute, which continued to place obstacles in my path, I was not going to be able to cope alone. Consequently, I got in touch with the healer. She had nothing against collaborating, it is true, but did not understand my concerns and did not see why Filippa still needed her medication, for the time being at any rate. Instead, she tried to calm me down by showing me Filippa's horoscope. This indicated a severe crisis was to be expected at any time but that a radical improvement would follow in the autumn – when in reality, after the therapy was broken off, and despite the continuing flower therapy, Filippa did have a breakdown. I also looked into the literature about the Bach flower therapy and found that I could give my unreserved support to the mother's experiment with the treatment since the subtle effects of the prescribed substances might very well have a positive effect on the therapeutic process. At the same time I sought out a doctor who might be sympathetic towards Frau L.'s anxiety and mistrust of medication; someone competent to treat Filippa's illness medically with psychological understanding as well as being open to Frau L.'s transference wish for a 'platonic relationship' to a father-figure. It was clear to me that in this situation I would not be able to persuade Frau L. to return to the neuro-paediatrician who had treated Filippa previously. My search for a doctor was also a sign that I was overstrained and that I did not want to have to bear the responsibility for this therapy alone. As my situation in the Institute had become untenable, I felt that things were getting on top of me.

Hitherto, Frau L. had always found in male doctors the contact with reality she found so difficult and worrying. In her phantasy, doctors, men, were omniscient and omnipotent (just as, as a child, she had phantasised about her dead father); they mastered medicine (and thus her mother's euphoria or depression, as she had experienced it in her childhood with their lover), and Filippa's former doctor had taken over this role unconsciously by pronouncing with God-like absoluteness the diagnosis and prognosis with which he wanted to pin Frau L. to her non-existent reality that left her no room for hope. Frau L. sensed this but, alone, she was incapable of seeing the danger realistically and at the same time of having hope. As a medical lay person I could not help her. So for the sake of her hopes for Filippa, she had to turn away from the killing reality of the doctor's diagnosis of inexorable fate towards the hope which she could only find in euphoric denial and in the promises of treatment which had introduced her to the realm of magic and miraculous healing on the fringes of society.

In her phases of denial, Frau L. was seeking, through this treatment, her mother's euphoria again; euphoria in which she had taken flight as a child from the coldness and hardness of the grandmother who was more adapted to reality.

For Filippa, however, this always meant the collapse of her hope – by her denial, her mother was not only hurting her psychical integrity, by burdening her with her own denied and projected affects, but her body itself. Left to the mercy of her fits and overpowering affects, without the support of medication, Filippa lost all her capacity for resistance. In such phases of the mother's denial, Filippa's condition deteriorated rapidly and so drastically – probably intensified by a period of illness – that her mother was eventually driven back into the arms of the hope-killing doctor, representing reality. This meant a repeated humiliation for Frau L. and a shock for Filippa that was likely to trigger another episode of illness. Each time, during these phases, Frau L. would break off contact completely with the doctor or with the healer respectively to devote herself completely to the other person, probably out of unconscious disappointment that they had not succeeded in acting as mediators between reality and hope. Frau L. now turned to me with this wish for mediation. I could sense how she was anxiously watching to see if I continued to be on her side or whether I would take sides with the doctor or the healer, and whether I would take her perceptions and phantasies of the devil in Filippa and the harmfulness of chemical drugs just as seriously as her wish to have contact with reality.

I did not find it difficult to take Frau L. seriously. I could understand her criticism of orthodox medicine which reduced Filippa's problem to human-genetic and chemo-physical factors, whereas Frau L.'s correct observation that when Filippa was having a fit she acted as if someone was clinging onto her back meant nothing. The validity of Frau L.'s criticism was not diminished in any way by the fact that it was motivated by her childhood experiences. But I also feared that Filippa was still far from being able to defend herself against the fits with her own resources and that the renewed attacks would undermine the gains she had made in music therapy. I thus stood between the child who urgently needed her medication, however problematic it was, and the mother who was trying, through Filippa, to free her own mother from her dreadful, and eventually fatal addiction to medi-cation, as she had tried to do in vain as a child. As much as I understood her, since it was Filippa's life that was at stake, I felt obliged to take sides. (This was another reason why it would have been good at this time of crisis for me to be able to work together with a doctor, for it was understandable that it was difficult for Frau L. to put up with my taking sides.) I spent a lot of time explaining to her why I did not approve of her decision in spite of understanding her motives; and, that Filippa would still need her medica-tion for some time to come even if a gradual reduction might be possible. Although I repeatedly made it clear how well I understood her reasons, I could sense how these discussions put more of a strain on our relationship and her trust in me than she could tolerate.

As can be seen from the 'Notes on Family L.', Filippa took the only path open to her which promised some sort of deliverance; that is, withdrawal, compliantly abandoning herself. Only in the music therapy sessions did her will to live continue to flicker and even then it did so more weakly and rarely. At home and at the kindergarten, after initially falling back once again – in protest – into her old wildness, she became so quiet that her mother was very relieved: her difficult Filippa was being good and with-drawn – it must be the miracle promised by the healer. However, the caregivers in the kindergarten were so horrified by this withdrawal that they withheld their support for Frau L. and considered reporting her for dangerous bodily harm. Although we had worked together well up till then, I now felt abandoned by them in my efforts to find a solution.

During this period Filippa developed a few peculiar habits: for the most part she only whispered, did not laugh cheerfully and clearly any more but giggled in an artificial, old-maidish way 'heeheeheehee'. It took her longer and longer in the music therapy session to thaw out and to participate as she had done before, and she had very little zest left. The only expression of anger that remained for a while was a teeth-gnashing smile while clasping my face in both her hands. If we played together on her favourite instrument, the temple blocks, she whispered 'not too hard' and only tapped very lightly on it.

The consequence of this withdrawal, of course, was that the fits gradually became less frequent. In spite of being very sad about Filippa's self-reduction, which was the price she had to pay for this progress, I was also quite pleased that Filippa had such a good sense of the connection between her 'too hard' feelings and the fits, and that she had better not play 'too hard' any more, as long as she had to manage without the support of medication and as long as she was unable to live without this support.

The healer now believed, anyway, that the miracle had happened and that, because of her belief in miracles, Frau L. was unable to see that the music therapy and the work she had been doing on herself had borne fruit here, too. Instead she was enormously thankful to the miraculous healer. She must have found me untrustworthy with my warnings and I found it difficult to get it across to her that it was not a miracle but only difficult and tiring work that had helped and that would help in the future. In the end, I could hardly believe myself – the counter-transference feelings with people with learning disabilities are always the same, i.e. false modesty, by means of which the therapist seeks to escape the parents' expectation of a miracle – that Filippa had been able to make use of the therapeutic help I was able to give her to do so much work on herself.

I came to the conclusion that reducing medication partially – not stopping altogether – might have been a good idea; I would not have come to this conclusion had it not been for Frau L.'s actions. She had noticed something that I had not been able to see but unfortunately had taken things too far; Filippa had started to bring her experience of the illness and the fits into our sessions and to work on this. At the beginning of one of these sessions, shortly after I had noticed from her skin changes that she had clearly suffered another episode of her illness, she came in, as always now, whispering, tired and oppressed; naturally, she had experienced the episode again as a punishment for her recent outbursts of anger.

> She spoke of 'sleeping' and wanted me to cover her with a blanket.
> 'Sing *Frau!*'
> 'Poor little girl, she's so sad, so tired, and would like to go to sleep.'
> 'No, not sleep!'
> She cried out again, clearly and energetically, no longer whispering. Sing *Frau . . . girl . . . Frau.*'
> 'Little girl, dainty girl, would like to *live* very much, would like so much to be strong, healthy and to become a big, grown-up woman!'

Filippa assented heartily and gave me a hearty hug, and then asked me to sing the same words again. Then she ground her teeth fiercely and I sang:

'Who was so nasty and hurt Filippa so much? The nasty, nasty illness. The little girl wants to defend herself and be strong against the illness.'

She now began playing a peek-a-boo game. I interpreted this game to her as a dramatisation of her experience during one of her attacks – during an attack she also suddenly 'goes away'. She became much happier, began playing almost like before, laughing and enjoying herself, with me running after her: she ran away from me into a corner where I then caught her.

In the next sessions – meanwhile she had been taken off the medication completely – this game in which I ran after her became more important and also more threatening. When I caught her in the corner, she screwed up her face with anxiety and I felt helpless as if I had the role of the illness that was persecuting her. When I suggested that we wanted together to try to run away she accepted thankfully. 'Get out', she demanded, and 'Mummy' – how right she was: if she really wanted to get out of the vicious circle of illness and psychical disaster, then the only way was via Mummy.

Once I was present when she had an attack. Again she said to me: 'Sing'. When I asked her again if she wanted to sleep she was able to cry out convincingly, 'No'; when I followed this up, however, by saying that she wanted to live, she hardly seemed to hear me. Instead, she asked me to continue singing to her: 'Sing *Frau* . . . girl . . . nasty . . . afraid' – I sang to her about the illness and the poor little girl's dreadful fear and then she began shaking with her pupils wide open with fear as if in unspeakable horror, turning round as if death was literally pressing hard on her heels.

I had another talk with her mother, this time in her home. Frau L. showed me her new apartment and Filippa followed close behind me as we went around, still as a shadow, oppressed, and, at times, going 'heeheeheehee' in an artificial way. Then, as her mother left us alone for a moment, she sat down right beside me. I promised her that when I spoke to her mother I would do everything I could to persuade the latter to give her her medicine again. This was what Filippa wanted to hear. She stood up and went off quietly leaving me alone with her mother.

I told the mother how I felt about Filippa's withdrawal and the concerns I had about it. I urged her once again to see a doctor and promised her that I would try to get the doctor to understand her reservations regarding medication. Frau L. became more and more worried and depressed; I had never seen her like this before. She made up her mind to go and see the doctor whom I had recommended with Filippa.

The same day Filippa had a session again. She was much less depressed than before. She was even able to show a bit of anger again. When I did not accept one of her habits – giving a kiss, which she had recently used to try and suppress her anger – by offering her my hand instead of my cheek and clapping it, she did the same, saying 'Hit Mummy'. Then we played on the temple blocks. 'Too hard?' I asked, and she replied: 'Yes, it is!' She got louder again, then almost joyful as we began chasing each other around; finally, she once again had something about her of the zestful girl she was before the disaster. The mother's willingness to relax her denial for a while and to look at the danger Filippa was in was such a relief to Filippa that she could at last be joyful again.

Admittedly this did not last long. After this session Filippa did not have any further attacks for two weeks. It was a period when some sessions had to be missed due to public holidays and vacations which I had to comply with because of room availability (I was now working privately in a school). Moreover, Frau L. had been unable to get an appointment with the doctor. When I saw them both again, they had not been to the doctor, denial had gained the upper hand again, supported by a conversation Frau L. had had with the healer. The latter had strengthened Frau L.'s belief in a 'miracle' and this belief was reinforced by the fact that Filippa had had no attacks during the last two weeks.

Generally speaking, Filippa seemed to regain her composure during the coming period. Her attacks became much rarer after we had been able to work through them in the peek-a-boo game and after her fear of the illness had been given expression both in the chasing game and in my singing. Admittedly, she still came across as being depressed but she nonetheless thawed out a little during our sessions. Once, I noticed that for the first time since the beginning of the therapy she forgot to say: 'Turn on the light!' I had never understood this injunction before, and had just done the things she requested, but now I understood it. As was often the case, I had some chocolate with me, and that day she wanted to eat a particularly large amount. I told her that the chocolate was 'just for her'. 'For me,' she said, and laughed, 'for me!' And now she did want the light on! 'Ligh' on' 'Ligh' on!' – 'Me on!' This was a new form of ego expression. Now she could be 'I', not just in exceptional situations when she felt understood, but at any time. The chocolate now became very important for her and she kept repeating proudly, 'For me'. In everyday life, too, she now began experimenting with 'I'.

With Frau L., too, there were now a few sessions which were not coloured by my worries and her defensiveness against contact but where she felt understood and closer to me again. I had supported her own wish to have treatment with the healer too and she now had the feeling she was making progress. 'It's all because of the little bottles', she said, meaning the Bach flower remedies. She then asked if I believed in spirits. I said no, but that I held such metaphorical language to be very important as long as we had no other possibility of putting experiences, for which orthodox medicine has no name, into words. She was very relieved by my point of view which did not question the reality of her experiences but neither did it banish them to the world of spirits. Once again the contact between us was good but I could sense that our talks could not heal the breach of mistrust caused by my insisting on medical treatment for Filippa as well as by my being thrown out of the Institute. She felt that I was weak and was at the mercy of an arbitrary superior; and, anyway, I must have been wrong since a 'miracle' seemed to have happened: for the first time in her life Filippa was having fewer attacks, even without medication, than ever before.

Filippa continued to work but was still subdued and often very oppressed. She seemed to have less vital energy than when she was under medical treatment (a 'secondary effect' of which, as a rule, is to dampen one's spirits). The 'sleeping' game now acquired two meanings: abandoning herself or hope. In the game of pursuit I was the illness pursuing her into dead ends. She cried painfully when I approached her but she could not stand it either when I tried to step out of this role. Getting more and more desperate, she would finally run out into the street and throw herself on the road. 'Tired, sleep.' When I dragged her out of the path of oncoming cars, she would scream and kick at me in desperate anger.

Sometimes, though, she also wanted to sleep and then I had to make a bed for us out of cushions, surrounded by her favourite instruments, on which we then lay, covering ourselves with a blanket. I then had to sing to her and she felt good, laughed and began – cautiously, was it allowed? – pawing my breasts with her hands. 'A sweet', she said or 'juice'. Since the long summer holidays were coming, I no longer offered her the baby bottle as play material.

This time it was particularly difficult to work through the impending holiday separation. It was far too long 'for Filippa', said Frau L., with audible anger in her voice. Although, at her request, I promised to write and also left her my holiday address, I did not feel good either about the idea of the long separation. The controversy over Filippa's medication had undermined our relationship and the healer's promise of a miracle was enticing. On top of this, Frau L. was going to have to pay for the therapy herself after the holidays (hitherto the Institute had financed the therapy); and, even with the low fee which I requested, this would be difficult for her as she was on public assistance. It was also uncertain – and I had had to inform her about this – how long I would be able to continue working in her place of residence. This was because I had to look for a new position and because the room in the school where I had been working since my departure from the Institute had only been allotted to me temporarily. I hoped, however, and I tried to explain this to Frau L., to be able to continue working with Filippa at least until she was able to accept a parting gift from me as a transitional object (perhaps a Filippa-doll), and until I had found someone who could take over the therapy. Owing to all these uncertainties I feared that Frau L.'s denial might become excessively strong again. This was reinforced by several factors: Filippa rarely had convulsions now, and when she did, they were very mild ones; she caused no more difficulties at home, spoke more and better, and had also begun playing a bit again. I wondered whether Frau L.'s relationship with me was robust enough to withstand all this. (Had I not been dependent on the school premises, I would have tried to find a better bridging solution.) When I spoke to Filippa about the long school holidays during which she would have to wait for me, she also seemed not to want to know about it – she probably sensed my uncertainty and her mother's ambivalence only too well.

During the second half of the holidays, Frau L. wrote to me saying that she wanted to break off the music therapy as she had now decided to move away from the small town where she lived – she had already found a flat somewhere else. She had already spoken to me several times of her idea of moving out of the town where things were going so badly for her, but also of her wish to give her eldest son a better school education and to find a school of anthroposophy for Filippa. This sudden decision looked to me, however, like a flight from the difficult encounter with a therapist who had disappointed her so much. In the letter she asked to speak with me again by telephone. I respected her decision although when we spoke on the telephone I noticed that she might well have been prepared to let me talk her out of it. In view of all the uncertainties and difficulties, I could not see any possibility of offering her a meaningful alternative to her decision. I could not have promised her anything at all. Through her sudden decision against our agreement to try to at least to make a meaningful transition for Filippa possible, all my discouragement, worry and exhaustion of the last months gained the upper hand over my readiness to work; I suddenly felt tired, too tired even to think about arranging a final session.

On the day Filippa would normally have had her first session after the holidays, I was told, on arriving at the school, that a few minutes before Filippa had been walking around alone and had obviously been waiting for me until someone found her and picked her up. So, despite having 'no sense of time', she had run away from home on time for her session and had been looking for me.

So I telephoned Frau L. and arranged for Filippa to come for a last session.

Filippa arrived at the school playground for this last session with her head bowed, holding her mother's hand. Only when her mother greeted me did she look up and see me. Whereupon she broke loose, ran over to me, throwing her arms round me full of endless despair. She had a desperately sad and hopeless expression on her face and just spoke in whispers. She wanted me to play music to her while she sucked a sweet and then she said quietly: 'Dietmut – music – tomorrow, too'. I told her that unfortunately it would not be possible. She took no notice and after a while she again said: 'Music – Dietmut is here – tomorrow'. Once again I had to tell her that it was the last time we would be making music. After a period of silence she held out the drumstick to me which she had previously used to make music and threw her sweet on the floor. 'Tired, sleep,' she whispered desperately sadly. 'Poor Filippa, are you so sad that you just want to sleep?' I said, and asked if I should fetch the blanket to put over her. At first, she did not react at all but later she said: 'Blanket' and nodded her head. When I brought her the blanket she did not look at it (of course not, since this 'sleeping' with me under the blanket is also no longer possible), but said, 'Drink water'. As I did not have a cup at hand, I showed her how she could drink out of my hand; she gulped it down and then said, 'Milk'. She drank it slowly in big gulps which she kept in her mouth as long as possible. 'You want to hold on to the good milk as long as possible because this is indeed our last session.' When she heard her mother coming outside, she left of her own accord, without saying good-bye.

At home – I heard this from the mother later – she later went wild.

Addendum: five months later Frau L. wrote to me asking if she could phone me. She said that soon after her last music therapy session Filippa had again had such frequent and severe convulsions that she had gone to see the doctor whom I had recommended. After a period free of convulsions due to medication, the attacks had begun again so that the dose had to be increased. Recently Filippa's father had been to visit and since then, in spite of higher doses of medication, her attacks had been just as frequent and severe as before. I gave Frau L. the name of a community practice for child psychiatry and child psychotherapy, which had recently been opened near where they were now living, in the hope that they would make use of this resource.

Chapter 9

The infantocidal introject[1]

Psychoanalysis has always striven to reconstruct damaged human subjectivity. However, with a few exceptions, mentally retarded people have long been excluded from this enterprise. This happened – and still happens – as a matter of course, as if such a state of affairs required no justification and could not be questioned. Ever since precise diagnostic methods were developed to establish the existence of abnormal physical conditions, there seems to have been no further need to enquire whether learning disability might be understood as resulting from social and psychological developmental difficulties. It has been taken for granted that learning disability is a deficient state in which psychodynamics play but a minor role and where development is irrevocably determined by organic conditions. Reflecting on the psychodynamics and socialisation of learning disability has seemed more or less pointless. Consequently, most psychoanalysts believe that learning disabled people cannot be understood and treated psychoanalytically and that psychoanalytic theory cannot contribute to an understanding of their specific mental states.

In this book I am presenting an attempt to understand mental retardation in terms of psychoanalysis and sociopsychology. My approach differs from that of others such as Gaedt (1990) and Sinason (1992), in as far as I do not differentiate between a primary handicap that is meant as organical bedrock and a secondary handicap which may or may not overlay the former due to social discrimination. Although I do not follow Mannoni in her Lacanian orientation, I agree with her view that learning disability cannot be divided into an organical and a psychological constituting component. Like Mannoni (1972), I assume that it is developed from the very outset of the process of socialisation in which the death wishes of caregivers triggered by diagnostic information or some – often minute – unusual and frightening ways in the infant's gestures, some 'uncanny' (in the sense of Freud's 'unheimlich', 1919a) perception of the infant are the driving forces of this socialisation process.

There is a strong argument to back up Mannoni's and my view. In his book, *Descartes' Error*, Damasio (1994) presents rich material suggesting that mind and body are not as clearly distinct as we might think. In the past few years psychoanalysis has been increasingly involved in a discussion with neurophysiology, thus in some way returning to a lifelong conviction of Freud himself, who always believed that one day the insights of psychoanalytic metapsychology might be unified with concepts of modern neurophysiology (cf. Lorenzer 2002; Solms & Kaplan-Solms 2000). The insights gained in this interdisciplinary discussion are apt to shed new light onto the old philosophical question of the mind–body relationship. Today we are aware of how the structure of the human brain is developed in close interaction with the environment. If this is so it must concern our ideas about learning disability, too. The differentiation between organical and psychological roots of mental conditions, between primary and secondary handicap, cannot be taken for granted. Therefore, neither 'brain damage of unknown origin' nor any other kind of physical alteration can serve as a passe-partout explanation for 'primary handicap' any longer.

On an individual level, learning disability may be understood as an impairment of the capacity to symbolise which is systematically developed in interaction with the 'organisers' of the 'institution learning disability'. It becomes almost irreversibly 'organised' in a process similar to that which, according to Balint (1957), is called 'organising illnesses' in the interaction between the patient and his or her consultant. This 'organisation' leads to a situation where autonomous imaginative capacity and symbolic interaction is inhibited or destroyed. As a consequence of this deficiency of symbolic capacity, the learning disabled ego is condemned to passivity and silence – a silence which has its counterpart in the silence of mainstream psychoanalysis on the subject. I therefore am inclined to understand the latter as an expression of collective counter-transference containing unconscious death wishes.

I shall go into some metapsychological detail, investigating the well-known phenomenon that the lives of learning disabled people are ruled by stereotyped behaviour and repetitions to a much larger extent than those of 'normal' people. My claim is that the common root of these repetitions and stereotypes is similar to what Freud called the repetition compulsion (1919b). Stereotyped behaviour is repetition compulsion in its most archaic form, to be sure. In presenting three typical cases, I shall try to design models of how such stereotyped behaviour may develop during the socialisation process of learning disability. Two of the cases were reported to me in a supervision group meeting, the last one stems from my own experience.

Mr K. is a good-looking man who at first sight does not appear disabled. There is little information about his childhood. He was left by his mother and brought up in various homes and institutions. He is known by those close to him as somebody who regularly gets himself into impossible situations. As he does not appear disabled, he awakens hopes and illusory ideas about his competence and independence, especially in his employers.

He then attempts to live up to these expectations, trying to conceal all signs of failure. To sustain his employers' hopes he has to use lies and pretensions. Quite regularly, these situations result in a complete breakdown in which he is unmasked and ridiculed as a confidence trickster. He is then not only dropped abruptly by the disillusioned and disappointed employer, but also severely reprimanded and humiliated.

Lars is a five-year-old boy who terrorises his family with his compulsions. For hours he will stay in the toilet room, flushing the toilet over and over again. When the toilet is not absolutely clean he bursts into tantrums. In his psychotherapeutic sessions he kneels in front of the toilet, flushing it or dipping the toilet brush slightly into the water and watching the drops drip down. We know a few details about his family background. His mother is second wife to his father, whose former wife hung herself during postnatal depression. His mother experienced a first pregnancy which was terminated in the fifth month after an amniocentesis had indicated that the baby would be born with a disability. The following pregnancy seemed normal but was terminated by premature birth in the fifth month. Lars survived with the help of an incubator. During his infancy he went through several operations. Twice he had to suffer the laying and undoing of an artificial bowel exit.

Hans is a young man who cannot speak and has little understanding of language. He has developed a symptom which makes everyone shrink away from him in disgust. He regurgitates and ruminates for long hours every day and sometimes spits over the person who has to take care of him. He provokes this regurgitation and occasional vomiting by pressing his thighs into his stomach in the crouching position. Often his caregivers try to make him stretch and relax but to no avail. While the case was reported to me, I listened with growing disgust, if not panic. I have always tried to avoid people with such symptoms but this time I could no longer do so. Just after I had been told about Hans, he entered the room and, as if he knew that I had been asked to help his caregivers understand him better, immediately got onto the sofa in a crouching position and began to regurgitate. I felt massive ambivalence: on the one hand, everything in me wanted to flee; on the other hand, I wanted to see the task that I had been given through and demonstrate psychoanalytic understanding even under extreme conditions. In this ambivalent state, I tried to make contact with Hans, which promptly misfired: I moved towards him too quickly and addressed him by his name. He got up abuptly and left the room. I had obviously frightened him.

Before I proceed to interpret the examples, let me make a few theoretical points. My thoughts on the 'organisation' of learning disability and the 'infantocidal introject', which will be developed here, are mainly based upon Harold Lincke's (a Swiss psychoanalyst and biologist) studies on introject formation. Lincke (1971) notes a critical situation which must inevitably arise time and again during development. This situation is that biologically based inner impulses occur according to a fixed schedule which is far ahead of motor development, so that the young individual is not yet in a position to translate these impulses into real life actions in an appropriate way. Hence, a dangerous contradiction arises between the impulse and its potential for realisation. Lincke mentions, for example, early contradictory impulses betweeen tearing the prey apart and devouring it and the concomitant social situation where the only available prey would be the mother, upon whom the child is totally dependent for all his or her vital functions at this stage. This model of an oral conflict situation resulting from the disharmony of human development assumes that, as the impulse to bite occurs, a biologically based natural inhibition mechanism is activated, namely the inhibition to bite members of the same species. A successful outcome of socialisation makes it necessary that according to this biological inhibition mechanism and through the mediation of caring interaction, the actual realisation of the impulse is inhibited thus being internalised, 'devoured', and becomes an intrapsychic possibility for a potential symbolic interaction pattern, an introject. In such an introject instinctive impulses are united with inhibitory mechanisms, thus making them independent of outside-world stimuli. If this process of introjection succeeds it will constitute the elements of a growing capacity for imagination independent of situations.

In accordance with this model of introject formation, but going beyond the generally unavoidable developmental crises, I propose that there are crisis situations specific for the socialisation of infants and young children who become learning disabled. Their outcome will not be situation-independent imagination, but the opposite. The introject formations created here will be likely to impair symbolic competence rather than to open mental spaces.

If for any reason during early interaction, the infant's activities, his or her spontaneous gestures, endanger his or her life by triggering death wishes in the early caregivers, the innate biological mechanisms for responding to life-threatening situations – physiological anxiety responses (Stern 1972) – will be aroused. This will immobilise the infant where the realisation of his or her intentions is concerned, an experience which may lead to a choking of vitality and a channelling of the development of the situation-independent imaginative faculty in a more or less drastically hampering way. The result of such a process would be an 'organisation' in the sense of merging physiological anxiety responses with intentional gestures. The introjects would forfeit at least part of their stimulus autonomy and the interaction forms would remain bound to stimulus–response mechanisms. Such interaction forms would essentially remain unsymbolised and permanently unavailable for symbolisation, as there is no room for symbolisation between stimulus and response.

The outcome of this process would, on the one hand, be a progressive, that is, healthy one because it would ensure the survival of the individual faced with a given threat. In this sense, the resulting disability could not be called a psychical illness. On the other hand, the 'organisation', that is, the fact that vital life impulses must remain at least partially withdrawn from the sphere of autonomous imaginative faculty, would hamper the individual's intellectual, social and motor development towards autonomy, at least to some extent, and could thus be called pathological.

From ethology, we are familiar with flight instincts and death-feigning reflexes as reactions to situations of acute threat. In what follows, I shall refer to the proposed instinctive response pattern of infants facing acute threat by their prototypes in the animal world – although I do not claim that this is correct from an empirical–biological standpoint – because the idea of the death-feigning reflex or flight instinct is more appropriate than the concept of physiological anxiety responses to make us aware of the affective catastrophe which I regard as the central driving force in the socialisation of learning disability. In the case of learning disabled development, death-feigning and flight impulses are to be triggered simultaneously with vital impulses such as instinctive search motions, spontaneous intentional gestures aiming to satisfy basic life needs. In the most severe cases they can even be triggered simultaneously with vegetative impulses. Such a process must appear as organic damage since mental space, the internalised 'potential space' (Winnicott 1960), in which a disorder could manifest itself as a mental one, has not yet been established. Vegetative impulses and early intentional gestures which have merged with a death-feigning reflex in such a way will be internalised and become independent psychophysical entities in the course of introject formation. However, the death-feigning reflex remains melded with these vital impulses and thus becomes generalised. Due to this the whole complex now remains tied to regularly recurring reflex-triggering internal stimuli. Vegetative impulses and spontaneous gestures thus become reflex cues. The symbolic autonomy of those introject complexes is incomplete and thus all participation in social and intellectual interaction involves the uncontrollable dynamics of the reflex. The result is a behaviour pattern which must seem at first sight meaningless.

Following these introductory remarks, let us now look at our three cases:

Mr K.

Due to the fact that I know very little about Mr K.'s early years I have to rely solely upon the scene which was reported to me in order to reconstruct his early experience. In Mr K.'s enactment we find a situation dominated by the disintegration of illusion and the ensuing feelings of shame, exposure, humiliation, unbearable loneliness and helplessness: a lone individual suddenly standing naked before the eyes of the whole world. On the other hand, there is the awful disillusionment of the counterparts who have now to recognise that they have supported a phantom and who feel driven towards punishing Mr K. in a devastating way.

This situative structure may guide us towards constructing a model of the 'original case' of Mr K.'s repetition compulsion. First of all we can directly trace the situation back to the mother–child relationship: we may imagine a maniacal activity, early intervention programmes dominating this relationship – followed by devastating disillusionment, which led the mother to abandon her child. If we consider the earliest interactions we can construct a scenery in which the 'sparkle in mother's eye', when confronted with the reality of this child, was turned into its opposite – shame.

The well-known metaphor of the 'sparkle in mother's eye' stands for the moment of recognition, of motherly intunement: the child is 'o.k.', is biologically and socially 'right', the mother can give his or her existence meaning within her own conceptions, it fits with her idea of it. With this 'sparkle' the mother reflects to the child that his or her biological inheritance – with Bion (1962) we speak of preconceptions – can be contained in her social world. It means that she can pick up and understand his or her gesture as an expression of intentional participation in the interaction between them. From Winnicott (1960) we learn that 'the true self becomes a living reality only if the mother is repeatedly successful in responding to the spontaneous gesture . . . of the infant' (p. 145).

In the primary interaction of the child K. with his mother this process seems to have failed. The mother in this scene was for some reason not able to see her newly born child as a magnificent product of an act of love. Fear and confusion may have led her to see this child more as physical evidence of her disgrace and her being at the mercy of someone else. It is as if looking upon her newborn child, she reconstructed the act of procreation as being an extremely humiliating experience of being raped, and as if this newborn baby – the product of this act – was unbearable evidence of her own helplessness and disgrace. Perhaps this mother had experienced pregnancy as a manifestation of her personal integrity and omnipotence, and this was shattered in a traumatic way at birth. Thus, the first interactions, that is, each simple act of putting on nappies, holding the infant or breast feeding would be influenced by the fact that in her child the mother sees the embodiment of her own helplessness and humiliation. In the face of this disillusionment the only possible reaction for the mother, as I see it, is to become numb inside. This numbness encompasses two aspects. First, she becomes numb just as she became numb in the 'primal scene'. Second, since she is now in an active position, the presence of the child that bears such significance must trigger the inner impulse to destroy the manifestation of her shame, and she goes numb in order not to become aware of this impulse to kill. Thus the infant K. will not only be unable to create the 'illusion', that is, a subjective feeling of being all right with his mother, he will also have to react to a life-threatening situation. The only means of reacting available to the infant will be the death-feigning reflex.

In the scene of Mr K.'s repetition compulsion, we re-encounter these impulses – first idealisation, the disillusionment, helplessness and shame and resulting hatred and killing impulses – in the form of the counter-transference of those individuals who fall for Mr K.'s ploys. In the actual scene we discover the mother figure becoming petrified with fright, re-enacted by the persistant refusal of Mr K.'s counterparts to admit that Mr K. is not how they imagined him to be in their grandiose efforts to assist him. This denial, the fearful immobilisation of the mother in the first instance, encompassing a murderous phantasy, must trigger the death-feigning reflex in the child, which at the same time – and this makes the physical reflex twice as powerful – is a mimetic banishing adaptation to the mother's fear. The child can only ward off the mother's fears in embodying them, in accepting a completely passive role insofar as he is containing the mother's projective identification: she is seeing him as a monster, and therefore he must become a monster and act as such.

This, as a result of successful projective defence, will cause a certain feeling of relief in the mother. The mother–child pair will partially regain its ability to act. Vital impulses are stirring again under the petrified surface. Since the 'illusion' is indispensable, the spontaneous gesture which is coming to life again will now trigger the flight instinct. The mother–child pair must now proceed to manic activity in order to fake the 'illusion'. Both mother and child will make use of the fading numbness to initiate hectic activity directed at warding off perception of the horror which has occurred by making it look as if nothing had ever happened, as if grandiose integrity had never been endangered.

Thus the first impulse of the child is alloyed with a death-feigning reflex. The second impulse, the feeling of life stirring beneath the frozen surface, can only occur now on the basis of the suspension of the infant's ability for spontaneous interaction. And this is where the impulse to flight must be organised, creating yet another reflex-bound structure. What actually should have been elevated to gestural-symbolic potency, is withdrawn into the somatic non-symbolisable sphere through alloyment with physical reflexes. By means of this introject, the death-feigning reflex and the impulse to flight will remain a necessity of quasi-organic character in all Mr K.'s intentional social interactions in the future.

Lars

In this example we have more information to draw upon in order to understand the scene of the child's repetition compulsion. We can assume that because he was born in the fifth month of his mother's pregnancy he became in her unconscious phantasy the aborted foetus, her first child. It is quite likely that she experienced the premature birth as an equivalent to the abortion of her former pregnancy. In her eyes he must become a baby with a potential disability for two reasons: because of the real danger of damage through the premature birth, and because of the striking similarity between the artificial abortion and the spontaneous 'abortion'.

In the first interactions between Lars and his mother reality and horror are one and the same. In this child the mother faces what she cannot but conceive of as a result of her 'crime', the abortion. Knowing that this child is rather liable to developing a disability of some kind she will always unconsciously identify him with his aborted brother or sister. The terror this causes inside her will have a threatening impact on her child whose vitality is already weakened. Again, there will be a melding of intentional action with the death-feigning reflex.

We can easily recognise the death-feigning reflex in the child's compulsive behaviour. He behaves as if he were in a state of numbness. The specific scenery of the toilet room might have its origins in several sources. How can we interpret this? It seems more than likely that in this place (in German there is a word signifying both, abortion and toilet: 'Abort') during care-giving activities the mother's traumatic memories concerning the 'Abort' were specifically activated. At the same time the toilet room might have reminded Lars of his early days in the sterile atmosphere of the hospital. Thus, faced with his mother's horror, he tried to cling to something known, something that at least had secured his survival, if only in total passivity and submission to the machine. Thus, surviving and fear of death become one and the same. Faced with mother's horror, his reaction will be death-feigning. In becoming numb he will mimic the mother's visions of horror. And like in the situation described before, we can imagine that this mimicking is giving way to the mother's projective identification, thus creating some moment of relief in which mother and child will be able to organise their flight impulses. They can now use the toilet room with all its impacts of potential meaning as a prerequisite of their common uncon-scious phantasm. Thus they create the 'illusion', Lars' specific form of 'being biologically and socially right'. In this context his panic caused by traces of dirt in the toilet can now be understood as his fear to find himself in the toilet as an aborted foetus.

Hans

In my contact with Hans, the only chance I saw for understanding was by attempting to form a relationship with him in which the symptom would be integrated. So the first step was to establish a symbolic space which could be the basis for an understanding. Obviously, such a construction of symbolic space from almost total destruction demands certain prerequisites; at least a firm hold on theory which can offer a containing function and substitute for the hold lacking in the subject, who is held captive in his stereotypes as far as language and scenic structure are concerned.

My first, unsuccessful encounter with Hans affords only a vague idea of what the meaning of his behaviour might be. The feeling of disgust emerging within myself and identificatory retching reflexes produced feelings of panic. By treating Hans too brashly, I drove him away. Here, one might think of an abortion phantasy, the desire to rid oneself through vigorous movements of the feeling of an alien element rising up threateningly within oneself. Certainly this interpretation is vague since the scene provides only sparse information. A deeper understanding is only possible from an analysis of a further encounter which I had with Hans after overcoming my feelings of disgust, and which had a positive outcome.

Hans had retired to his room and I found him there crouching on his bed, ruminating continuously. Alone with him in his room, I withdrew into a corner to be as far away from him as possible and first tried to control my feelings of repulsion by breathing deeply in and out. I concentrated on this until my panic subsided and I felt a little calmer. I also began talking to myself – first, because it helped me to keep calm, and second, to try and make sense of this unbearable situation in which I found myself locked up in a room with someone I dreaded. I verbalised what I felt: the uncanniness of the situation, my panic, then the gradual lessening of my feelings of nausea through regular breathing, the feeling that through the nausea and disgust Hans existed inside me; the idea that his feelings were contained in my own body; namely, nausea as a kind of inner pressure which sought relief through burping.

As I became aware of this projective identification process I began to talk about the need for relief, not only for me but also for Hans. I told him that I had the impression that he had never known what a relief it could be to burp (since I had to assume that Hans' grasp of everyday language was very limited, I did not try to use simple 'disabled-appropriate' words but spoke to him instead as I would with an infant who has ears for the emotional content of the spoken word, which he can understand quite well in his own way long before the meaning of words becomes important to him (cf. Eliacheff 1993)). When I had said all this, the situation changed radically: I was no longer dominated by disgust. I still felt it but had gained some distance from it in that I now found it meaningful. Achieving greater calmness enabled me to attempt to make another initial contact with Hans: I repeatedly threw a ball to him and then went over to pick it up. This time my approaching him did not drive him away. Instead he allowed it to happen, risked glancing at the ball, and finally tried to take hold of it. Then he glanced at me out of the corner of his eye, finally took the ball and let go of it again when I made a gesture for him to do so. As soon as he would release the ball – which I interpreted to him as the burping and spitting of an infant needing to expel the excess inside him (which was too much for him, just as I had been 'too much' for him in our first unsuccessful meeting) – the situation also changed for Hans. He lay down and carefully pulled his blanket over his whole body including his head. His posture was almost the same as it was at the beginning: hands and legs drawn into the body with shoulders rounded – the embryonic position. However, there was one important difference: his head was no longer drawn in and he was now generally relaxed. He stopped ruminating and I heard him breathing deeply and regularly. I sat down next to him, breathing together with him and all the while talking to him about this. He responded by scratching his bed and so I did likewise. A dialogue of great intensity and beauty developed from this scratching and breathing. I gently touched his feet and then his back which was covered by the blanket. I started to feel like a pregnant woman caressing her child tucked away safely in her belly while communicating with it in a vegetative way. I no longer experienced Hans through feelings of disgust and nausea in myself but as a tenderly cathected love object. Our dialogue lasted for some time; finally Hans poked his head out from beneath the blanket and inspected the room with a look of quiet curiosity as if he were looking at it for the very first time.

From my affective involvement, this encounter with Hans can easily be interpreted as a pregnancy scenario, and not only because I eventually phantasised I was pregnant myself. Regurgitation, pressure on the stomach, the desire to breathe deeply – all are vegetative expressions of a pregnancy and birth scene. Hans' eventual emergence from under his bed cover and his calm and attentive look also resembled a birth scene. Thus, one is tempted to look for the first breakdown in the interaction between Hans and his mother during pregnancy and to regard it as the prototype for the failure of my first attempt to approach him. In the first scene, I tried to ward off the inner pressure filling me with panic by removing Hans from my perception – by 'aborting' him. From this we may be led to reconstruct the 'primal scene' of his repetition compulsion as a pregnancy scene, in which the mother felt that the foetus growing inside her was a foreign body creating panic and nausea, threatening her physical and mental integrity and that she must destroy it by vomiting or, more actively, by making strenuous movements (just like my first approachment) which would lead to a miscarriage.

However, the fact that Hans was able to create a regressive scene relatively quickly, making it possible for both of us to achieve contact, suggests a different interpretation. This interpretation would be that he fell back on an interaction form that had been successful during pregnancy but for some reason either came to an end after birth or acquired a destructive context at a later point in time. Perhaps it was an encounter accompanied by feelings of uncanniness and insecurity during or after birth which first caused the mother to retrospectively invest a normal feeling of ambivalence towards pregnancy with feelings of panic and disgust, feelings which I had for Hans when we first met. This could have led the mother to react with panic and repulsion to the normal burping and spitting of her infant, insofar as it had become an expression of a killing phantasy through the process of identification. This in turn caused the vital expressions of letting go, releasing and spitting out to become associated with the death-feigning reflex in the infant. This merging of vegetative impulses and anxiety response now had even more drastic consequences as in the case of Mr K. and Lars; namely, an almost complete destruction of symbolic capacity. In the cases of Mr K. and of Lars, the death-feigning reflex was alloyed with an intentional gesture; in other words, an active impulse which was not completely indispensable as such. In their cases, the satisfaction of physical needs was not fundamentally called into question when the impulse became immobilised in the death-feigning reflex. In Hans' case, a vitally indispensable vegetative expression, burping and vomiting, formed an indissoluble bond with the death-feigning reflex. Thus, the vegetative impulse had to find expression in the symptom of rumination in which the irreconcilable contradiction between life needs and mortal threat is maintained. The indispensability of vegetative expression becomes apparent in the perpetual repetition of rumination. Death-feigning is realised by the symptom substituting almost totally for active participation in life and (symbolic) interaction.[2]

Facit: Mr K.'s early interaction form has enabled him to proceed to the phallic phase; in Lars' case we can recognise strong anal features; in the case of Hans, with its welding of vegetative impulses and the death-feigning reflex, the development seems to have been arrested in the oral phase. It seems likely that such processes of phantasmatic derailment involving not only early intentional gestures but also vegetative impulses will have the severest impact on the development of symbolic capacity.

None of the three cases seems to contain triangular, let alone oedipal traits, indispensable prerequisites for autonomous intellectual capacity. Landauer (1938), as well as Mannoni (1972), has observed the lack of triangular moments in the instinctual drive structure of learning disabled people. Triangular structures require the dissolution of stimulus–response patterns into symbolic formations, while what I call 'infantocidal introject' is organised in the exact opposite way: a reflex-bound, organismic structure.

Epilogue: Solidarity

After visiting Inge for the last time, I dreamt about her at night. From the dream I simply remembered one question: is it possible to be friends with a person who has a learning disability? In the dream I answered the question affirmatively and I can still remember well the warm sense of joy which I had. It was a wishful, unrealisable dream. Inge was more aware of this than I was, when she turned to leave me for the last time. What I would have liked to happen with her would not have been possible without a protective framework.

A simpler visiting arrangement would have left both of us dissatisfied; it would simply have nourished the unrealisable wish for more. So I respected her decision and never visited her again. I have had to learn to live with my sadness about it.

I have written about two broken off therapies here, but also about all the positive developments that occur in therapeutic failures. This failure taught me a lot about the institution 'Learning Disability'. Resistance of a private nature, such as the dreamed of friendship with Inge, would have been of no avail against it. Solidarity is only possible as a critique of the institution, and we shall always have to accept that the institution stands like a fence between ourselves and someone like Inge, and that we are obliged to stand by helplessly in face of the untold unhappiness or ruin of individual cases.

Failure not only familiarised me with the institution 'Learning Disability', as I encountered it in my work, but also, and more importantly, as I discovered it, and continue to discover it, in myself; for I was implicated in the failure and not a mere victim. It seemed obvious that the unacceptable living conditions in the institution were to blame for the fact that there was no likelihood of a fundamental change in Inge, and that the constant overstrain I suffered from, and which eventually forced me to give up, was also, in part, attributable to this. It also seemed clear that the unreasonable working conditions at the Institute for Outpatient Music Therapy were responsible for Filippa's therapy being broken off and it was easy to make the Institute's management into a scapegoat – a role it played with great bravura. I do not wish to deny the reality of such external pressures. It would be omnipotent of me to think that I could have done things better at the time. Nevertheless, if I needed to make the Institute a scapegoat then it was because I projected my own reservations, ambivalence, feelings of impotence onto them, which unconsciously affected and impaired my work with Inge and Filippa. I knew beforehand, or at least suspected, there were unpleasant aspects about the Institute and I was not at all sure that I would be able to find suitable conditions for my work there; yet I began the therapies in the hope that I would have the strength and possibilities necessary for them. I denied my ambivalence and put too much strain on myself: it was not really possible to carry out the therapies under the conditions that prevailed. But as I began them I held on to the mad hope, coloured by omnipotent phantasies, that some kind of miracle might happen and so made myself a victim along with my patients. My work with Inge suffered from this particularly. The phantasy of being a victim meant I had the tendency to be blind to the children's anger towards me – anger I aroused and which my work situation made me provoke in them. I did not want to see that, for them, I myself was a representative of the institution 'Learning Disability', inflicting its judgement on them, and that the only chance of showing solidarity would have been to accept this role attributed to me. Only by recognising the fact that as an agent of the institution I necessarily participated in its rigidity, would I be able to succeed in psychotherapy with people with learning disabilities by providing them with the space for working through the introjected phantasm. This demands a considerable readiness for self-criticism and an ability to tolerate a good deal of shame and sadness. Only in this way, however, is it possible to remove the veil of individuality covering the omnipotent phantasies, showing them up for what they really are: a reflex response to the inconceivable horror inflicted by the institution 'Learning Disability'.

Inge's falling ill so often, and particularly the sad end, could probably have been avoided if I had understood that she had quite likely sensed my ambivalence as well as the fact that I was inwardly saying good-bye. I could not have spared her this but it is possible that she might have been better able to preserve the inner world of experience she had acquired in the music therapy. This had happened with Wilfried – and in this case it was a carer who backed up my perception and gave me the solid support I needed.

With Filippa I had somewhat more experience. I was familiar with the problem of the pain of leaving, the anger involved in separations, and knew better how to manage this – not, however, in our last session. In this session we were both in despair, we were both victims; I could not find a way of interpreting her anger towards me for leaving her. If she had been able to get mad with me, perhaps her wild tantrum at home after the last session could have been avoided. But it would not have saved her from her breakdown. This book is 'work in progress' and is not based on decades of experience. The experiences which I have explored in it were, in part, only acquired as I was writing it – or to put it another way: I have written up my experiences of the institution 'Learning Disability' as I was going along in order to give myself the space and opportunity for showing solidarity with those who have been hopelessly left behind by our advances in understanding.

As I have been writing the book, it has been instructive and helpful to me to be able to read parts of the text or discuss individual ideas with colleagues or other people who expressed interest. There have been some, particularly as I was beginning the book, who vehemently contested the validity of my ideas, obliging me repeatedly to be more precise in what I was putting forward; there have been others, on the other hand, who have followed my writing with curiosity and open-mindedness and who have given me courage by supporting me in periods of doubt. There have also been colleagues, at times, who have reproached me for forcing doors that are already open. What I am saying is by no means new for them and is already being practised. So much the better, I tell myself, and I ask those amongst my readers for whom this is the case to show forbearance. The militant tone is a response to the hurtful experiences I have had in my encounter with the institution 'Learning Disability', and even though some progress has been made in recent years there is still a great deal which justly deserves to be struggled against. The extremes of evil also help sharpen one's perceptions for the falseness in what is otherwise full of good intention.

The need to show solidarity with minorities and fringe groups is something which critical intellectuals have become increasingly aware of. Intellectuals seldom give much thought to those who have learning disabilities – unless they are autistic children – with whom they have little or no contact either through their work or privately. What is worrying, especially for intellectuals whose narcissism is based on their mental power, is the confrontation with the projections located in the institution 'Learning Disability'. I am all the more moved when I occasionally come across a hero or heroine in literature who has learning disabilities. I have not found many: I have learnt more about epilepsy from *The Idiot* by Dostoevsky, a novel about a person with epilepsy who, because of his illness was regarded as having learning disabilities, than from many specialised textbooks. In *A Personal Matter* by Kenzaburo Oe, the author describes bluntly a father's crisis after his son was born with a brain hernia, which almost resulted in an attempt to kill him. Finally, I have discovered an early short story by Gabriel Garcia Marquez relating a black slave's attempt to show solidarity for his white owners' daughter who had learning disabilities. This story is called 'Nabo'.

After an accident in which he suffered a skull-brain-trauma, Nabo, the black slave, has been living bound and locked up in a room. He cannot live like this but neither can he die – for he has lost something he wants to find; he cannot and will not give up the search. 'The girl', the master's daughter, who has a learning disability and is now grown up, has been sitting for many years in the living-room where she was once parked like a permanent piece of furniture. She has no name. She drools and does not speak, and her sole activity is listening to music. Her parents had long since

> grown used to the idea that the girl would never be able to walk, would never recognize anyone, would always be the little dead and lonely girl who listened to the gramophone looking coldly at the wall until we lifted her out of her chair and took her to her room. Then she ceased to pain us, but Nabo [before his accident, D.N.] was still faithful, punctual, cranking the gramophone. [. . .] One day, when the boy was in the stable, someone beside the gramophone said: 'Nabo!' We were on the veranda, not concerned about something no one could have said. But when we heard it a second time: 'Nabo!' we raised our heads and asked: 'Who's with the girl?' One day, three weeks later, the gramophone began to play again while Nabo was in the stable, which no one could account for. They asked Nabo: 'The gramophone's playing. Can't you hear it?' Nabo said he could. And they asked him: 'Who wound it up?' And he, shrugging his shoulders said: 'The girl. She's been winding it for a long time now.

As Nabo, having been kicked on the forehead by the master's horse, was dozing 'brutishly' in the locked room, 'the girl' wound her gramophone up again and destroyed it, overwinding it for the first time, precisely on the day Nabo broke out, in order, finally, to die – something they had been waiting for for a long time.

> And then the door gave way and the huge bestial Negro, with the harsh scar marked on his forehead, [. . .] came out stumbling over the furniture, [. . .] passed by the girl, who remained seated, [. . .] (when she saw the unchained black force she remembered something that at one time must have been a word), [. . .] and, leaving behind catastrophe, dissolution and chaos like a blindfolded bull in a roomful of lamps, he reached the backyard [. . .] before he finally found the stable doors and pushed them, too soon, falling inside on his face, in his death agony perhaps, but still confused by that fierce animalness that, a half-second before, had prevented him from hearing the girl who raised the crank when she heard him pass and remembered, drooling, [. . .] the only word she had ever learned to say in her life, and she shouted it from the living room: 'Nabo! Nabo!'

Such close observation by a writer is a sign of hope. When literature is successful in bringing to light again, in an artistic form, that which is hidden from our consciousness by the institution 'Learning Disability' as something belonging to the order of personal fate, then the individual omnipotent phantasies of those who try to desert can be recognised for what they are: scars of forgotten humanity. The story offers hope that those who show solidarity will perhaps not always end up like Nabo, foundering and leaving behind catastrophe, dissolution and chaos in the 'room full of lamps' of our enlightened world, because 'the girl' may be able to discover her name, and the 'huge bestial negro', his rightful place, in our world.

Notes and references

Chapter 1

1 The German here is *Geistigbehindertsein* (literally: 'being mentally handicapped'). In view of the fact that the term 'mental handicap' has been officially replaced in the UK (since 1992) by the politically correct term 'learning disability', I have, after considerable discussion, and with the author's agreement, translated accordingly throughout this book. The reader should bear in mind, however, that the book was written in the late 1980s and that the terminology in the German editions has remained unchanged. Equally, the author's formative experiences of working with people with learning disabilities were acquired in a large old-fashioned institution of the kind that no longer exists in the United Kingdom [transl. note].

2 An allusion to Luke 14, 11 [transl. note].

3 'Früherkennungs- und Frühförderungsinstitute' [transl. note].

4 From the preface (p. 10) to Maud Mannoni's *Das zurückgebliebene Kind und seine Mutter*, 1972. Original title: *L'Enfant arriéré et sa mère*, 1964.

5 In Germany there has been a move away from saying 'geistig behindert' (two words: mentally handicapped) to saying 'geistigbehindert' [one word] in a well-meaning attempt to get away from the emphasis on mental defect by transforming the words into a term. In so doing, another implication of the term is conveyed which tends to set 'geistigbehinderte' apart as a species, showing that when there is no reflection on the mechanisms of the institution 'mental handicap/learning disability', these mechanisms continue to work unconsciously, undermining the positive intentions of those concerned [author's note].

6 The word 'Mongol' is preserved here intentionally by the author but the usual term now is of course 'Down's syndrome' [transl. note].

7 The German here is: '*der Gnade der späten Geburt*'. It means that those who were born after the Nazi era do not bear direct responsibility for the crimes committed at that time [transl. note].

8 A 'life not worthy of being lived' – a well-known expression used by the Nazis [transl. note].

9 See Wunder, M. & Steck, U. (1982) *Sie nennen es Fürsorge*. Verlagsgesellschaft Gesundheit mbH, Berlin.

10 'Der Schoss ist fruchtbar noch, aus dem dies kroch' [transl. note].

11 Original edition: Horkheimer & Adorno, *Dialektik der Aufkädrung* (1944).

12 See Kulke, Christine (1985) *Rationalität und sinnliche Vernunft. Frauen in der patriarchalen Realität.*

13 Extracts from a radio programme by Fredi Saal, quoted from: *Einladung zur Bundesarbeitstagung 1988 of the DGMT*, *'Arbeitsgruppe 8'*.
14 From the preface (p. 12) to the German edition of *L'enfant arriéré et sa mère* (Mannoni, 1964).
15 Personal communication.
16 See Mentzos, S. (1987) *Interpersonale und institutionalisierte Abwehr*.
17 The work of A. Lorenzer has not yet been translated into English. However, a concise English summary of his work is available on the internet: Schaffrik, T. (2002) (http://bidok.uibk.ac.at).
18 In *Sprachzerstörung und Rekonstruktion* (1973).
19 *'Deserteurinnen'*, i.e. those who do not toe the institutional line. My inverted commas [transl. note].
20 *Zivildienst*: instead of military service [transl. note].

Chapter 2

1 Stoeckenius, M. & Barbuceanu, G., 1983.
2 'Learning disability – formative processes and acts of defence' [my transl.].
3 In *Wege aus der Isolation*, p. 77. Ed. Ulrich Kasztantowicz (Elbert, 1982).
4 Bach, Heinz (1979) *Familien mit geistigbehinderten Kindern*, p. 2.
5 Häusler, Ingrid (1979) *Kein Kind zum Vorzeigen*, p. 65.
6 Prekop, Irina (1979) *Wir haben ein behindertes Kind*, p. 98.
7 Müller-Garnn, Ruth (1977) . . . *Und halte dich an meiner Hand. Die Geschichte eines Sorgenkindes*, p. 98.
8 Ibid., p. 15.
9 Ibid., p. 88.
10 Ibid., p. 86.
11 Ibid., p. 93ff.
12 Erdheim, Mario (1982), p. 291.
13 Ruppert, Joanna, *Warum gerade ich?*, p. 46ff.
14 Ibid., p. 102ff.
15 Ibid., p. 104.
16 Ibid., p. 105.
17 Melton, David (1969) *Todd*, p. 14.
18 Ibid., p. 22.
19 Balint, Michael (1957) *The Doctor, His Patient, and the Illness*, p. 25.
20 Ibid., p. 18.
21 Ibid., p. 20.
22 German: *Der gesellschaftliche Mordauftrag*.
23 Bach, Heinz (1979) *Familien mit geistigbehinderten Kindern*, p. 2.
24 Lüdeke, Hermann (1985) 'Der unerwartete und ungewisse Abschied' in *Der Nervenarzt*, vol. 56, p. 641.

Chapter 3

1 Horkheimer, M. & Adorno, Th. W. (1944) *Dialectic of Enlightenment*, pp. 256–7 [transl. John Cumming].
2 Spitz, R. (1963) *The First Year of Life. A Psychoanalytic Study of Normal and Deviant Development of Object Relations*, p. 134.
3 Balint, M. (1968) *The Basic Fault – Therapeutic Aspects of Regression*, p. 136.

4 Ibid., p. 136.
5 In his lecture at the Marburger Symposium for Psychoanalysis, 1962.
6 Lorenzer, A. (1971) *Zur Begründung einer materialistischen Sozialisationstheorie.*
7 Mahler, M. (1968) *On Human Symbiosis and the Vicissitudes of Individuation:* Vol. 1, *Infantile Psychosis,* p. 12.
8 Lorenzer, A. (1981) *Das Konzil der Buchhalter,* p. 137ff.
9 Winnicott, D. W. (1971) *Playing and Reality.*
10 Spitz, R. op. cit.
11 Jegge, J. (1983) *Dummheit ist lernbar* [my transl.].
12 Mahler, M. op. cit., p. 71.
13 Spitz, R. op. cit., p. 278.
14 Spitz, R. op. cit., p. 286.
15 Bettelheim, B. (1974) *The Empty Fortress: Infantile Autism and the Birth of the Self* (German edn), p. 168.
16 Ibid,. p. 165.
17 Ibid., p. 166.
18 Schorsch, E. & Becker, N. (1977) *Angst, Lust, Zerstörung. Zur Psychodynamik sexueller Tötungen,* p. 131 [my transl.].
19 Mannoni, M. (1972) *The Retarded Child and His Mother.*
20 Ibid., p. xxiii.
21 Ibid., pp. 7–8.
22 Hundley, J. M. (1974) *Der kleine Außenseiter* (German edn) [my transl.].
23 Ibid., p. 6.
24 Ibid., p. 101.
25 Ibid., p. 7.
26 Ibid., p. 16.
27 Ibid., p. 18.
28 In England, by the Mental Health Act of 1983 [transl. note].
29 Hundley, J. M. op. cit., p. 7ff.
30 Ibid., p. 8.
31 Winnicott, D. W. (1975) *Through Paediatrics to Psychoanalysis* (German edn), pp. 55–6.
32 Pedrina, F. (1984) 'Psychotherapie mit einem Säugling', in *Arbeitshefte für 'Kinderpsychoanalyse',* vol. 4, p. 90 [my transl.].

Chapter 4

1 An investigation into the interdependence of the Enlightenment and changed attitudes towards learning disabled people can be found in: Inghwio aus der Schmitten (1985) *Schwachsinnig in Salzburg.* Werkstattbuch im Umbruch, Salzburg.
2 From Ruppert, J. *Mehr als ich erwarten konnte.*
3 Ruppert, J. *Warum gerade ich?* p. 102.
4 I should like to thank Rezia Bücklers for letting me have the manuscript of her report.
5 Holthaus, Hanni, in Speck, O. & Warnke, A. (Eds) (1983) *Frühforderung mit den Eltern,* p. 22.
6 Hunt, N. (1966) *The World of Nigel Hunt.*
7 This is what a child's mother told me in an assessment interview.
8 Adorno, Theodore W. (1951) *Minima Moralia,* p. 59.

9 Park, C. (1973) *Eine Seele lernt leben.*
10 Selfe, L. (1977) *Nadia. A Case of Extraordinary Drawing Ability in an Autistic Child.* Academic Press, London.
11 Park, C. op. cit., p. 111.
12 Kaufmann, B. N. (1981).
13 Ibid., pp. 18ff.
14 Sennett, R. (1977) *The Fall of Public Man.* Knopf, New York.
15 Wendeler, J. 'Neuere Forschungsergebnisse' in J. K. Wing (Ed.) (1973) *Früh-kindlicher Autismus*, p. 296.
16 Cornell, P. H. 'Medezinische Behandlung' in J. K. Wing (Ed.) (1973).
17 Tinbergen, N. & Tinbergen, E. A. (1984) *Autismus bei Kindern* [my transl.].
18 Kaufmann, B. N. op. cit., p. 25.
19 Bettelheim, B. (1974) *The Empty Fortress: Infantile Autism and the Birth of the Self* (German edn), p. 46.
20 Ibid.
21 Ibid. p. 404.
22 Häusler, Ingrid (1979) *Kein Kind zum Vorzeigen.*
23 Ibid., p. 14.
24 Ibid., p. 15.
25 Ibid., p. 24.
26 Ibid., p. 24.
27 Ibid., p. 15.
28 Ibid., p. 13.
29 Ibid., p. 120.
30 Ibid., p. 60.
31 Ibid., p. 76.
32 Ibid., p. 76.
33 Ibid., p. 67.
34 Ibid., p. 19.
35 Ibid., p. 133.
36 Ibid., p. 15.
37 *Autism*, Vol. 4, 1977, p. 13.

Chapter 5

1 Aly, M., Aly G. & Tumler M. (1981) *Kopfkorrektur.*
2 Gottwald, P. & Redlin, W. (1975) *Verhaltenstherapie bei geistig behinderten Kindern*, p. 10ff.
3 Ibid., p. 23.
4 Ibid., p. 25.
5 Lane, R. (1984) *Robby.*
6 Ibid., p. 46.
7 Ibid., p. 46.
8 Ibid., p. 18.
9 Ibid., p. 61ff.
10 Ibid., p. 63ff.
11 Ibid., p. 69.
12 Häusler, Ingrid (1979) *Kein Kund zum Vorzeigen.*
13 Ibid., p. 27.
14 Ibid., p. 18.
15 Ibid., p. 98.

16 Ibid., p. 105.
17 Ibid., p. 101.
18 Gottwald, P. & Redlin, W. op. cit., p. 27.
19 Ibid., p. 46.
20 Winnicott, D. W. (1958) *Collected Papers: Through Paediatrics to Psychoanalysis*, p. 200.
21 Ibid., p. 199.
22 Bach, Heinz (1981) *Früherziehungsprogramme*, p. 23.
23 Thurmair, M. 'Aufgabe und Dilemma der Elternarbeit in der pädagogischen Frühförderung' in Speck, O. & Warnke, A. (1983), p. 35.
24 Ibid., p. 36.
25 Cf. Landauer, Karl, 'Zur psychosexuellen Genese der Dummheit', in *Psyche*, vol. 6 (1970).
26 Bach, Heinz op. cit., p. 13.
27 Speck, O. & Warnke, A. (1983) *Früförderung mit den Eltern*.
28 Ibid., p. 24.
29 Bach, Heinz op. cit., p. 13.
30 Ruppert, Hans and Christa, 'Das Prager Eltern-Kind-Programm', *Geistige Behinderung*, vol. 4, p. 2ff.
31 Ohlmeier, Gertrud (1983) *Früförderung behinderter Kinder*.
32 Sachers, Hannelore 'Die Situation des geistigbehinderten Säuglings' in Bach, Heinz op. cit., p. 21.
33 Thurmair, op. cit., p. 36.
34 Holthaus, Hanni, in Speck, O. & Warnke, A. (Eds) (1983) *Frühförderung mit den Eltern*, p. 21.
35 Aly *et al.* op. cit., p. 56.
36 Thurmair, M. op. cit., p. 34.
37 Ibid., p. 40.
38 Holthaus, Hanni op. cit., p. 22.
39 Ibid., p. 24.
40 Bach, Heinz op. cit., p. 20.
41 An allusion to Grimm's Fairy Tales [transl. note].
42 Bach, Heinz op. cit., p. 11.
43 Ruppert, Hand and Christa op. cit., p. 27.
44 Kautter, H., Klein, G., Laupheimer, W., & Wiegand, H.-S. (1983) 'Ganzheit und Selbstgestaltung als zwei Leitgedanken eines Handlungsforschungsprojekts zur Frühförderung' in *Frühförderung interdisziplinär*, pp. 6–19.

Chapter 6

1 Balint, M. (1968) *The Basic Fault: Therapeutic Aspects of Regression*, p. 136.
2 Ibid., p. 136.
3 Niedecken, D. (1988) *Einsätze – Material und Beziehungsfigur im musikalischen Produzieren*, p. 117ff.
4 Winnicott, D. W. (1971) *Playing and Reality*, p. 64.

Chapter 7

1 An old-fashioned German song she remembered from her early years [transl. note].

Chapter 8

1 The German here is *Den Tod im Nacken*. During her fits the girl would literally keep looking over her shoulder, turning round and round, as if she had something clinging to her back.

Chapter 9

1 This essay was first published in German in *Forum der Psychoanalyse*, vol. 13: 241–262, 1997. The English version was revised by the author for this publication.
2 In the case of Hans there are certain hints which may back up my reconstructions and metapsychological reflections. The relationship between Hans and his caregivers was radically changed after I had talked to them about the encounter I had had with him, and about my understanding of it. His symptom became meaningful in everyday interaction: in starting to ruminate he was able to let them know that he wanted to be left alone. More than a year after I first met him I learned that his symptom had almost disappeared and that he had found other means of expressing his wish to be by himself.

Bibliography

Adorno, T. W. (1951). *Minima Moralia – Reflections from Damaged Life*. Translated by E. F. N. Jephcott. Verso, London 1974.

Aly, M., Aly, G., Tumler, M. (1981). *Kopfkorektur – oder der Zwang, gesund zu sein. Ein behindertes Kind zwischen Therapie und Altag*. Rotbuch-Verlag, Berlin.

Autismus, Zeitschrift des Bundesverbandes Hilfe für das autistische Kind e.V., Hamburg, vol. 4, 1977.

Bach, H. (Ed.) (1979). *Familien mit geistigbehinderten Kindern. Untersuchungen zur psychischen, sozialen und ökonomischen Lage*. Wiss. Verlag Spiess, Berlin.

Bach, H. (1981). *Früherziehungsprogramme für geistigbehinderte und entwicklungsverzögerte Säuglinge und Kleinkinder*. Wiss. Verlag Spiess, Berlin.

Balint, M. (1957). *The Doctor, His Patient and the Illness*. IUP, New York.

Balint, M. (1968). *The Basic Fault – Therapeutic Aspects of Regression*. Tavistock, London.

Bettelheim, B. (1974). *The Empty Fortress: Infantile Autism and the Birth of the Self* (German edn). Free Press, New York.

Bion, W. (1962). *Learning from Experience*. Heinemann, London.

Damasio, A. R. (1994). *Descartes' Error. Emotion, Reason and the Human Brain*. G. P. Putnam's Sons, New York.

Elbert, J. (1982). 'Geistige Behinderung – Formierungsprozesse und Akte der Gegenwehr' in Kasztantowicz, U. (Ed.), *Wege aus der Isolation. Konzepte und Analysen der Integration Behinderter in Dänemark, Norwegen, Italien und Frankreich*. Schindele, Heidelberg.

Eliacheff, C. (1993). *A corps et à cris. Etre psychanalyste avec les tout-petits*. Odile Jacob, Paris.

Erdheim, M. (1982). *Die gesellschaftliche Produktion von Unbewußtheit*. Suhrkamp, Frankfurt.

Freud, S. (1919a). 'The Uncanny' in Strachey, J. (Ed.), *Standard Edition of the Complete Psychological Works of Sigmund Freud*. London, Hogarth Press, 1953–73, vol. 17, p. 217.

Freud, S. (1919b). 'Beyond the Pleasure Principle' in Strachey, J. (Ed.), *Standard Edition of the Complete Psychological Works of Sigmund Freud*. London, Hogarth Press, 1953–73, vol. 17, p. 18.

Gaedt, C. (1990). *Selbstentwertung – depressive Inszenierungen bei Menschen mit geistiger Behinderung*. Evangelische Stiftung Neuerkerode, Sickte.

Gottwald, P., Redlin, W. (1975). *Verhaltenstherapie bei geistig behinderten Kindern. Grundlagen, Ergebnisse und Probleme der Verhaltenstherapie retardierter, autistischer und schizophrener Kinder.* Vandenhoeck & Ruprecht, Göttingen.

Groef, J. de, Heinemann, E. (1999). *Psychoanalysis and Mental Handicap.* Free Association Books, London.

Häusler, I. (1979). *Kein Kind zum Vorzeigen? Bericht über eine Behinderung.* Rowohlt, Reinbek bei Hamburg.

Kautter, H., Klein, G., Laupheimer, W., Wiegand, H.-S. (1983). 'Ganzheit und Selbstgestaltung als zwei Leitgedanken eines Handlungsforschungsprojekts zue Frühförderung' in *Frühförderung interdisziplinär*, pp. 6–19.

Holthaus, H. (1983). 'Brief einer Mutter' in Speck, O., Warnke, A. (Eds) (1983), *Frühförderung mit den Eltern. Behindertenhilfe durch Erziehung, Unterricht und Therapie.* Ernst Reinhardt, Munich.

Horkheimer, M., Adorno, T. W. (1944). *Dialectic of Enlightenment.* Translation by John Cumming. Continuum, New York 1988.

Hundley, J. M. (1974). *Der kleine Außenseiter* (German edn). *Die Geschichte eines autistischen Kindes.* Otto-Meier-Verlag, Ravensburg.

Hunt, N. (1966). *The World of Nigel Hunt: Diary of a Mongoloid Youth.* Darwen Finlayson, UK.

Jegge, J. (1981). *Dummheit ist lernbar.* Zytglogge, Basle.

Kaufmann, B. N. (1981). *Ein neuer Tag. Wie wir unser Sorgenkind heilten.* DVA, Stuttgart.

Korff-Sausse, S. (1996). *Le miroir brisé.* Calmann-Lévy, Paris.

Kulke, C. (Ed.) (1985). *Rationalität und sinnliche Vernunft. Frauen in der patriarchalen Realität.* Centaurus, Berlin.

Landauer, K. (1938). 'Zur psychosexuellen Genese der Dummheit', reprinted in: *Psyche*, vol. 6, 1970.

Lane, R. (1984). *Robby.* Scherz, Berne.

Lincke, H. (1971). 'Der Ursprung des Ichs', in *Psyche*, 25: 1–30.

Lorenzer, A. (1970). *Kritik des psychoanalytischen Symbolbegriffs.* Suhrkamp, Frankfurt.

Lorenzer, A. (1971). *Zur Begründung einer materialistischen Sozialisationstheorie.* Suhrkamp, Frankfurt.

Lorenzer, A. (1973). *Über den Gegenstand der Psychanalyse oder: Sprache und Interaktion.* Suhrkamp, Frankfurt.

Lorenzer, A. (1973). *Sprachzerstörung und Rekonstruktion.* Fischer, Frankfurt.

Lorenzer, A. (1981). *Das Konzil der Buchhalter.* Fischer, Frankfurt.

Lorenzer, A. (2002). *Sprache, Symbol und Unbewußtes.* Klett-Cotta, Stuttgart.

Lüdeke, H. (1985). 'Der unerwartete und ungewisse Abschied. Probleme von Angehörigen apallischer Patienten' in *Der Nervenarzt*, vol. 56, 641–54.

Mahler, M. S. (1968). *The Selected Papers of Margaret Mahler*, vol. 1, *Infantile Psychosis and Early Contributions.* International University Press, New York.

Mannoni, M. (1972). *The Backward Child and his Mother: A Psychoanalytic Study.* Translated by A. M. Sheridan Smith, London, Tavistock. Original title (1964), *L'Enfant arriéré et sa mère.*

Mannoni, M. (1976). *Un lieu pour vivre.* Coll. 'Le champ freudian'. Seuil, Paris.

Melton, D. (1969). *Todd. Ein Bericht von der Heilung eines hirngeschädigten Kindes.* Herder, Freiburg.

Mentzos, S. (1987). *Interpersonale und institutionalisierte Abwehr*. Suhrkamp, Frankfurt.

Müller-Garnn, R. (1977). *. . . und halte dich an meiner Hand. Die Geschichte eines Sorgenkindes*. Echter Verlag, Würzburg.

Niedecken, D. (1988). *Einsätze – Material und Beziehungsfigur im musikalischen Produzieren*. VSA, Hamburg.

Niedecken, D. (1999). 'The "Organisation" of Mental Retardation', in de Groef & Heinemann, *Psychoanalysis and Mental Handicap*. Free Association Books, London.

Ohlmeier, G. (1983). *Frühförderung behinderter Kinder*. Verlag Modernes Lernen, Dortmund.

Park, C. C. (1973). *Eine Seele lernt leben*. Scherz-Verlag, Bern.

Pedrina, F. (1984). 'Psychotherapie mit einem Säugling' in *Arbeitshefte für Kinderpsychoanalyse*, vol. 4, 90–103.

Prekop, I. (1979). *Wir haben ein behindertes Kind*. Kösel-Verlag, Stuttgart.

Ruppert, H., Ruppert, C. 'Das Prager Eltern-Kind-Programm', *Geistige Behinderung*, vol. 4, p. 2ff.

Ruppert, J. *Mehr als ich erwarten konnte*. Spee-Verlag, Trier.

Ruppert, J. *Warum gerade ich? Einer Mutter überwindet Resignation und Verzweiflung*. Spee-Verlag, Trier.

Schaffrik, T. (2001). *The Work of Alfred Lorenzer: An Introduction*. (Dissertation submitted at the Psycho-Analysis Unit, University College London.)

Schorsch, E., Becker, N. (1977). *Angst, Lust, Zerstörung*. Rowohlt, Reinbek bei Hamburg.

Selfe, L. (1978). *Nadia. A Case of Extraordinary Drawing Ability in an Autistic Child*. Academic Press, London.

Sennett, R. (1977). *The Fall of Public Man*. Knopf, New York.

Sinason, V. (1992). *Mental Handicap and the Human Condition*. Free Association Books, London.

Solms, M., Kaplan-Solms, K. (2000). *Clinical Studies in Neuro-Psychoanalysis. Introduction to a Depth Neuropsychology*. Karnac, London.

Speck, O., Warnke, A. (Eds) (1983). *Frühforderung mit den Eltern. Behindertenhilfe durch Erziehung, Unterricht und Therapie*. Ernst Reinhardt Verlag, Munich.

Spitz, R. (1963). *The First Year of Life. A Psychoanalytic Study of Normal and Deviant Development of Object Relations*. International Universities Press, Madison, CT.

Stern, M. (1972). 'Trauma, Todesangst und Furcht vor dem Tod', in *Psyche*, 26: 901–28.

Stoeckenius, M., Barbuceanu, G. (1983). *Schwachsinn unklarer Genese. Ein Hauptanliegen humangenetischer Beratung*. Birkhäuser-Verlag, Stuttgart.

Tinbergen, N., Tinbergen, E. A. (1984). *Autismus bei Kindern*. Paul Parey, Berlin.

Thurmair, M. (1983). 'Aufgabe und Dilemma der Elternarbeit in der pädagogischen Frühförderung' in Speck, O., Warnke, A. (Eds) *Frühförderung mit den Eltern. Behindertenhilfe durch Erziehung, Unterricht und Therapie*. Ernst Reinhardt Verlag, Munich.

Wing, J. K. (Ed.) (1973). *Frühkindlicher Autismus*. Scherz Verlag, Ravensburg.

Winnicott, D. W. (1960). 'Ego Distortion in Terms of True and False Self' in

Maturational Processes and the Facilitating Environment, Hogarth, London, 1965, pp. 14–52.

Winnicott, D. W. (1975). *Collected Papers: Through Paediatrics to Psychoanalysis* (German edn). Tavistock, London.

Winnicott, D. W. (1971). *Playing and Reality*. Tavistock, London.

Wunder, M., Steck, U. (1982). *Sie nennen es Fürsorge*. Verlagsgesellschaft Gesundheit mbH, Berlin.

Index